RUSH

RUSH

LIFE, LIBERTY AND THE PURSUIT OF EXCELLENCE

ROBERT FREEDMAN

Algora Publishing
New York

Library of Congress Cataloging-in-Publication Data —

Freedman, Robert, 1960- author.
  Rush: life, liberty and the pursuit of excellence / Robert Freedman.
      pages cm
  Includes bibliographical references.
    ISBN 978-1-62894-085-5 (hard cover: alk. paper) — ISBN 978-1-62894-084-8 (soft
cover: alk. paper) — ISBN 978-1-62894-086-2 (ebook) 1. Rush (Musical group)—Criticism
and interpretation. 2. Rock music—History and criticism. I. Title.
    ML421.R87F74 2014
    782.42166092'2—dc23
                            2014026842

Front cover photo credit: John Patuto, Cygnus-X1

Printed in the United States

To the letters S and E

Table of Contents

FOREWORD

Ed Senger, Rush is a Band

> "I believed what I was told. I thought it was a good life, I
> thought I was happy. Then I found something that changed it all."
>
> —*Anonymous, 2112*

Like so many other fans, my obsession with Rush began with this simple,
4-digit number: *2112*. One rainy afternoon in the fall of 1982, when I was 12, I
discovered a beat-up cassette tape of Rush's *2112* in a cave behind a waterfall—
okay, it was my older brother's closet, but you get the picture. After several listens
on my mono-speaker cassette player I was hooked. What struck me about the
music was the power of the lyrics and the emotion in which they were delivered.

The lyrics told a story of discovery, hope, rejection, and despair. These were
themes I could relate to, and they were told it in such a way that I felt I was
being spoken to, like the song was written for me. In the weeks that followed I
devoured Rush's catalog and would forever be changed by it.

Although I loved the music and recognized the musicianship behind it, the
lyrics were what ultimately drove my fascination with the band. The messages
of individualism and humanism, often conveyed in stories of science-fiction and
fantasy, resonated with me as a teenager. Whenever I was down, I'd listen to
Rush as a pick-me-up, or as a form of musical therapy, and whenever I needed
strength I would turn to the band for inspiration. There was just so much to
think about in what was being said. Whenever a new album came out, I would
pore over Neil Peart's lyrics before listening to a single note, conducting my own
philosophical analysis of them.

After speaking to many other fans over the years, from my vantage point as
editor and publisher of *Rush is a Band*, I've learned I'm not alone in this practice.

Trying to understand what Rush is saying is half the enjoyment of listening to the music. So, it stands to reason that there have been a number of books written over the years just on the band's lyrics. Robert Freedman's book, *Rush: Life, Liberty and the Pursuit of Excellence*, fits squarely into this genre and is an important addition to it, but it also tries to take lyrical interpretation one step further by bringing together all the different treatments into one grand, unifying theme, Aristotelian individualism, and then showing the historical context into which the band falls.

Whether he's looking at Aristotle, Ayn Rand, humanism, or critics' responses to Rush over the years, Freedman brings it all together in a comprehensive history of Rush's lyrical philosophy and does so in an accessible, down-to-earth manner that I think any Rush fan will enjoy.

—*Ed Stenger*

Neil Peart

Alex Lifeson

Geddy Lee

Photos by John Patuto, Cygnus-X1.

PREFACE

> The difficult thing about music writing, in the end, is not to describe a sound but to describe a human being. It's tricky work, presumptuous in the case of the living and speculative in the case of the dead.
>
> —Alex Ross, *Listen to This*

It's a remarkable turn of events that Rush is in the Rock and Roll Hall of Fame. While its brand of hard rock has long had a large and loyal following worldwide, the band has never been "canonical" to many music critics—that is, representative of what's best about rock and roll. Not only did the band, when it was building its audience in the late 1970s and early 1980s, lack groove, but its spirit of rebellion seemed almost to be going in the wrong direction. While other bands were singing about smiling on your brother and getting together to love one another, it was exhorting people to pull themselves up by their bootstraps and get on with their lives, come what may.

But a lot has changed in the 40 years since the band first came onto the scene from its roots as a Toronto bar band. Today, the forty-somethings that make up its core fan base are moving into positions of power in business, government, academia, entertainment, and the arts and they want their band, the mythmaker of their generation, to be given its due. Maybe that's why, when the Rock and Roll Hall of Fame in 2012 opened its selection process to the public for the first time, Rush was the biggest vote-getter of all the contenders. The people had been given a chance to speak and a band that leaves so many baby boomers mystified is joined with the likes of Jimi Hendrix and Led Zeppelin in the Pantheon of rock.

Rush really is a mythmaker for a generation. Its tales of the individual against society, cast in the robes of science fiction and fantasy in the band's early years, formed the perfect backdrop for the first generation growing up on video games and harnessing the Internet. It's all about the individual empowered: armed with sense and liberty, together each of us helps create a world that's a perfect sphere, heart and mind united.

There are plenty of books available today on Rush: biographies, lyrical interpretations, and scholarly essays. As I write this, more are on the way. This book is intended to organize the band's ideas under a single philosophical framework to show how the band is in fact canonical—maybe not in the mainstream-rock sense but in the intellectual sense. Rush's lyrics over the decades put its point of view firmly in the great Western intellectual tradition of Aristotle, John Locke, and Adam Smith. So when you listen to the band's 165 original compositions, you're hearing the same ideas that animated Thomas Paine and Thomas Jefferson—only a lot louder.

Alex Ross, the fine music critic for *The New Yorker*, says it's presumptuous for critics like him to interpret the work of the living. But that doesn't make the critic's job any less necessary. The artists themselves are not the best guides to their music, because they can never know with certainty that their audience is hearing the same thing they're saying. It's the critics who help them know whether they're making that connection.

In the case of Rush, it's pretty clear that what Rush is saying and what their audience is hearing are one and the same thing, and this book is the case I've built to show that.

—*Robert Freedman, Alexandria, Va.*

Introduction: Clear Enough

> I truly believed that if I could just *express* things well enough—injustice, narrow-mindedness, destructive and thoughtless behavior—people would recognize their own folly, and change.
>
> —*Neil Peart*, Roadshow

When Rush started out as a Toronto bar band in the early 1970s, playing clubs like Abbey Road, the Colonial Tavern, and the Piccadilly Tube on the city's main strip, Yonge Street,[1] the focus was only on the music, not the lyrics.

"Most of the lyrics were just what rhymed, whatever fit in," says the band's original drummer, the late John Rutsey. "We never really spent much time at all on the lyrics."[2]

It shows.

"Hey, now, baby / Well, I like your smile / Won't you come and talk to me / For a little while?"

That stanza's from "In the Mood" by Geddy Lee, the band's vocalist and bass player, who says it was the first song he ever wrote.

Other pieces from their early days are equally nondescript, with lines like "I'm runnin' here / I'm runnin' there / I'm lookin' for a girl," from "Need Some Love," and "Ooh, said I, I'm comin' out to get you / Ooh, sit down, I'm comin' out to find you," from "Finding My Way," both of which appeared on the band's 1974 debut album, *Rush*.

Whatever the band is on its first album—"Led Zeppelin junior," as one critic

---

1 Bill Banasiewicz, *Rush Visions: The Official Biography*. New York: Omnibus Press, 1988, page 9.
2 Rutsey's and other band members' comments about the dashed-off nature of early Rush lyrics is in *Visions*, page 10, and in Martin Popoff, *Contents Under Pressure*. Toronto: ECW Press, 2004, p. 13.

called them, or "high energy rock," as another did,[1]—no one would accuse them of striving for lofty lyrical heights. The only exception is "Working Man," the piece that won them initial attention on the radio. Its aggressive, meaty guitar riff and high-octane vocals caught the attention of Cleveland WMMS program director Donna Halper and impressed their future Mercury label rep Cliff Burnstein.[2] "I get up at seven, yeah / And I go to work at nine / I got no time for livin' / Yes, I'm workin' all the time."

Maybe not much better than "I'm runnin' here / I'm runnin' there / I'm lookin' for a girl," but it's *about* something: the day-to-day grind of bringing home a paycheck and wondering whether this is all there is to life for a young man.

Had Rush carried on in this fashion, it's a question whether they would have achieved the success they've had over their 40-year career or whether, as one early critic put it, they would have simply flamed out. "The only weakness with all of this has to do with the lyrics," Jim Knippenberg of the *Cincinnati Enquirer* said after he watched one of the band's early shows. "They could use some polish. And a little variety. Perhaps some getting away from the 'love is the thing' and 'let's boogie' for a time."[3]

Knippenberg was prescient, because all that changed once Neil Peart, a drummer with an insatiable appetite for thinking about the world, came on board.

Rutsey, a diabetic who was conflicted about whether the rock and roll lifestyle was for him and who wrestled with creative differences with his band mates, left in late 1974, just before they were to start on their first tour, as opening act for Manfred Mann and Uriah Heep in Pittsburgh at the Civic Arena.

His departure forced Lee and Alex Lifeson, the band's guitarist, to find a replacement without delay, and of course this is where Peart steps in, the tale well-told how he pulled up in an old clunker with his drums stuffed in garbage pails and earned himself the job. "After I heard Neil play, there was no one else who could come after the guy," Lee says.[4]

At first Peart was impressive simply because of his drumming: powerful and versatile, and for that he's been duly recognized, called by some fellow drummers nothing less than the world's greatest living rock drummer. Not all drummers would agree with that, of course, and certainly few critics

1 Rush as junior Led Zeppelin comes from listeners mistaking the band for Led Zeppelin when they first hear "Working Man" on the radio in Cleveland and critics, including Larry Rohter of *The Washington Post*, comparing their sound to Zeppelin. These points are made in Robert Telleria. *Rush Tribute: Merely Players.* Kingston: Quarry Press, 2002, page 28.
2 The role of Donna Halper at WMMS in highlighting the band and Burnstein's quote about "Working Man" being a "motherfucker" are in Telleria, *Merely Players*, page 19.
3 Telleria, *Merely Players*, page 24.
4 Banasiewicz, *Visions*, page 16.

would, but there's little doubt of the impact he's had on his craft.[1]

But Peart also brought his lyric-writing to the mix, and that really changed everything. Once the three of them started writing songs together, while driving from date to date on that first 1974 tour,[2] the breadth and depth of what their songs were about suddenly exploded, and the range and complexity of the music exploded as well. It was as if, musically, Lee and Lifeson wanted to up their game in the same way Peart had helped them up their lyrics, and that was reflected in the band's second album, *Fly by Night*, released in 1975.

"A real unity of purpose was beginning to develop," Peart has written of those first months traveling together. "We were pooling our creative resources, and exploring each other's aptitudes and personalities."[3]

The ABCs of the Peart effect

You can really hear the change in the band's music in two early bootleg recordings that were turned into a commercial CD in 2012, called *ABC 1974*, with the "ABC" standing for "Agora Ballroom Cleveland." The CD is divided into two sections, both of which are based on live recordings at the Agora Ballroom, the first from a 1974 show, while the band was touring to promote their debut album, and the second from a 1975 show, while they were promoting *Fly by Night*.

Peart is behind the drum kit for both shows, so when you listen to the CD you hear his influence throughout. But the lyrical change between the 1974 songs and the 1975 tracks is unmistakable. Suddenly the music has a completely new complexity, the pieces far more composed, the bluesy jamming de-emphasized, and, most importantly, the words coming out of Lee's mouth are no longer just ad hoc accompaniment to the music; they're actually words that say something and that you want to hear.

In short, with Peart now picking up the wordsmithing, a job he says he took only because neither Lee nor Lifeson had any interest in it,[4] Rush was transformed from an exciting but conventional hard rock band with a facility for odd time signatures to a newly interesting musical enterprise with a piercing point of view.

This isn't to say that critics suddenly began to pay the band respect because of Peart. Indeed, as the band's biographies have made clear, Peart in some ways was as much a liability as an asset, his lyric writing scoffed at, sneered at, and laughed at by not one but two and maybe even three

---

1 Peart's influence on other drummers is at, among other places, *The Rush Forum* http://www.therushforum.com/index.php?/topic/13877-peter-criss-praises-neil-peart/ retrieved December 10, 2012, and *Rush is a Band*: http://www.rushisaband.com/blog/2011/03/21/2514/Foo-Fighters-discuss-Rush-influence-on-new-single-Rope retrieved December 10, 2012.
2 Popoff, *Contents Under Pressure*, page 24.
3 Banasiewicz, *Visions*, page 18.
4 Telleria, *Merely Players*, page 21.

generations of music critics. The now-defunct *Blender* magazine notoriously voted Peart the second-worst rock lyricist of all time (Sting was voted the first)[1], and critics have tripped over themselves dismissing his lyrics in the most pointed way. Steve Weitzman in *Circus* magazine called them "caca"[2] and Jon Pareles of the *New York Times* called them "screeds"[3] in two examples.

Of course, it wasn't just Peart's lyrics that inspired critics to compete amongst themselves to dismiss the band; Lee's vocals were also the target of a spirited competition to find the most memorable put-down. The music critic of the *London Globe & Mail* uproariously compared Lee's singing to "the damned howling in Hades,"[4] John Griffin of the *Montreal Gazette* says he sounds like a "guinea pig with an amphetamine habit,"[5] and Dan Nooger of *Circus* says of his singing, if it got any higher, it would only be intelligible to "dogs and extraterrestrials."[6]

So, the band in its early years, although it was building a sizable fan base, remained something outside the mainstream, at least in the eyes of some of the music industry's most well-known critics, including *Rolling Stone's* Robert Christgau and David Wild, neither of whom could ever reconcile themselves to the band's sound.[7]

Of course, fast forward to today and the story's quite a bit different, with even mainstream critics having come around. *Rolling Stone*, long thought of as the band's nemesis with its sometimes harsh snubs of their music, in early 2012 came out with an admiring feature, and, a few months later, the Rock and Roll Hall of Fame, founded by *Rolling Stone* publisher Jann Wenner, nominated and then inducted the band into its hallowed halls (or "hollow" halls, as some critics call it).

In truth, Peart is not a natural poet, and his lyrics are far from eloquent. Bob Dylan is a poet. Fellow Canadian Neil Young has been called a poet. Roger Waters of Pink Floyd, John Lennon, Pete Townsend—these are rock poets, many critics would agree. Peart, by contrast, although he writes in many poetic verse forms,[8] is really a prose writer, and that might explain why

---

1 The *Blender* worst-lyricist list was published October 9, 2007. It's referenced at Rush is a band: http://www.rushisaband.com/display.php?id=1251 retrieved December 13, 2012.
2 Telleria, *Merely Players*, p. 46.
3 Chris McDonald, *Rush, Rock Music and the Middle Class*. Bloomington: Indiana University Press, 2009, p. 193.
4 Telleria, *Merely Players*, p. 28.
5 Referred to in "Rush: Power From the People," by David Fricke, *Rolling Stone*, May 28, 1981.
6 Telleria, *Merely Players*, p. 25.
7 Ibid., p. 31.
8 Peart in his 2007 essay "The Game of Snakes and Arrows" talks about his experiments with different verse forms, using his rhyming dictionary as a guide. "The front of my rhyming dictionary had an index of traditional verse patterns, and I tried writing in some of them—as an exercise, like solving a crossword puzzle. Among sonnets, villanelles, and sestinas, I particularly liked a Malay form called the pantoum, and wrote several lyrics using that scheme, including 'The Larger Bowl.'"

so many critics never took to his style. In the early years, while the band's fan base was digging his style—these were the days of epic heroic tales like "The Necromancer" and "The Fountain of Lamneth" and short stories like "Red Barchetta" and "By-Tor and the Snow Dog"—the critics were just seeing cheesy tales of science fiction and fantasy. As *Blender* put it in its October 2007 smackdown, "richly awful tapestries of fantasy and science."[1]

If you don't count *Clockwork Angels*, the band's chart-topping concept album that came out in 2012, Peart pretty much packed away his science fiction and fantasy pen years ago, the last piece written in that genre, "Red Barchetta," about a futuristic car chase, coming out in 1981 on the band's popular *Moving Pictures* album.

But Peart never packed away his signature style, which is a kind of *prose* writing that looks at matters with an air of critical detachment, as if he's standing apart from the messy world around him and just explaining how things are and how they could be a whole lot better if people would just listen—listen to what he's saying. "I truly believed that if I could just *express* things well enough—injustice, narrow-mindedness, destructive and thoughtless behavior—people would recognize their own folly, and change," he says in his 2007 book *Roadshow* (ECW Press).[2]

"War Paint" from the band's 1989 album *Presto* is a great example of Peart's hunger to explain. Critics jumped on the album and on songs like "War Paint" as examples of everything the band was doing wrong in the mid-1980s, the band's middle period, as it's sometimes called, but the piece showcases the kind of critical writing that Peart does so well. "All puffed up with vanity / We see what we want to see / To the beautiful and the wise / The mirror always lies."

You can call the lyrics poetry if you want, but it's not in their meter or symbolism that their strength lies; it's in the qualities they share with prose writing. They don't invite you to tease out their meaning, the way a poem does. Their meaning is already pretty clear. They want to inform, educate, explain, analyze, and criticize. That's why Peart's lyrics have seemed to some to have a concrete, almost clunky quality to them. These are lyrics of a writer who wants to be *understood*.

In these lines he's describing young people's short-sightedness about what's important. They spend all their time thinking about how they look, whether they can attract the eyes of the ones they want to hang with, but they've completely misplaced their priorities. They should be uncovering who they are—living the examined life—so they can go out and take the world by the horns and thrive. Instead, their horizon doesn't extend past the next party.

---

1 The *Blender* worst-lyricist list was published October 9, 2007. It's referenced at Rush is a band: http://www.rushisaband.com/display.php?id=1251 retrieved December 13, 2012.
2 Neil Peart, *Roadshow: Landscape with Drums*. Toronto: ECW Press, 2007, page 21.

"Second Nature," on the band's 1987 *Hold Your Fire* album, another piece snubbed by critics, is also a good example. Here, Peart is using the motif of an open letter to entreat leaders of industry and government to think of the environment as something more than an afterthought. He's not saying that going for profit or political gain is a bad thing; he's just saying that one's planning horizon should be expansive enough to take in the big picture—and that's a goal we should all be capable of agreeing on. "A memo to a higher office / Open letter to the powers that be / To a god, a king, a head of state / A captain of industry / To the movers and the shakers / Can't everybody see? / It ought to be second nature / I mean, the places where we live / Let's talk about this sensibly / We're not insensitive / I know progress has no patience / But something's got to give."

Once again, we have Peart standing apart from the action in the lyrics and playing the role of commentator: "We all see the problem, don't we? Now let's see what we can do to fix it."

This kind of disinterest, or personal separation, is what defines Peart's lyric writing through its many stages, and arguably this is what psychology professor Mitch Earleywine is getting at in the 2011 book *Rush and Philosophy* (Open Court Press) when he says Rush's music serves as a kind of cognitive behavioral therapy to listeners. Earleywine, professor of clinical psychology at the University at Albany, State University of New York, says in his essay "Rush's Revolutionary Psychology" that listening to Rush is a bit like listening to a trusted therapist say to you, "The world is what it is. You need to find what you like to do and get out there and do it."

"Rush pairs music with words in a way that trains listeners in some of the key ideas in modern psychology," Earleywine says, "leading us to think clearly, responsibly, and happily."[1]

Although Earleywine doesn't make this connection, the reason Rush has this effect on listeners, you can argue, is because of the space Peart leaves in his lyrics for you to insert yourself and apply what's being said to your own situation. Although Peart makes it clear he's writing from his own experience, he's not turning the magnifying glass onto himself while he explores his emotions. Rather, he's taking himself out of the picture and universalizing his experience into a generalization that listeners can relate to. Instead of, "I need to get out there and be my own person!" he says, "You need to get out there and be your own person!"

"The beauty of all these tunes," Earleywine says, "comes in the way they are the incarnation of their own recommendations."[2]

There are exceptions to everything, and there are exceptions to this disinterested approach, too. "Limelight," the band's big hit on *Moving Pictures*, is autobiographical. It looks at the problem people face when they're in the limelight and fans breach their personal space. As Peart has said in many

1 Jim Berti and Durrell Bowman, eds., *Rush and Philosophy: Heart and Mind United.* Chicago: Open Court, 2011, page 89.
2 Ibid., page 100.

interviews, the song is about his discomfort when fans act like they know him. And it would have been explicitly autobiographical except that, at Lee's suggestion, the word "I" was changed to "one,"[1] so it comes across in a more universalized way: "One must put up barriers / To keep oneself intact."

Many of the pieces on the band's 2007 *Vapor Trails* album, released after the band took a five-year hiatus while Peart pulled his life back together after a string of personal losses, are similarly inward-gazing. But even here, the pieces are not the emotional stream of poetic consciousness you might expect from a person trying to come to grips with matters. They remain written in a way that provides plenty of room for you, as listener, to insert yourself and relate what Peart is writing to your own experience.

"Like the rat in a maze who says / 'Watch me choose my own direction' / Are you under the illusion / The path is winding your way?".

This stanza is from "The Stars Look Down," a bleak look at how the heavens can often seem to look on with complete indifference to our personal pain, whether deserved or not. That's certainly how you would expect to feel if you're the victim of what appears to be random misfortune, but in the way the feeling is related in the piece, we're invited to share in Peart's observations about it without entering his personal space, because the piece, while written from his personal experience, isn't about him but about the universalizable experience of feeling that way. He brings you into the piece by asking you, "Are *you* under the illusion / The path is winding *your* way?"

Jim Berti, co-editor with Durrell Bowman of *Rush and Philosophy*, says in his essay "Ghost Riding on the Razor's Edge" that he took a lot of solace in Peart's lyrics in 2009 when he was dealing with his own issues. At one point, he says, "I was experiencing my own personal Hell, a dark period that [stretched] the line of physical and mental breakdown. As I have done so often during rough patches in life, I turned to Rush to help me through. . . . I'm not saying that my problems were the same as Peart's, but I shared the same feelings . . . and hearing Peart's story told through music was the perfect combination of emotional and physical release for me."[2]

Although Berti doesn't frame it in these terms, one can certainly make the case that he would not have found the same solace if the lyrics were too me-focused—that is, focused on the writer's emotional experience without regard to how listeners are supposed to relate to it, which is the way so many musicians approach lyric writing. I don't intend to be critical of Lifeson, whose focus all along has been on the band's music and who has never fancied himself a lyricist, but you can see the difference in how Peart approaches writing lyrics compared to how Lifeson approaches it, in the few times he's contributed the lyrics for Rush and for his own 1996 solo album, *Victor*.

Here's a stanza from "Lessons," one of the pieces on the backside of the band's breakout *2112* album, released in 1976. Lifeson is given sole credit for

1 Telleria, *Merely Players*, page 178.
2 Berti and Bowman, *Rush and Philosophy*, pages 119-120.

the piece. "Sweet memories / I never thought it would be like this / Reminding me / Just how close I came to missing / I know that / This is the way for me to go / You'll be there / When you know what I know / And I know."

These are perfectly fine lyrics and you can find lyrics of this style in lots of pop and rock songs. Just consider for a moment "Sam's Town" by The Killers on their 2006 album of the same name. "Why do you waste my time? / Is the answer to the question on your mind / And I'm so sick of all my judges / So scared of what they'll find."

Both of these cases show inward-looking and personal lyrics, with veiled emotional meaning that's clearly important to the writer but leaves little chance for the listener to find a place for himself in them. We see this in any writing in which the writer is talking about something personal to himself and is exercising the need to express something about himself without regard to whether it makes any sense to the reader or listener.

The lyrics on Lifeson's solo album, *Victor*, are very much of this nature. "What if I wasn't so scared? / Why can't I be brave? / I've forgotten all that we've shared / You can't give me what I crave."

Again, perfectly fine lyrics and of a type that you see in many pop and rock songs, but this stanza, taken from "Promise," is almost too personal and self-absorbed to invite a third-party—that is, the listener—into the conversation. It seems like Lifeson is having a personal conversation with his wife or someone else and we're invited to listen in, but we're not sure we should intrude.

In truth, in addition to being the band's "musical scientist," as his band mates have called him, Lifeson is a genuinely funny writer. Some of his "essays" in the band's tour books over the years are gems, so he certainly knows how to connect with an audience. Here's an excerpt from his equipment list in Rush's 1982 *Signals* tour book:

> I've broken down the equipment I'm using into three categories: amplification, guitarification and effectification. It is truly an amazing coincidence how similar all three categories are to each other. For instance, through my keen sense of awareness, I've noticed all three have a series of knobs. Also the amps and assorted effects all have glowing lights.
>
> The amps I'm using are four Marshall Combos, which we jokingly refer to as the Marshall Combos.
>
> For effects, I have many: a Westinghouse Blender, two Amana Freezers, a gas pedal, a flower pedal, Maestro Parametric Filter, cigarette filter, six nozzles, three lungs, and an M.X.R. Micro Amp. All of these effects are capable of producing a wide range of sounds. Some are scary while some are awful. I prefer the scary sounds.[1]

1 You can access the *Signals* tour book at *Rush Vault*: http://rushvault. com/2011/03/13/signals-tour-book/ retrieved December 14, 2012.

In any case, given Peart's approach to lyric-writing, it doesn't come as a surprise that he's found great success with his prose writing, something he took up early in his career with Rush but which, as he describes it in interviews and in his essays, didn't come to much until he hit on a genre that he felt really suited him, which is a kind of adventure travel memoir. As we know from his own remarks on the matter, he self-published a few short travel memoirs in the 1980s for family and friends[1] while he perfected his literary approach and then went for broke with publication in 1996 of a travel memoir about his bicycle trip through Cameroon with a small tour group, *The Masked Rider* (Rounder Books).

Following publication of that book, he limited his writing to letters and journaling while he came to grips with the death of his daughter, in 1997, and then his wife, in 1998. But once he returned to the band and started writing again, his literary output was prodigious: *Ghost Rider*, about motorcycling in the wake of his personal losses, in 2002; *Traveling Music*, about the development of his musical tastes, in 2004; and *Roadshow*, about the band's 30-year anniversary tour, in 2007.

Meanwhile, he published more of this type of travel-memoir writing when he launched his blog, *News, Weather & Sports*, in 2005, and with the compilation of his monthly blog posts into his book *Far and Away* in 2010. All of the books were published by ECW Press in Toronto.

These travel memoirs are important to mention because they provide the perfect bookend to the approach Peart has taken over the years in his lyric writing. They're personal, yes, and they're based on his experiences, but his point never gets lost in a vague miasma of emotions and unresolved psychological issues. He keeps himself far enough in the distance that we, as readers, can insert ourselves in his place and see things from his point of view. We're not onlookers as he tries to discover himself; he's discovered himself already and now he's inviting us along for the ride while he talks about what he's found significant and why, and it makes for compelling reading—and, in the case of his lyrics, compelling listening. Peart is an accomplished writer.

What it's all about: personal stewardship

So, the arrival of Peart helped Lee and Lifeson take their music to a new level. But what does that mean? What was Rush talking about once Peart came on board and they began talking to their listeners in a meaningful way?

Well, the short answer is, they were talking about individualism. You hear a lot in the media about Rush's libertarianism, but really what Rush has been about from the beginning is individualism. This is simply the idea that each of us is a sovereign and, as such, we have certain inalienable rights—

---

1 You can see all of Peart's self-published travel memoirs at 2112.net: http://www.2112.net/powerwindows/main/PeartsWritings.htm retrieved December 10, 2012. They are *Riding the Golden Lion* (1985), *The Orient Express* (1987), *Pedals Over The Pyrenees: Spain and Spokes and Trains* (1988), *Raindance Over the Rockies: Across the Mountains by Bicycle* (1988), *The African Drum* (1988).

but also certain responsibilities. And almost everything Geddy Lee sings about, when he sings lyrics written by Peart, which is 90 percent of the time, touches in some way on individualism.

The idea of individualism is so basic to our way of life, at least in the West, that it almost seems meaningless, like the idea of air: it's all around us and life depends on it and we just take it for granted so there's really not that much to say about it.

While the notion of individualism has been widespread since the eighteenth century, with the Enlightenment, the idea of each of us possessing personal sovereignty will always have to compete with the needs of society, which in every social group requires some agreed-upon bounds of conduct. Battles continue to rage over what a state can and can't compel us to do. Do we have an unbreachable right to own a gun? Do we have a right to an abortion? At what point does personal sovereignty end and state sovereignty take over? The issues related to individualism are far from settled.

Peart made these issues that relate to our personal sovereignty a key theme of the band's music. And that is rather unique in the world of rock music.

To be sure, other bands and musicians have touched on themes of individualism and indeed have been "political" in the sense that they have taken a position on how things should be run. Think of the progressive social consciousness in much of the folk rock in the 1960s, with the likes of Peter Ochs ("I Ain't Marching Anymore"), Joan Baez ("We shall Overcome"), and Judy Collins ("Turn! Turn! Turn!") channeling the old heroes like Woody Guthrie ("Vigilante Man") and Pete Seeger ("If I had a Hammer"). It's not just the folk rockers who do this, of course. Bruce Springsteen, John Lennon, U2, REM—any number of pop and rock acts have built social consciousness into their music in a big way.

On the other side of the political spectrum we have acts like The Bobby Fuller Four singing "I fought the Law," Sammy Hagar singing "I Can't Drive 55," and The Kinks singing "20th Century Man" to remind us that the meeting place between our rights as an individual and the rights of the society in which we live is in a constant state of flux. Sometimes the line moves to the left a bit, as it did in the 1960s and 1970s, in the United States, Canada, and the U.K., and sometimes it moves to the right a bit, as it did beginning in the 1980s, again, whether in the U.S., Canada, and the U.K.

But Peart's take on individualism isn't a political one. Of course, there's often a political element to it, because ultimately our individual rights are part of a larger political conversation. That's why when Peart writes in "Second Nature," the Rush piece in the form of an open letter, there's a political element to it. He's writing to private and public leaders and asking them to find the middle ground that will enable the private sector to continue doing its thing while keeping in mind the public-interest aspect of our environment. He knows "perfect's not for real," he says, but can't we still "make a deal"?

But mostly Peart's take on individualism, particularly in the early years, is a *moral* one. It's about the battle each of us faces as we wrestle with how to strike a balance in our own lives, whether to seize our sovereignty and be a leader or to let it wither on the vine while we allow ourselves to be led. We all think of ourselves as leaders of our own lives, but really in many small ways we prefer to abdicate responsibility for ourselves to others. On the surface this seems political: I can't find a job, therefore the government should try to help me get a job or at least pay me unemployment while I look. I'm sick and my illness can easily wipe me out financially, therefore the government at a minimum should step in so I don't lose my ability to support myself. I want to smoke pot and I don't feel I should be at risk of getting arrested for it since I'm not hurting anyone else, so the government should legalize pot.

Peart's approach to these issues asks not so much whether government intervention is right or wrong than, what kind of person am I? At the end of the day, do I have the strength of character to steer my ship through the shoals of life and take responsibility for myself, regardless of the outcome and regardless of how interventionist or non-interventionist my government is? In other words, this isn't about me versus the government; it's about me versus me. Do I have what Aristotle called *virtue*?

This is the mistake that is made so often in the media when music critics and reporters throw out shorthand references to Rush as a libertarian band. They see far-right politicians and commentators like Rand Paul and Rush Limbaugh quoting from or using Rush music for their own didactic purposes and they give a knowing wink and nod and say, "Rush, the libertarian rock band."

But as Steven Horwitz makes clear in his essay in *Rush and Philosophy*, "Rush's Libertarianism Never Fit the Plan," although Peart incorporated libertarian references in some of his earliest work with Lee and Lifeson, the band is really not an avatar of libertarian values. What it really is, Horwitz says, is an avatar of individualist values, which is not reducible to libertarianism.

"Even where Peart seems to reject elements of libertarianism . . . he still holds on to a very clear commitment to the dignity and centrality of the individual and the individual's ability to achieve greatness and overcome tragedy," Horwitz says. "What we might call Rush's 'individualism' (and I do think *this* is a description that applies to all three band members) provides the overarching philosophical theme of their career, from their own choices as a band to the lyrical content." [Emphasis supplied.][1] Horwitz is the Charles A. Dana Professor of Economics at St. Lawrence University in Canton, N.Y.

Indeed, as another *Rush and Philosophy* contributor shows, Rush is a carrier of Aristotelian virtue ethics. Neil Florek, a philosophy professor at Purdue University, in his essay "Free Wills and Sweet Miracles," shows how much

---

1 Berti and Bowman, *Rush and Philosophy*, page 270.

of what Rush sings about is virtuous living under an Aristotelian framework. He identifies a number of the Aristotelian virtues, like courage, justice, moderation in Rush's music, and adds a couple more that can be found in it that are uniquely Rushian: persistence and what he calls "prudent non-conformity."

As he puts it, "Like the most important, influential philosophers of the Western world, Rush's music expresses a conception of how best to live to become excellent, happy persons," says Florek.[1]

Thus, what you have in Rush's lyrics is Peart's brand of disinterested commentary about right living from an Aristotelian virtue perspective, and, whether it's early Rush or late Rush, it's there like bedrock: everything Rush sings about, whether it concerns relationships, environmentalism, the social order, or religion, among the big variety of topics the band hits, it's all laid on top of this bedrock of Aristotelian virtue ethics, which in turn is the bedrock for individualism.

As we'll see, this is where the band's connection to Ayn Rand comes in. Just as it has been linked to libertarianism, the band has been called Randian for its adherence, in its earliest years, to the ideas of the 1950s-era Objectivist philosopher who made her name with her big, thick novels about self-reliant movers and shakers who don't need namby-pamby government stepping in to make the world a kinder, gentler place for everyone.

But although early on Peart did make explicit references to her work, not only is he not her "disciple," as he has put it, but the philosophy in Rush's music has little in common with what Rand's Objectivist vision is all about. Rather, both Rand's Objectivism and Rush's individualism are grounded in Aristotelianism, so commentators routinely conflate the two and say they are talking about the same thing. But they merely share this common ancestor. Their viewpoints are actually quite a bit different.

As Deena and Michael Weinstein put it in "Neil Peart versus Ayn Rand" in *Rush and Philosophy*, the two Rush songs most closely associated with Rand, the band's 1975 "Anthem" on *Fly by Night* and the 1976 breakout "2112," ultimately go in directions that is diametrically opposed to Rand. "[W]hatever [Peart's] intentions happened to be when he wrote the lyrics . . . the protagonist of "2112" would be anathema to Rand," the Weinsteins say.[2] Deena is professor of sociology at DePaul University and Michael is professor of political science at Purdue University.

Politically, rather than channeling Rand's brand of libertarianism (a term Rand wouldn't use), in which the smallest government is the best government, otherwise the state will impede the sovereignty of the individual, Rush is channeling the classical liberalism of our Western heroes like John Locke and Adam Smith.

Classical liberalism is a term that applies to the Enlightenment principles that form the framework of the Constitution in the United States and the

1 Ibid., page 140.
2 Ibid., page 285.

Declaration of the Rights of Man and of the Citizen in France. In fact, you can say that classical liberalism is really the governing philosophy of every Western democracy today.

It's simply the view that we as individuals consent to give up some of our natural rights to take advantages of the benefits that come from organizing ourselves into a governed society. "Every man, by consenting with others to make one body politic under one government, puts himself under an obligation to every one of that society, to submit to the determination of the majority, and to be concluded by it,"[1] Locke says in the second treatise of his 1689 classic, *Two Treatises of Government*.

It's very much an individualistic governing model, because the sovereignty of the individual remains sacrosanct. And yet classical liberalism isn't as extreme as libertarianism, because, under it, the amount of rights we're willing to give up isn't based on some set amount—government can do these things and no more—but rather is a fluid, constantly adjusting amount based on what we (democratically) agree we want our government to do for us. As Locke puts it, we "give up all the power necessary to the ends for which [we] unite into society."[2]

In Locke's classical liberal view, even though there's no formula for how much in rights individuals are willing to give up for the benefits of society, there are certain inviolable limits that no society can breach, at least systematically, and these are our rights to life, liberty, and the pursuit of property ("happiness" in the U.S. Constitution). To the extent a society tries to breach these rights, which are inalienable, individuals have the right—even the duty—to overthrow the government. Locke puts it this way:

> [I]f a long train of abuses, prevarications and artifices, all tending the same way, make the design visible to the people, and they cannot but feel what they lie under, and see whither they are going; it is not to be wondered, that they should then rouse themselves, and endeavour to put the rule into such hands which may secure to them the ends for which government was at first erected.[3]

Finding the point of trade-off between our rights and those of the society is really the political program of Rush, not Randian extremism. That's why you can go back to songs like "Second Nature" and see Peart searching for where to plant the line between our individual sovereignty and government sovereignty. Where that line should be is no simple question, and it can't be glibly answered. Ideally, it's where the parties agree to draw it and with the understanding that our inalienable rights will be left standing.

Thus, with Rush, Aristotelian virtue ethics serve as the foundation for

---

1 John Locke, *Two Treatises of Government* and *A Letter Concerning Toleration*, Ian Shapiro, ed. New Haven: Yale University Press, 2003, page 112.
2 Ibid., page 113.
3 Ibid., page 160.

individualism, which serves as the foundation for classical liberalism. This takes us to one more spot on Peart's philosophical road map: humanism.

Much has been made of Peart's humanism in recent years, principally because it plays such a major theme in the band's 2007 *Snakes & Arrows* album (and, as we'll see, *Clockwork Angels*) and he's long dabbled in the topic in his prose writing. There are many types of humanism, including some that don't rule out the notion of God, but in general humanism is simply the view that the world is what we see before us and our sense of morality flows from that and not from some type of intervention from a deity that we can't account for in the natural world. What's important for our purposes is that right and wrong under humanism is grounded in the idea of human flourishing, meaning that humanism shares the same individualist bedrock of Aristotelian virtue ethics. That's why it seems to flow so naturally out of what Rush has been singing about all along. Chris McDonald, an ethnomusicology instructor at Cape Breton University in Nova Scotia, talks about Rush's humanism in "Enlightened Thoughts, Mystic Words" in *Rush and Philosophy*.

And so we come to the point of this book. In the pages ahead, we'll be looking into the philosophies that build the foundation of Rush's Aristotelian point of view, as expressed over the band's recording history. These include individualism (each of us is our own sovereign), classical liberalism (we voluntarily give up some of our sovereignty to live together in society), and humanism (the world is running according to its natural laws so all this business about God intervening in the world is beside the point).

Along the way we'll even look a little at the Objectivism of Ayn Rand, what we might call a very overcooked version of Aristotelianism.

What's most interesting is how the philosophies line up so nicely in the words and music of Rush—a testament to an admirable consistency on the part of Peart's thinking over the years even as his (and the band's) ideas continue to evolve in interesting ways. But what never changes lyrically in Rush's music is the individualism of Aristotle. For planting your own philosophical flag and standing your moral ground, you would be hard pressed to find a better starting point than that.

Chapter 1. And the World Is Set in Motion

> I was brought up to believe
> The universe has a plan
> We are only human
> It's not ours to understand
> — "Brought Up to Believe," *Clockwork Angels, 2012*

Hold Your Fire from 1987 is rarely mentioned among Rush's more memorable albums. The trio from Canada that helped create progressive metal in the late 1970s with their breakout "2112" concept piece and gave us radio hits like "Tom Sawyer" and "Limelight" were trying to find their legs at a time when synthetic pop acts like George Michael and Kenny G. were topping the charts. The one piece from their 1987 album to get radio play, "Time Stand Still," shows, in its pop-sounding melody and use of backing vocals by Aimee Mann of 'Til Tuesday, a willingness to abandon metal completely and stretch their idea of progressivism.

Only the album's opening piece, "Force 10," a last-minute addition to force a tenth title onto the tracklist (when people were still listening to music on cassette tapes), has the kind of hard-rock edge that the band's fan base tended to like.

Lyrically, drummer and main wordsmith Neil Peart was at his most earnest, and not necessarily in a good way. In "Tai' Shan," a piece that includes a sampled Japanese shakuhachi flute to evoke a sense of otherness, Peart recounts a climb he took two years earlier to a sacred Chinese site, Mount Tai, where visitors are said to have mystical experiences upon reaching the top. "High on the sacred mountain / Up the seven thousand stairs / In the golden light of autumn / There was magic in the air."

A little sophomoric, you might say of the lyrics. Rather pedestrian.

"You're supposed to be crappy when you make your first three or four records,"

Geddy Lee, the band's vocalist and bass player, says in a March 2009 *Blender* magazine interview. "When I listen to ['Tai' Shan'] it's like, 'Bzzt. Error.' We should have known better."[1]

But the album includes a very interesting piece. "Prime Mover" touches on a subject that you won't find many rock bands taking a stab at: teleology.

Teleology is the old Greek discipline of trying to articulate the design and purpose of the universe. In the most famous teleological argument of all time, depicted by Raphael on the ceiling of the Pope's private library in the Vatican,[2] you have Plato, pointing upward, positing the existence of a demiurge, and Aristotle, gesturing toward the ground, positing the existence of a prime mover.

Plato says this demiurge (or *demiourge*, "worker of the people"), which you can picture as an old bearded watchmaker, sets the gears and wheels of the world in motion. He's like a god, only with limited powers: a craftsman who sits between eternity, the world of Plato's timeless and ideal Forms, and the heavens, a replica of that ideal world here in our material world. Once he sets the gears and wheels of the world in motion, that's it. He can no more alter the trajectory of events than you or I can. If it helps, you can think of Plato's idea of the demiurge as the source of deism, the idea that God created the world but doesn't intervene in its affairs now that it's up and running.

Aristotle's prime mover is quite a bit different. Instead of *pushing* the world into existence by setting substance into motion, he *pulls* the world into existence by motivating, or inspiring, change, in the same way a saucer of milk motivates a cat to get up from her nap to slake her thirst. As Aristotle puts it in his *Metaphysics*, "[T]he object of desire and the object of thought move in this way; they move without being moved. The primary objects of desire and of thought are one and the same. . . . [T]he thinking is the starting-point."[3]

Aristotle's view is in many respects more intellectually satisfying than Plato's, because substance in the world is striving *toward* something, rather than just being a passive recipient *of* something. (For a really interesting contemporary take on this idea, read *What Technology Wants* (Viking Adult: 2010), by *Wired* magazine co-founder Kevin Kelly.) What's more, Aristotle makes room for the idea of chance, so the world isn't completely determined. As he puts it in his *Metaphysics*, "It is obvious that there are principles and

---

1 Geddy Lee calling "Tai' Shan" an error is in "Dear Superstar: Geddy Lee" in the March 2009 issue of *Blender* (which ceased publication one month later) and featured under the same title simultaneously in sister magazine *Maxim*.

2 The painting in which Plato is pointing upward, and Aristotle downward, is "The School of Athens" and is considered Raphael's masterpiece. Note that in Raphael's depiction of Plato, he's holding his *Timaeus*, which is the dialogue in which the demiurge is featured. You can learn more about the painting in Georgio Vasari's "Raphael of Urbino," in *Lives of the Artists*, Vol. I. Oxford: Oxford University Press, 1998.

3 Aristotle's passage on the object of desire and object of thought being one and the same is in his *Metaphysics*, 1072a26-31. Note that all references to Aristotle's texts are to Ross, W.D. *Aristotle's Metaphysics*, Vols. I and II. Oxford: Oxford University Press, 1948, and I'm using the Bekker number system.

causes, which are generable and destructible apart from the actual processes of generation and destruction, for if this is not true, everything will be of necessity."[1]

No excuse to get wild

What makes Rush's song "Prime Mover" interesting is that it tries to encapsulate the different perspectives of this teleological debate into five and a half minutes of rock, and it's pretty good rock at that. Rush is saying the world spins like a Platonic top that's been set in motion by its craftsman and is now just whirling randomly, with no purpose or aim. As Lee sings, "From the point of ignition / To the final drive / The point of the journey is not to arrive."

Two other verses make the same point about the lack of destination. "From a point on the compass / To magnetic north / The point of the needle moving back and forth" and "From the point of entry / Until the candle is burned / The point of departure is not to return."

These lines are all about randomness and existential absurdity, a theme Rush picks up again quite a number of times in later years, including in the title piece to its 1991 album *Roll the Bones*, when it asks, "Why are we here? / Because we're here / Roll the bones / Why does it happen? / Because it happens / Roll the bones."

In "Prime Mover," we're given a clear picture of the existential absurdity of our world, and then, at the bridge, or middle eight portion of the song, the point of view shifts from a neutral, omniscient narrator to the Platonic watchmaker who crafts everything. "I set the wheels in motion / Turn up all the machines / Activate the programs / And run behind the scene / I set the clouds in motion / Turn up light and sound / Activate the window / And watch the world go 'round."

Setting the wheels in motion, setting the clouds in motion, turning up light and sound . . . it all sounds a little like a creationist narrative, although of a very different kind than Genesis. It's the demiurge, who has one foot in eternity and the other in the material world, who creates the material world, but all he's doing is interpreting eternity as best he can using the gears and wheels of materiality to replicate the world of the gods in a very mechanical way. As Plato says of the demiurge in his *Timaeus*, he "resolves to have a moving image of eternity."[2]

So far, "Prime Mover" sounds like it has a lot to do with Plato's teleological theory and little to do with Aristotle. But Aristotle comes in when the piece talks about how we're supposed to *act* in this randomly spinning world.

---

1 Aristotle on there being principles and causes outside the process of generation and destruction (that is, chance) is in his *Metaphysics*, 1027a29.
2 Plato's passage about the demiurge making an image of eternity based in time is in his *Timaeus*, 37c-39e. Timaeus references are to Zeyl, D. J., trans. Plato: *Timaeus*. Indianapolis: Hackett, 1974, and I'm using the Stephanus pagination system.

On the one hand, we're spinning randomly to nowhere and it's all outside of our control. On the other hand, this existential reality doesn't mean we can just do what we want. It's true no one's minding the store, but if we run around willy-nilly, with no moral compass to guide us, our lives will be miserable and we'll make the lives of everyone around us miserable as well. Quality of life matters. It's not enough to hang on for the ride. If we want to achieve happiness and avoid existential despair, we have to temper our fun with a rational governor. That means editing our actions: putting up a "rational resistance to an unwise urge," as we hear in the song, or exercising "rational responses" to "force a change of plans."

Aristotle encapsulates this rational governor, or moral editing process, in which we use our reason to override our impulses, in two key words in his ethical philosophy: *akrasia* and *eudaimonia*.[1]

Akrasia is about our desire to pursue immediate pleasure (literally, "lack of mastery" over oneself), and *eudaimonia* is about our reaching true happiness, or excellence, an end-point requiring us to hold our pleasure-seeking in check.

With *eudaimonia*, it's not that we want to live our life as an old scold. Rather, we want to pursue life in a way that enables us to realize our true nature, our final cause, which is the source of true happiness and the antidote to existential despair. And we can't do that if we allow our lives to be completely subject to *akrasia*. So we seek balance, which Aristotle defines as the "mean" between deficiency and excess, as determined by our use of reason in pursuit of our true nature.

Purdue University Philosophy Professor Neil Florek does a good job describing *eudaimonia* in his essay "Free Wills and Sweet Miracles" in *Rush and Philosophy*. First, he says, it's up to each of us, using our reason, to determine how we ought to live, what we're aiming for, and what our ultimate goal is. Although he doesn't use these terms, this is very much like us acting as our own prime mover in that it's up to us to seek out our highest end. In that way our thoughts are volitional, like the prime mover's, because it's the thoughts that compel us or motivate us to achieve our highest end.

Once we identify what our end is, we seek to achieve it by developing our critical character traits, or virtues—prudence, justice, courage, moderation, and pride, among them—to their "peak form," as Florek puts it.[2]

In other words, first we will the end, and then we will the means to the end.

Of course, at the same time, we can't just elbow others out of our way as we pursue our ends. Those around us must be able to pursue their ends equally without hindrance from us or anyone else, because it's only when we're all treating one another with respect that our polis, or community, can thrive. To Aristotle, a thriving polis is what our individual freedom

---

1 Aristotle talks of eudaimonia (happiness) and akrasia (lack of mastery or incontinence) throughout his *Nicomachean Ethics*. His idea that happiness is an activity of the soul in accordance with virtue is summed up at 1098a16-19. "[H]uman good turns out to be activity of soul in accordance with virtue . . . in a complete life."
2 Berti and Bowman, *Rush and Philosophy*, pages 140-141.

is all about. Polis is "prior" to family and to individual. "[T]he state is by nature clearly prior to the family and to the individual, since the whole is of necessity prior to the part" is how Aristotle puts it in his *Politics*.[1]

Plato's moral view is quite a bit different. Although the polis is prior to the individual in his view as well, the way you achieve a strong polis is entirely different, and it's in this difference that we see so much of the power of Rush's lyrics.

On the idea that Aristotle and Plato see the role of the individual in society quite a bit differently, with Aristotle seeing the need for more individual autonomy vs. Plato's more restrictive view, it's worth quoting Zeller at some length:

> In this [Aristotle's] opposition to the Platonic socialism we shall not only recognize Aristotle's practical sense, his clear insight into the laws and conditions of actual life, his aversion to all ethical one-sidedness and his deep knowledge of human nature and of social life, but we shall not fail to observe that here, as in Plato, the political views are closely connected with the principles of the metaphysical system. Plato had demanded the abolition of all private possession and the suppression of all individual interests, because it is only in the Idea or Universal that he acknowledges any title to true reality. Aristotle refuses to follow him here. To him the Individual is the primary reality, and has the first claim to recognition. In his metaphysics individual things are regarded, not as the mere shadows of the idea, but as independent realities; universal conceptions not as independent substances, but as the expression for the common peculiarity of a number of individuals. Similarly in his moral philosophy he transfers the ultimate end of human action and social institutions from the State to the individual, and looks for its attainment in his free self-development. The highest aim of the State consists in the happiness of its citizens. The good of the whole rests upon the good of the citizens who compose it. In like manner must the action by which it is to be attained proceed from the individual of his own free will. It is only from within through culture and education, and not by compulsory institutions, that the unity of the State can be secured. In politics as in metaphysics the central point with Plato is the Universal, with Aristotle the Individual. The former demands that the whole should realize its ends without regard to the interests of individuals: the latter that it should be reared upon the satisfaction of all individual interests that have a true title to be regarded.
>
> — Costelloe, B.F.C., and J.H. Muirhead, trans. *Aristotle and the Earlier Peripatetics: Being a Translation from Zeller's 'Philosophy of the Greeks,'* Vol. II. London: Longman, Greens, and Co., 1897, pp. 224-226.

---

1 Aristotle's notion that the polis, or whole, takes priority to the individual, or part, is in his *Politics*, 1253a18-20.

As Plato sees it, in contrast to Aristotle, the rational governor we use to edit our actions shouldn't be used to help us achieve our own chosen ends. That would just produce chaos, because everyone will be acting in their own selfish interests. Rather, our rational governor should be used to conform our lives to our society's chosen ends, as determined by our leader, what Plato calls the philosopher-king.

The philosopher-king is the wisest man in the society and he dedicates his life to making the social order run as much like clockwork as possible. He is thus empowered to make the rules—not just for his own benefit, but for the benefit of everybody—and it's your responsibility as a member of the polis to do what he says and ask no questions, because you can't be expected to have the same insight he has. As Rush says in "Brought Up to Believe," one of the pieces from its 2012 album *Clockwork Angels*, the way of the world is "not ours to understand."

Thus, if you're deemed a worker by the philosopher-king, that's what you are, and your happiness comes from being the best worker you can be. If you're deemed a warrior (also called an auxiliary), your happiness is based on your fulfilling that role as best you can. And if you're deemed a leader, or guardian, you devote your life to making yourself knowledgeable so you can act with appropriate wisdom.[1] With everyone in society performing their roles as best they can, everyone is happy and the society is in balance, or "just," as Plato puts it. "When the trader, the auxiliary, and the guardian each do their own business, that is justice, and will make the city [society] just," Plato says in his *Republic*.[2]

Well, there's no doubt on which side Rush falls on these two different moral views: Aristotle's. We're all our own prime mover, and even if the world turns out to be existentially absurd, each of us has the freedom to discover and pursue our ultimate goal, and in so doing, we help strengthen the world around us.

Making sense of existential absurdity

"Prime Mover" is certainly one of the more thoughtful songs of a band that's known for having a rather philosophical take on things, and by some measure you can say it encapsulates the whole of Rush's view of the world. To take some liberties, if you could set down in one short paragraph the

---

1 The idea in Plato that the ideal society is divided into three parts (leaders, warriors, and workers) is known as the three classes of a just society. The portion of Plato's *Republic* dealing with rule of the philosophers is at 5.471c—5.502c.

2 Plato's view that achieving the ideal state requires it to be led by philosopher-kings is in his *Republic*, 5.473d. "[T]hose whom we now call our kings and rulers take to the pursuit of philosophy seriously and adequately, and there is a conjunction of these two things, political power and philosophic intelligence, while the motley horde of the natures who at present pursue either apart from the other are compulsorily excluded . . . ."

band's philosophy, as expressed over its 40-year career recording music, it might look something like this:

> We're in this world by chance. No one's in control. So, by all means let's have fun. But to really enjoy ourselves, we have to act responsibly. Otherwise, we'll be in the gutter by the time we're 25 and in the process we'll have dragged down those we love and respect, and, more broadly, made the world a worse place for everyone. For that reason, we have to think about our goals and act accordingly. If we approach life in this way, even if the world is existentially absurd, we at least have our own purpose. That purpose is to become the best person we can be. If each person pursues the goal of becoming the best person he or she can be, each of us will be capable of conferring on and receiving from others love and respect, and the world, as the ultimate beneficiary, will be the best it can be.

On this view, when Peart says in "Freewill," Rush's big radio hit from 1980, that he will "choose free will," he's saying he will determine what to strive for and how he will get there, even if the world itself is existentially absurd (an "aimless dance," as he calls the world in the song). He will *not* pursue a Platonic end in which he does what he's told to do by the powers that be, who claim to know the purpose of the world. Rather, he will be his own prime mover and seek out his own end. As Florek says of this exercise of individualism, "What we're really choosing when we 'choose free will' are autonomy and responsibility. . . . We must develop our capacity for rational self-direction (autonomy) and take responsibility for our own faults, strengths, failures, and successes."[1]

Peart revisited this idea in much more depth 25 years later, in Rush's *Clockwork Angels* album, which the band released in mid-2012 to much fanfare. (And much success, as it is. It debuted at No. 1 in Canada, the band's home country, No. 2 in the U.S. on the Billboard Top 200 chart, No. 1 on Amazon's best seller list for music, and No. 3 on iTunes.)[2]

Over the course of the album's 12 tracks, the world is presented as a randomly spinning top to nowhere, set in motion by something very much like Plato's demiurge and ruled by something very much like one of his philosopher-kings, in the character of an old bearded watchmaker. The world is not under the watchmaker's control, but he would very much have his subjects believe that it is. With this as the context, we meet our hero, Owen Hardy, whose passion, or *akrasia*, drives him to adventure but whose sense of reason, or rationality, enables him to reach a state of *eudaimonia*.

---

1 Berti and Bowman, *Rush and Philosophy*, page 142.
2 The debut chart position of *Clockwork Angels* is at Rush is a Band: http://www.rushisaband.com/blog/2012/06/20/3171/Rushs-Clockwork-Angels-debuts-at-2-on-the-Billboard-200 retrieved June 20, 2012.

In the end, he achieves true happiness and lives out his life in peace and harmony in a simple garden, basking in the love and respect of others.

Thus, in a world that's both completely determined and existentially absurd, our hero, acting as his own prime mover and taking advantage of the windows of opportunity provided by chance, exercises free will in pursuit of his goals. Put another way, we have an Aristotelian self-mover who breaks free of the duties imposed on him by the Platonic society into which he was born and achieves true happiness.

Against this framework, the album-length tale, which Peart says he based loosely on Voltaire's 1759 satire *Candide*, also serves as a scalding humanistic critique of religion in general and what might be called Leibnizian Christianity in particular. Leibnizian Christianity is the idea, formulated by the German mathematician and philosopher Gottfried Leibniz in his 1710 book *Theodicy*, that ours is the best of all possible worlds because it was created by God, whose omnipresence and omnipotence make it impossible for Him to create anything but the most perfect world.

(The full title of Leibniz's book is *Essays of Theodicy on the Goodness of God, the Freedom of Man and the Origin of Evil*. He also talks about this being the best of all possible worlds in his most famous work, *Monodology*, which lays out his metaphysical theory that the universe is comprised of unchangeable building blocks, called monads, that act in harmony with one another.)

With *Candide*, Voltaire mercilessly smashes the idea that ours is the best of all possible worlds, and with *Clockwork Angels*, Peart does the same thing, although he has the advantage of doing it in collaboration with his two band mates, Lee and Lifeson, because he gets to do it to some really epic music.

From Aristotle to Locke to Rand to Rush

The philosophies of Plato and Aristotle are huge mountain ranges, and in talking about aspects of their moral viewpoints it's hard to do more than just scratch the surface. But the broad outlines of the differences in the two approaches to ethics are clear: Plato is very much the philosopher of collectivism and Aristotle the philosopher of individualism.

With Plato, it's all about the society: you adapt yourself to society with the aim of furthering its goals as defined by the leader, the philosopher-king. It's about fitting in, doing your part, and in return receiving the benefits of the society whose bounty you help create. If you are in the leadership, your role is to lead; if you are in the auxiliary, your role is to protect; and if you are in the working class, your role is to produce. The world is the way it is and we can only passively play the role we are destined to play, and it's simply not our place to ask any questions about it.

That's not to say there isn't social mobility. But it's the role of the leadership to determine who exercises mobility and to what station in life they move. The leaders are the ones who are wise and whose temperament, intellect, training, and moral compass make them uniquely qualified to make decisions solely for the benefit of society.

If this sounds a lot like a totalitarian society, that's because it is. Plato is one of our greatest thinkers ever, but you can't sugarcoat this: he was no democrat. His republic is really a classic dictatorship. Probably no one has expressed this better than Karl Popper, the eminent twentieth-century British philosopher, who says in his 1962 book *The Open Society and Its Enemies: The Spell of Plato* (Princeton University Press), that Plato mistrusted individual freedom. "Excellent as Plato's sociological diagnosis was, his own development proves that the therapy he recommended [i.e., his *Republic*] is worse than the evil he tried to combat. . . . It seems to me to be a consistent and hardly refutable interpretation of the material to present Plato as a totalitarian party-politician, unsuccessful in his immediate and practical undertakings, but in the long run only too successful in his propaganda." Indeed, "Far from being morally superior to totalitarianism, Plato's political programme is fundamentally identical with it."[1]

Eduard Zeller, whose 1881 work *The Philosophy of Greeks in Their Historical Development* (Longmans, Green, and Co.) remains one of the standards of its genre, makes the exact same point:

> Plato had demanded the abolition of all private possession and the suppression of all individual interests, because it is only in the Idea or Universal that he acknowledges any title to true reality. . . . [And he] demands that the whole should realize its ends without regard to the interests of individuals.[2]

But Plato's totalitarianism isn't like any we're familiar with, because in his world his dictatorship is truly benevolent. As he sees it, leaders really *are* concerned for the welfare of the society. The people who make up the leadership genuinely *are* the right people for the job based on their temperament, intellect, training, and moral vision. The person who sits on top of this society genuinely *is* a philosopher-king, whose life is dedicated to using his knowledge and wisdom for the betterment of society as a whole. He's not out to live richly on the backs of the peasants, with a wink and a nod to social values; he's out to create a truly harmonious society. As Plato puts it in his *Republic*, no one who is a ruler would ever "consider and enjoin his own advantage but that of the one whom he rules and for whom he exercises his craft, and he keeps his eyes fixed on that and on what is advantageous and suitable to that in all that he says and does."[3]

1 The Karl Popper quote is from his book *The Open Society and Its Enemies: The Spell of Plato*. Princeton: Princeton University Press, 1962, and draws together passages on pages 87, 169, and 200.
2 B.F.C. Costelloe and J.H. Muirhead, trans. *Aristotle and the Earlier Peripatetics: Being a Translation from Zeller's 'Philosophy of the Greeks,'* Vol. II. London: Longman, Greens, and Co., 1897, pages 224-226.
3 The idea in Plato that the philosopher-kings only act on the needs of their society and not to their own advantage is in the *Republic*, 1.342e.

Pardon my reaction

It's hard to look at Plato's *Republic* and not, for lack of a more eloquent way of putting it, snort through your nose, as George Orwell was surely doing when he wrote his 1945 classic *Animal Farm*. The idea that the leaders of a socialist society will actually govern in the interests of the society seems naïve, to say the least. Creating a society in which leaders set aside their own ambitions to use their intellect and training for the benefit of society and not themselves is hardly plausible, and certainly not something we've seen in the real world, not in our lifetime and not historically.

What's more, even if such a society were to be successfully organized, is it plausible to think of the people as happy or fulfilled under such an arrangement? What about ambition? What about striving to make your mark? Can we really check our egos at the door and happily toil on behalf of the whole rather than for ourselves? In contrast to Plato, Aristotle clearly saw that burying our ambitions in this way simply isn't in our nature, because for all of us, no matter what our station in life, "living well and doing well"[1] is the universal goal, the object to which we're constantly being pulled by our nature. Whereas for Plato, the happiness level of any individual, regardless of his station in life, is simply not important, because it's only the overall smooth workings of the society that matter. "Our aim in founding the state [is] not the disproportionate happiness of any one class, but the greatest happiness of the whole."[2]

That's harsh—if you have the misfortune of being born a worker.

Even if the society's leaders are true philosopher-kings *and* the people are genuinely happy toiling for the good of the whole, the economic success or failure of the society to provide for its people depends entirely on the wisdom of the leaders. And it was the key insight of Austrian School economists like Ludwig von Mises and his 1974 Nobel Prize-winning student Friedrich Hayek that—regardless of what you think of the modern libertarianism that grew out of their work—even the wisest and most benevolent leaders simply can never know enough to manage a complex economy for optimal growth. It's simply not humanly possible. Because of the way information and knowledge is dispersed throughout an economy, only a market mechanism can lead to the efficient allocation of resources and the accurate setting of prices.

"It is through the mutually adjusted efforts of many people that more knowledge is utilized than any one individual possesses or than it is possible to synthesize intellectually," Hayek says in his 1960 book *The Constitution of Liberty* (University of Chicago Press), "and it is through such utilization of

---

1 Aristotle's "living well and doing well" quote is in his *Nicomachean Ethics*, 1095a18-19.
2 Plato on happiness for the whole rather than for the individual is in his *Republic*, 4.420b.

dispersed knowledge that achievements are made possible, greater than any single mind can foresee."[1]

Compared to Plato, the view of Aristotle, whom we can say without equivocation was an early free-marketer, is much more realistic and fulfilling. In his view, we're all running around trying to find ourselves, discover what's important to us and what we're best at. We're working for ourselves, and by doing so, it's the society as a whole that benefits, à la Adam Smith and his invisible hand of the market.

Again, it's Eduard Zeller who captures this idea in *The Philosophy of Greeks in Their Historical Development*:

> To [Aristotle] the Individual is the primary reality, and has the first claim to recognition . . . . [I]n his moral philosophy he transfers the ultimate end of human action and social institutions from the state to the individual, and looks for its attainment in his free self-development. The highest aim of the state consists in the happiness of its citizens. The good of the whole rests upon the good of the citizens who compose it. In like manner must the action by which it is to be attained proceed from the individual of his own free will. It is only from within through culture and education, and not by compulsory institutions, that the unity of the state can be secured. [2]

Anyone familiar with Rush's music over its 40-year career will recognize the Aristotelian roots of the lyrics. In song after song, whether it's to be your own change-maker in "Something for Nothing," on the band's *2112* album, or to let yourself think big in "Caravan," in *Clockwork Angels*, the message that we get is pure Aristotle: identify your goals, make your mark, live for yourself, go out and achieve, and everyone else will benefit by your doing so.

This is what Aristotle's virtuousness is all about. It's all about the kind of person you develop into over the course of your life as you first seek your own ends, rather than passively accept your role in life, and then summon, or will, the power to achieve them.

This Aristotelian attitude is arguably one of the characteristics of Rush that has made the band so intuitively attractive, even to listeners who've never had the vocabulary to articulate what they hear in the music. Who doesn't want to have the freedom to find his or her aims in life and then will the power to achieve them? That's certainly been Rush's message throughout its career. And that's what we'll be looking at next.

---

1 Friedrich Hayek, *The Constitution of Liberty*. Chicago: University of Chicago Press, 1960, page 82.
2 B.F.C. Costelloe and J.H. Muirhead, *Aristotle and the Earlier Peripatetics*, Vol. II, pp. 224-226.

Chapter 2. Individualism: Some Geddit, Some Don't

> I'm old enough not to care too much
> About what you think of me
> But I'm young enough to remember the future
> And the way things ought to be
> —"Cut to the Chase," *Counterparts, 1993*

Since the late 1970s Rush's music has been typecast by many in the media as right-wing or libertarian. "Right-wing Canadian prog-metal heroes" is how *Time Out*, London's entertainment guide, put it rather characteristically in a 2004 article.[1] Or the *National Review*: "Before there was Rush Limbaugh, there was Rush, a Canadian band whose lyrics are often libertarian."[2]

The libertarian reference makes sense, because you can find libertarian ideas in the band's music, particularly in the early years, and Peart to this day describes himself variously as a "quasi-libertarian," "bleeding-heart libertarian," or "left-leaning" libertarian.[3]

But the right-wing label has never made much sense. To be sure, libertarianism is a right-of-center political and economic philosophy, because it shares with the right a preference for small government. But the two couldn't be more different on social matters.

Libertarianism is socially progressive. It holds that people should be allowed to do what they want as long as they don't impede the ability of others to do what they want. So on all those hot-button social issues like same-sex marriage,

---

1 Neil Peart, *Roadshow: Landscape with Drums*. Toronto: ECW Press, 2007, page 312.
2 "Rockin' the Right: The 50 Greatest Conservative Rock Songs," *National Review*, May 26, 2006.
3 You can find Peart's various descriptions of himself as a libertarian in Neil Peart, *Far and Away: A Prize Every Time*. Toronto: ECW Press, 2011, pages 88 and 261, and in Peart, *Roadshow*, page 313, among other places.

separation of church and state, drug use, capital punishment, right to die, abortion, immigration, and others, libertarians, if they're true to their creed, fall in the same camp as liberals. Live and let live.

That's a far cry from the sniffy intolerance of the right wing, whose partisans want to keep men from marrying men or women from marrying women even though such unions have no impact on anyone's lives but those involved.

In any case, one of the consequences of having your name bandied about as right-wing or libertarian is that you end up in sometimes strange and maybe not always welcomed company. A good example is when Kate Zernike of the *Washington Post* came out with *Boiling Mad* (Times Books), her 2010 book on the Tea Party. In her description of a campaign stop by Rand Paul, the Tea Party favorite from Kentucky who went on to win a seat in the U.S. Senate the year her book came out, she tossed off the libertarian label as if it were an understood fact about the band, even though a critical look at the band's music will show a far more nuanced and complicated viewpoint.

> Paul stayed long at every stop, and he gave expansive, sometimes rambling answers. His message was more apocalyptic than the usual uplift of the politician's speech. "The end is coming, the times are growing short to fix the situation," he said ominously. He often quoted Thomas Paine—"These are the times that try men's souls"—or the Canadian band Rush, known for their libertarian views: "Glittering prizes and endless compromises / Shatter the illusion of integrity." The glittering prizes, Paul told the audience outside Ol' Harvey's, were the pork-barrel projects that politicians bring home even though there is no money to pay for them. It was like the last days of Rome, he told the audience, where leaders used bread and circuses to placate the mob.[1]

By all indications, Rand Paul is indeed enthralled with the band. This will be old news to Rush fans, but during his 2010 run for office he liked to have his speeches introduced by Rush's big 1981 hit "Tom Sawyer," and he even went further than simply having the music playing when he took the podium; he liked to use Rush's music in his speeches didactically—that is, to explain his position on issues. In one instance that became something of an Internet meme, he used one of Rush's more commercially popular songs, "The Trees," from 1977, as a jumping off point for talking about the differences between equality of opportunity, which he likes, and equality of outcome, which he doesn't.

"I do like the lyrics to a song," he said at one of his campaign stops, "and I'd like to tell you, this is a song called 'Trees,' by Rush."

The song has something of a cartoonish feel to it and in fact Peart says he was thinking of Dr. Seuss-like trees arguing with one another when he wrote

1 Kate Zernike, *Boiling Mad: Inside Tea Party America.* New York: Times Books, 2010, page 171.

the lyrics. It's about the maples getting upset at the oaks for hogging all the sunlight, and, in a plot development straight out of *Atlas Shrugged*, Ayn Rand's 1957 anti-collectivism novel, the maples retaliate by getting the government to make all the trees equal "by hatchet, axe, and saw."[1]

After quoting the opening verse—"There is unrest in the forest / There is trouble with the trees"—Paul explains how the song illustrates the difference between government policies that take an economically liberal approach (equality of outcome), and those that take an economically conservative approach (equality of opportunity).

What we see in the song, he says, is government stepping in and cutting all the trees to equal sizes, and that "is what happens if you want equal outcomes."[2]

Whatever you think of the song, and whatever you think of Paul, you can't deny that the tree analogy is spot-on for launching into conservative talking points about the role of government in society, so it would be ungenerous to fault Paul using the piece in the way he did. But if you were a rock band, given the polarizing nature of his politics, would you want Rand Paul running around linking himself to your stuff like that? One wouldn't think so, and Rush made it clear it didn't.

Shortly after a video surfaced of Paul making this remark, Bob Farmer, attorney for Anthem Entertainment Group, Rush's management company, sent the Paul campaign a letter requesting that it stop using Rush's material at its events. "The public performance of Rush's music is not licensed for political purposes," Farmer said in his May 25, 2010, letter. "Accordingly, we hereby demand that Dr. Rand Paul and the Rand Paul For U.S. Senate campaign immediately stop all use of Rush's music and remove all references to Rush and their music in all campaign materials. In addition, all videos using Rush music (such as the one noted above) must be removed."[3]

The videos were in fact removed (to the extent you can remove anything from the Internet) but Paul continues to use Rush as his music of choice at his political appearances. As recently as his 2012 Republican National Convention appearance in Tampa, Fla., in which he was featured as a keynote speaker on the third night, he took the stage to the opening beats

---

1 The Maples' retaliation is also straight out of the 1962 Kurt Vonnegut short story "Harrison Bergeron," which Steven Horwitz points out in his essay "Rush's Libertarianism Never Fit the Plan," in Berti and Bowman, *Rush and Philosophy*, page 261. In the Vonnegut story, as Horwitz relates it, equality is maintained by forcing the strong to wear weights and the smart to hear disruptive buzzers in the ears.

2 The video of Rand Paul talking about "The Trees" is online at *The Week*, among other places: http://video.theweek.com/video/Rand-Pauls-spoken-word-of-Rush#c=VLJ3NTIL6ISG0TPQ&t=Rand%20Paul%20reads%20Rush%20lyrics%20at%20public%20event retrieved October 1, 2012.

3 You can read Bob Farmer's cease and desist letter to the Rand campaign at *Rush Vault*: http://rushvault.com/2011/09/24/one-year-later-is-rand-paul-still-rocking-to-rush/ retrieved November 1, 2012.

of . . . "Tom Sawyer."[1]

And it wasn't just Paul who did so. In both a funny and curious prelude to Paul's entrance that night, the Senate Minority Leader, Mitch McConnell (Ky.), arguably not the hippest cat to stride the Senate floor, was introduced in all his sniffiness to the same pounding beat of . . . "Tom Sawyer."

With friends like these . . .

The fact is, at least in the United States, more than a few conservative politicians, policymakers, and political commentators have attached themselves to the band in some fashion. And that's a weight the band must carry with it.

In what might be one of the more famous tweets among Rush fans, John Kasich, the Republican governor of Ohio, home of the Rock and Roll Hall of Fame, sent out a tweet in 2011 complaining that the Rock and Roll Hall of Fame had yet again passed over Rush for a nomination. "Just met w/Rock & Roll Hall of Fame board & demanded to know why @RushtheBand isn't in the @Rock_Hall of Fame," he said.[2]

Maybe Kasich, a former long-time congressman who chaired the influential House Budget Committee in the late 1990s, is more influential in the rock world[3] than was understood at the time, because lo and behold, the very next year, in 2012, Rush was indeed among the list of nominees, and it even went on to win induction. (Heart, Randy Newman, Public Enemy, and, posthumously, Donna Summer and Albert King, were the others.) Good job, Governor!

In any case, there are a couple of other prominent conservatives whose affinity for the band is instructive, starting with Neel Kashkari, the self-avowed "free-market Republican" who enjoyed his 15 minutes of fame when he was administrator of the much-criticized post-financial-meltdown bank bailout in the U.S. known as TARP, when George W. Bush was president.

The forty-something Kashkari, many might recall, endured a ribbing in the media in 2008 when a page from his 1991 yearbook from the tony private

1 A video of Paul taking the stage at the Republican National Convention in 2012 to the beat of "Tom Sawyer" is at *Rush Vault*: http://rushvault.com/2012/08/30/tom-sawyer-still-welcoming-in-rand-paul-at-events/ retrieved November 3, 2012.
2 Gov. John Kasich's Rush tweet is at *Rush is a Band*: http://www.rushisaband.com/blog/2011/05/17/2636/Ohio-governor-John-Kasich-wonders-why-Rush-isnt-in-the-Rock-Hall retrieved November 10, 2012.
3 Actually, it probably didn't hurt that a former Rush A&R representative, Cliff Burnstein, who had a big role in the band's first contract with a major American label, Mercury, had recently joined the Rock Hall nominating committee. No one in the music business has ever accused the Rock Hall of not being influenced by who sits on its nominating committee. It also probably didn't hurt that in 2012 the Rock Hall for the first time opened the process to outside voting. Although the outside votes only counted as one part of the selection process, it would be hard to ignore the nominee that got the most votes, and in 2012, it was Rush.

school Western Reserve Academy in Hudson, Ohio, became an Internet meme and spread word far and wide that he lists among his favorite quotes "A modern day warrior / Mean mean stride / Today's Tom Sawyer / Mean mean pride" from "Tom Sawyer," and the Shakespearean line incorporated by Rush into its 1981 radio hit "Limelight," "All the world's indeed a stage / And we are merely players."[1]

Not to pile onto Kashkari, who can't seem to catch a break, at least in the media, but he's probably not someone a band would go out of its way to cultivate as a celebrity fan,[2] if only because he's such a lightning rod for criticism from both the left and the right. The snarky news site *Gawker* seems to absolutely loathe him.[3]

This animosity doesn't seem to be spurred by his affection for Rush. But it might have something to do with how he, as an avowed "free-market Republican," could have even taken such a job as administrator of TARP when its very existence as a government program goes against everything a free-marketer is supposed to stand for.

The great sin of TARP ("Troubled Asset Relief Program"), to refresh your memory, wasn't just its Keynesian approach to solving the 2007 mortgage crisis; it was the cavalier way in which the big banks took some $700 billion in taxpayers' money to buy back the banks' worthless subprime loans, but instead of doing that (the goal was to put a price floor under the collapsing market for mortgage-backed securities), they bought back their own corporate stock! In other words, instead of using the money to shore up their bad debt, they used it to inflate their equity.[4]

It's worth mentioning one more high-profile right-leaning personality who advertises his fondness for the band, or at least uses the band's music to reinforce his philosophy, and that's none other than the other Rush—Rush Limbaugh.

It's painful to write this, but Limbaugh had Rush's "The Spirit of Radio" playing in the background when in 2012 he denounced Sandra Fluke for her stand on the use of public subsidies to fund contraception.

---

1 Neel Kashkari's yearbook page featuring his Rush quotes is at *Gawker*: http://gawker.com/5066012/neel-ferrari-kashkari-the-us-bailout-chiefs-epic-high-school-yearbook retrieved November 15, 2012.
2 While Kashkari might not be a sought-after endorser of Rush, Stephen Colbert arguably is, and he seems to be quite a fan, or at least his producer is, as we learn from Rush's July 16, 2008, appearance on the show, a video of which is at *Colbert Nation*: http://www.colbertnation.com/the-colbert-report-videos/176346/july-16-2008/rush-is-here retrieved November 17, 2012.
3 The snarky Kashkari references are at *Gawker*: http://gawker.com/5066012/neel-ferrari-kashkari-the-us-bailout-chiefs-epic-high-school-yearbook retrieved November 15, 2012.
4 The controversy over how banks used TARP funds vs. how they were intended to use them was covered quite a bit in 2009. Here are a few examples: "Bailout Is a Windfall to Banks, if Not to Borrowers," New York Times, January 17, 2009, and "Accountability for the Troubled Asset Relief Program: The Second Report of the Congressional Oversight Panel," January 9, 2009.

Fluke, you might recall, was the Georgetown University graduate student who earlier that year had testified before Congress in favor a federal rule requiring hospitals receiving federal funds, including church-affiliated hospitals like Georgetown University's, to pay for patients' birth control pills. Limbaugh, in his inimical way, demanded Fluke videotape herself having sex and post it online so taxpayers could get something for their money.

"Ms. Fluke and the rest of you feminazis, here's the deal," Limbaugh said on his February 29, 2012, show. "If we are going to pay for your contraception, and thus pay for you to have sex, we want something for it, and I'll tell you what it is. We want you to post the videos online so we can all watch."[1]

Once again, Bob Farmer, Rush's lawyer, trotted out his cease and desist letter. "The public performance of Rush's music is not . . . " yada, yada, yada. He sent the letter on March 6, 2012.[2]

Not only are they right wing, but they're fascist

Tracing the origins of a cultural trope is never easy to do, especially when it dates back to pre-Internet days. But the knowing nod to Rush as a right wing band surely got its biggest boost from what is widely recognized as the band's most infamous interview, with Barry Miles of New Musical Express, on May 18, 1978, when Miles called the band members' views "proto-fascist" and likened some of their stances to "shades of the 1,000-year Reich."[3]

The publication goes by its acronym, NME, which sounds like "enemy" when spoken out loud. And it was certainly Rush's enemy in this interview.

The piece came out after a long and, by Peart's account, stimulating conversation the band had had with Miles while they were in London in February on their *A Farewell to Kings* tour and were just about to come out with their *Hemispheres* album.

Hemispheres, it's worth noting, was released a few months later and was the band's seventh studio album. It helped solidify Rush as an originator of the progressive metal genre. Its side-long title piece, "Cygnus X-1 Book II: Hemispheres," was an extended metaphor about the battle between the two halves of our brain, the emotional, creative side and the rational, calculating side. The two sides battle to a draw and it takes a space traveler, whom we met on the closing track of the band's previous album, *A Farewell to Kings*, to bring the two sides together. He travels through the black hole Cygnus X-1

---

1 A video of Rush Limbaugh making his Sandra Fluke remark with "The spirit of Radio" playing in the background is at *Rush Vault*: http://rushvault. com/2012/03/07/memo-to-rush-limbaugh-rush-the-band-is-not-right-wing/ retrieved November 18, 2012.
2 Bob Farmer's cease-and-desist letter for Rush Limbaugh is at *Rush Vault*: http://rushvault.com/2012/03/07/memo-to-rush-limbaugh-rush-the-band-is-not-right-wing/ retrieved November 18, 2012.
3 A partial transcript of the Barry Miles NME interview with Rush, along with links to the actual article, is at *Rush Vault*: http://rushvault.com/2011/07/27/ barry-miles-big-mistake/ retrieved November 19, 2012.

to reach this battling world and do his good deed.

That surely sounds like a strange concept, and it is, but for many of the band's fans, it helped solidify what they like about Rush's music: it's highly conceptual, uses narrative story-telling, and really shakes the rafters.

In any case, on this 1978 tour, Rush was now a headline act, with London boogie rock band Tyla Gang opening for them on the U.K. dates, and it was attracting growing crowds. Miles, who went on to a notable career as a biographer of Bob Dylan, The Beatles, Frank Zappa, and other rock acts, as well as Beat Generation poets Allen Ginsberg, Jack Kerouac, and others, volunteered for the interview because of the band's Ayn Rand connection. As he puts it, "I got the job of interviewing Rush because I was the only one on NME who knew who Ayn Rand was—simple as that."

To be sure, the band had only itself to blame for this Ayn Rand connection. Peart at the time was genuinely interested in her philosophy and both intentionally and unintentionally was incorporating her ideas into the band's music. For a band to be talking about Ayn Rand in the late 1970s, when music critics and other rock bands and really the popular music industry as a whole were still in the throes of a 1960s counter-establishment ethos, was . . . courageous, to say the least. As Peart himself put it in a 1997 interview with *Liberty*, a libertarian journal, "There was a remarkable backlash, especially from the English press—this being the late 70s, when collectivism was still in style, especially among journalists."[1]

"The connection with Ayn Rand definitely was a media turnoff," says Cliff Burnstein, an A&R rep who at the time was with the band's American label, Mercury Records. "There was certainly a kind of association with the 50's, conservatism, the McCarthy years, all this stuff probably made the media think, 'Well, this is just not my kind of band.'" Burnstein made his remark in a 2010 DVD on the making of Rush's *2112* and *Moving Pictures* albums by Eagle Rock Entertainment.[2]

In a nutshell, Rand's philosophy is a brand of secular individualism, the polar opposite of the communitarian utopianism that you could find in the music of, say, Joan Baez, Phil Ochs, and, in his earliest incarnation, Bob Dylan, among other 1960s folk and rock idealists.

It's worth digressing a moment to talk about Rand here. To be fair to her, her philosophy is not at all unreasonable. Once you separate it from her as an individual and the rather ham-handed way in which she conveys it in her novels, you see it's not the kooky line of thought critics paint it as. Her philosophy is simply about the individual, driven by his own ambition, who identifies what he wants to do, does it, and helps lift up society as a whole as a result. The idea is that, when you step back and look at this picture from on

---

1 "Who is Neil Peart?" by Scott Bullock, *Liberty*, September 1997.
2 The Cliff Bernstein remark about the band's Ayn Rand connection any why that wasn't good can be found at *Objectivist Blogspot*: http://objectivish.blogspot.com/2010_09_01_archive.html retrieved November 22, 2012. It originally appeared in *2112-Moving Pictures*, a DVD by Eagle Rock Entertainment, released September 28, 2010.

high, and see the millions of people striving to achieve great things for their own self-centered reasons (and, importantly, secure in the rights to their intellectual property), you see Adam Smith's hidden hand of the marketplace at work and you get a very successful, Aristotelian-based society. And that's what Rand saw when she emigrated from her native communist Russia to the United States in 1926: a very successful society (at least, after it got through the Great Depression).

In short, with Rand, if you give credence to Adam Smith's invisible hand of the marketplace idea, which people in the United States generally do, at least in rhetoric, then you should have no quarrel with Rand, because all she did was build a philosophy around that idea.

The United States, in her view, despite its many and obvious shortcomings, was the closest thing to utopia on earth because of its emphasis on individualism. As she puts it in *Atlas Shrugged*, her most important work, "To the glory of mankind, there was, for the first and only time in history, a country of money—and I have no higher, more reverent tribute to pay to America," her character Francisco d'Antonia says in the novel, "for this means a country of reason, justice, freedom, production, achievement. For the first time, man's mind and money were set free, and there were no fortunes-by-conquest, but only fortunes-by-work; and instead of swordsmen and slaves, there appeared the real maker of wealth, the greatest worker, the highest type of human being—the self-made man—the American industrialist."[1]

Compared to utilitarianism, other secular ethical philosophies, and even Judeo-Christian moralities, with their reliance on the miraculous, Rand's Objectivism holds its own just fine, at least when it's understood to be a framework and not a set of rigid rules, and Rand does a much better job in her non-fiction writings defending her views than critics give her credit for. But, again, she tended to be dismissed by academics and often invited eye-rolling because of her over-cooked literary approach. Her characters, like John Galt of *Atlas Shrugged*, are simply ridiculous. "We, the men of the mind, are now on strike against you in the name of a single axiom, which is at the root of our moral code," Galt says in his dramatic, *64-page* (!) wrap-up speech, "the axiom that *existence exists*."[2]

People just don't *talk* like that. And—I'm not being flip here—her heroes come across as having clinical personality disorders. They simply cannot relate to ordinary people on an emotional level. In a typical moment, after a highly emotional outburst by his wife, Henry Rearden, one of the heroes of *Atlas Shrugged*, simply looks at his wife like she's an alien, "feeling nothing but the emptiness of wonder."[3]

The only thing that gets the motors of Rand's heroes revving is efficiency, and when they're in the presence of *that*, it's a sensuous, even fetishistic, experience: "She was flying [in a train car]. . . at a rate of 100 miles an hour,"

1 Ayn Rand, *Atlas Shrugged*. New York: Signet, 1957, page 384.
2 Ibid., *Atlas Shrugged*, page 929.
3 Ibid., *Atlas Shrugged*, page 489.

the narrator says of Dagny Taggart, the severely beautiful industrialist heroine who knows how to make the trains run on time and appreciates a hard, straight railroad shaft. "She leaned to an open window by her side and felt the wind of the speed blowing her hair of her forehead. She lay back, conscious of nothing but the pleasure it gave her."[1] La, la, la, I plug my ears. It's just too, too much.

In any event, it was against the background of this Randian connection that the NME interview took place, and what Miles took away from the conversation compared to what the band members took away from it were two very different things.

The article that came out is called "Is everybody feelin' all RIGHT? (Geddit . . . ?),"[2] and for Miles, what Peart and Lee said came across as outside the mainstream in the extreme, bordering on a radical right-wing ideology.

What the band appeared to be doing, as Miles described it in his narrative, was surreptitiously pushing their right-wing ideology onto tens of thousands of unsuspecting young men. As he put it, you have these three terribly nice Canadians—"polite, charming, even naive"—but they're "roaming the concert circuits preaching what to me seems like proto-fascism like a leper without a bell."

The band's sin, in his eyes, was its use of rock and roll, the music of social consciousness and rebellion, to extol a point of view that the board of directors of IBM would love:

Laissez-faire capitalism is good.
Private property is good.
Private charity is good.
State-owned business is bad.
Unions (big, government-supported ones) are bad (small ones are okay).
Taxes are bad.

Peart even committed the sin of saying that the anger and rage in punk rock, which at the time was exploding onto the scene throughout Europe and North America, might ostensibly have been directed at the rich and their capitalist money-making machines. But its underlying cause wasn't capitalist inequality at all but rather left-wing government policies that coddled people and sucked the oxygen out of the free-market economy.

As Peart had put it, "The reason that these kids are growing up and feeling that there's no future for them is because there simply isn't. If they don't join the union, and go to work with all their mates, then they're lost. There's nothing else they can do."

Miles, who wrote himself into the article as a first-person observer, said in response, "Fighting against socialism? I couldn't believe what I was hearing."

---

1 Ibid., *Atlas Shrugged*, page 226.
2 A partial transcript of the Barry Miles NME interview with Rush, along with links to the actual article, is at *Rush Vault*: http://rushvault.com/2011/07/27/barry-miles-big-mistake/ retrieved November 19, 2012.

Peart went on: "With overly prescriptive government, your freedom is negated. You have no freedom. You do what you're told to do: by the socialists, by the good of the people."

When Miles protested that the profit motive of multinational corporations would hardly make them trustworthy stewards of people's interests, Peart replied that labor flexibility is one of the beauties of capitalism. No one is being forced to work for a company whose policies are anathema to your values, he said. "You can just quit!"

Then, in what must be one of rock journalism's most stunning leaps of logic, Miles responded by equating capitalist freedom to quit and move to another job with Nazism:

> "So now I understood the freedom he was talking about," said Miles, "freedom for employers and those with money to do what they like and freedom for the workers to quit (and starve) or not. Work makes free. Didn't I remember that idea from somewhere? 'Work Makes Free.' Oh, yes, it was written over the main gateway to Auschwitz concentration camp."

Ouch!

Miles went on: "They are actually very nice guys. They don't sit there in jackboots pulling the wings off flies." But, he continued, that doesn't change the fact that they're preaching "what to me seems like proto-fascism."

Other writers, particularly in the U.K., picked up the right-wing label and perpetuated it, mainly in the 1980s and 1990s. A typical example is the way British music critic Paul Stump in his 1998 book on progressive rock, *The Music's All That Matters* (Quartet Books, 1997), summarized the band's music as "a social prescription of great toxicity."[1]

And outside of the music world there were the fringe groups, like the U.K. neo-Nazi group Young National Front, whose ears perked up at these references and in its magazine *Bulldog* called Rush's music "Nazi rock . . . Aryans and fascists who aren't afraid to admit it."[2]

"They were calling us 'Junior Fascists' and 'Hitler lovers,'" Peart would say years later. "It was a total shock to me."[3]

Peart went on to dismiss Miles as "a pasty, scruffy, humorless, left-wing 'intellectual,'" who had "written a sensationalized exposé, portraying us pretty much as standard-bearers for the Hitler Youth. To my shock and horror, he twisted the libertarian notions of an idealistic twenty-four-year-old drummer and lyricist into the darkly sardonic words above the gates of many Nazi concentration camps."[4]

1 The Paul Stump line about the "great toxicity" of Rush's music is in *The Music's All That Matters: A History of Progressive Rock*. London: Quartet Books, 1998, page 257.
2 The reference to the neo-Nazi Young National Front is in "Permanent Raves," by John Gill, *Sounds*, March 14, 1981.
3 "Who is Neil Peart?" by Scott Bullock, *Liberty*, September 1997.
4 Peart, *Roadshow*, page 313.

It was especially insulting to the Jewish Lee (born Gary Lee Weinrib), whose mother was interred in Bergen-Belsen, and his father in Dachau, during World War II. And both of them spent time in Auschwitz, which means both of them could very well have walked under the infamous gate that Miles had connected to their son's music.

Lee expressed his disgust years later in an interview with the British music magazine *Sounds*. "I got over that a long time ago but at the time it really bothered me. The guy who wrote that story. . . . Let's face it. He didn't know what the hell he was talking about."[1]

Miles in a June 2012 piece in another British magazine, *Mojo*, says he was "surprised by the furor" that his interview caused. But, he went on, "I stand by what I wrote. Societies that fail to protect the weak pave the way for fascism."[2]

Both Lee and Peart later tried to express their feelings about the Holocaust. On "Grace to Grace," the closing track of his 2000 solo album, *My Favorite Headache*, Lee talks about all the "eloquent stories" that will never get told because of the journey so many people took on those "hundred thousand miles of track" that led to the death camps.

"Along with most members of my family," Lee said in a *Rockline* interview shortly after his album came out, "my mom came over after the war and [she and my dad] went through their own private hell. She's conducted her life in a completely elegant and heroic way. She had most of her dreams stolen from her as a child and there are so many people like her that have gone through tragedies or wars or whatever and they pick up and just carry on."[3]

Partly inspired by the story of Lee's mother, Peart in Rush's "Red Sector A," on the band's 1984 album *Grace Under Pressure*, tries to put the listener in the place of survivors of the Holocaust and other acts of inhumane internment. At the time they're liberated, Peart said in interviews, prisoners often believe they're the last people left alive in the world. It's almost like a natural defense mechanism kicks in to protect them against the reality that people allow such terrible things to happen.

"When people were released from that kind of incredible confinement, and incredible inhumanity, they believed that no one else in the world existed," Peart said in a 2011 *In the Studio with Redbeard* radio interview, "because they couldn't believe that anyone else would let that go on."[4]

1 "Another Round of . . . RUSH 'N' ROULETTE," *Sounds*, May 7, 1988, page 22.
2 "Rush: Revenge of the Nerds," by Paul Elliott, in the June 2012 issue of *Mojo* magazine. In that same article, Lee was quoted as saying, "It didn't hurt our career per se, but it definitely hurt our image. And it just felt so cruel. But I think there was a huge divide between being a North American and being a Brit at that time. In Britain it was a very politically charged time."
3 *Rush Vault*: http://rushvault.com/2011/04/03/grace-to-grace-background/ retrieved November 15, 2012.
4 *Rush Vault*: http://rushvault.com/2012/02/04/red-sector-a-riffing-on-the-dignity-of-survival/ retrieved November 16, 2012.

Left as much as right

Lee's charge that Miles didn't know "what the hell he was talking about" is certainly right on the mark, at least on the question of whether Peart's views betrayed a right-wing ideology.

Whatever the Nazis were, they were no more right-wing than left-wing; typical of a fascist regime, they employed both wings in the service of their radical nationalism. Indeed, the consensus among historians is that, as a party, the Nazis never had a coherent economic philosophy. Like other fascist regimes, they mixed extensive social welfare programs and state-sponsored make-work programs with what remained of the hybrid capitalist-socialist economy under the Weimar Republic, which preceded the Nazis' rise to power in the 1930s.

As Stephen J. Lee and Paul Shuter say in their book *Weimar and Nazi Germany,* "The ideology of Nazism had no underlying economic component: there was no equivalent to the [Marxist] notion of political change occurring through the dialectical conflict between classes exerting their economic interest. Nazism was fundamentally racist and *völkisch* in its conception, and economic factors were always subordinate."[1]

In other words, the Nazis had no ideology beyond their authoritarian nationalism, racism, and militarism. They wanted to grow the economy so they could put the country on a war footing, and they didn't really care how it was done: right or left, they would deploy whatever economic prescriptions worked.

In Miles' defense, he arguably saw in Peart's remarks a sympathy for the kind of corporate socialism that's historically been at the heart of the fascist economic program. Under this view, corporations and the state work in concert with one another, with little sympathy for workers as a class, to further the prosperity of the state as a nationalist entity.

Plenty of what Peart said that day, such as his defense of factory owners' pursuit of wealth, would feed into this view. As Peart told Miles of the factory owner, he's "taking steps to achieve his needs, through his own initiative. . . . Private property is the most inviolable private right of all. If you own it, it's yours. Simple truth. If you own it, it belongs to you. You do what you want with it." That fits into fascists' heroic, social Darwinist ideal of the "economic warrior" who would exploit workers as needed to help the fascist state achieve greatness.

But the similarity ends there, because for an individualist like Peart, private-property rights are valued as a tool for helping individuals as they strive for self-perfection, not as a tool to exploit workers in the name of corporate-state efforts to achieve nationalist greatness.

For that reason, when Miles makes the leap from Peart's comment about labor flexibility to the "Work Makes Free" sign above the main gate

1 Stephen J. Lee, *European Dictatorships, 1918-1945.* 3rd ed. New York: Routledge, 1, page 223.

at Auschwitz, he could scarcely have had Peart's individualist frame of reference in mind.

Incidentally, "Work Makes Free" ("*Arbeit macht frei*") wasn't even a Nazi slogan; it was used as early as 1928 by the Weimar Republic in support of its public works program—that is, state-sponsored spending projects—to offset the economically punitive effects of the Treaty of Versailles after World War I. When the Nazis assumed power, they simply retained the phrase and cynically used it in support of their own economic priorities.[1]

Even from a political perspective, Miles' comment makes little sense, because everything Peart (and the other band members) talked about with him during the interview emphasized individualism—that is, maximum political *freedom*—and not the authoritarianism of the Nazis. As Peart had put it, "The government's only functions are to protect the rights of the individual."

You couldn't have a point of view more opposed to the totalitarianism of the Nazis than that. It's perhaps too obvious to even point this out, but in Nazi Germany under the concept of *Führerprinzip* the government did whatever Hitler and his ministers told it to do. And under the regime's *volksgerichtshof* court system, jurists could pretty much sentence to prison or even death anyone charged with political crimes. By some estimates, completely separate from the death camps and everything else that was going on, more than 7,000 German citizens were put to death simply for getting politically cross-eyed with the regime.

In short, whether it's from an economic, social, or political standpoint, Miles' linking of the individualism in Rush's music to fascism makes little sense. It appears to be as uninformed as it is repellent, yet the remark lingered for years, and unthinking journalists and music critics simply picked up the label and carried it forward. "With four or five music papers to fill every week, the often bitter and resentful scriveners could be as lazy, irresponsible, and shameless as their counterparts in the celebrity tabloids," Peart says in his book *Roadshow* of the British music press of the 1970s and 1980s when the right-wing label was bandied about most promiscuously.[2]

Of course, even by trying to show how wrong-headed Miles' remark is, you risk perpetuating the insult, because by treating it seriously, you're giving it validation it doesn't deserve. But it's important to at least mention Miles' interview, because it remains a chief link in the reason Rush has been stuck with the right-wing label for so much of its career.

---

1 Information on the origins of "Arbeit Macht Frei" is in a fact sheet by the same name on Princeton University's web site: http://www.princeton. edu/-achaney/tmve/wiki100k/docs/Arbeit_macht_frei.html retrieved December 1, 2012.
2 Peart, *Roadshow*, page 313.

Peart's chance at rebuttal

NME did eventually give Peart a chance to set the record straight. A little more than a year later, Peart was invited to talk with another writer from the publication, John Hamblett, who gave Peart plenty of space to vent. Peart had his say in the follow-up NME piece, "Rock Against Right-Wing Rock Being Called Fascist," which came out May 5, 1979. He said,

> That was a very dishonest article, . . . I was under the impression that Miles and I had gotten on very well. I even gave him my address in New York and told him to stop by any time he was in the neighbourhood. All that so-called political dialogue took place after the interview had finished; we were just chatting, really amenably, I thought, and he twisted it all round. I just feel that it was basically dishonest.

> All I was doing was taking up a contrary stance in what I considered to be an essentially philosophical argument," Peart went on, "and he made it appear to be political dogma . . . . He represented us as fascist fanatics . . . and if that were the case we would have the world's first Jewish Nazi bass player [laughs]. It's ludicrous. We're not fascists. We're not racists. I was very upset when I read that article. In America when you call someone a fascist it's the worst, y'know? It's the pits. But over here, I now realize, that in certain quarters anyone who isn't a socialist is, by definition, a fascist. [Laughs].[1]

As it happens, Hamblett turned out to be hardly more sympathetic to Peart and his band mates than Miles. Although he gave Peart all the space he wanted to air his complaint, he nevertheless conceded nothing, just as Miles hadn't, and indeed concluded his piece by referring back to Miles' warning: "Remember, as someone once said, 'The next time you see them, make sure you see them with your eyes open, and know what you see . . . .'"

The Randian thing: Guilty as charged

The other reason Rush has been tagged right-wing isn't quite so easy to dismiss, and that's because of the band's—really, Peart's—dalliance with Rand and libertarianism, both of which on economic matters fall on the right side of the political spectrum.[2]

---

1 The article in which Peart is given a chance to rebut Miles' "fascist" remark is in "Rock Against Right-Wing Rock Being Called Fascist," by John Hamblett, NME, May 5, 1979, page 7.
2 It's worth noting that Ayn Rand never considered herself a libertarian. In fact, in interviews and in her essays she dismissed libertarians as shameless copycats of her ideas. But her dismissal of libertarianism is more semantic and parochial than substantive. On the basis of what they're aiming for,

Again, Peart today by his own admission doesn't consider himself a hard-core libertarian. He's said in numerous interviews that he sees himself as something of a libertarian-liberal hybrid, a "bleeding-heart libertarian," who believes in the ideals of small government and maximum freedom of individuals to rise or fall on their own merit, but he also says he believes in a social safety net so people have some place to turn for help when no other help is available.

As he put it in an August 2012 interview for *Maclean's* magazine, Canada's newsweekly, "I still totally believe in individual rights and individual responsibility and in choosing to do good . . . . Pure libertarianism believes that people will be generous and help each other. Well, they won't. I wish it were so, and I live that way. I help panhandlers, but other people are, "Oh, look at that—why doesn't he get a job?" While I believe in all that freedom, I also believe that no one should suffer needlessly."[1]

But that's today. Back in the 1970s and early 1980s, Peart was drinking liberally from the Fountain of Lamneth and made no bones about the idea that each of us must embark upon our own journey of discovery, confront the world in all its evil and temptation, and build for ourselves the life we choose, without looking to government for our identity and welfare.

In talking about his conversion to libertarianism as a teenager, Peart told Roy MacGregor for his 1978 cover feature on Rush in *Macleans* that he at first thought he was a socialist, "like everyone else seemed to." But over time he realized he was just miming the zeitgeist of the 1960s. "Now I think socialism is entirely wrong by virtue of man himself. It cannot work. It is simply impossible to say all men are brothers or that all men are created equal. They are not. Your basic responsibility is to yourself."[2]

In another interview, this one in 1997 with the libertarian publication *Liberty*, Peart said, "Howard Roark stood as a role model for me—as exactly the way I already was living. [Howard Roark is one of the main characters in Ayn Rand's 1943 novel *The Fountainhead*.] Even at that tender age [18] I already felt that. And it was intuitive or instinctive or inbred stubbornness or whatever, but I had already made those choices and suffered for them."[3]

Lee got caught up in the Randian thing, too, a bit, although it's hard to say how much he would have thought about it if it weren't for the influence of Peart.

---

libertarianism and her Objectivism are very similar. The main difference is in philosophical foundations. Objectivism is based on a metaphysical theory that Rand elucidates over her career, while libertarianism is based in a political philosophy, and in the United States the key document is the Constitution.

1 Peart talks about his continuing left-leaning libertarianism in "Neil Peart on introverts, learning to improvise, and why people should be nicer to one another," by Mike Doherty, Maclean's, August 13, 2012.

2 "To Hell with Bob Dylan, Meet Rush," by Roy MacGregor, *Maclean's*, January 23, 1978, page 26. Also online at *Rush is a Band:* http://www.rushisaband.com/display.php?id=2213 retrieved November 16, 2012.

3 "Who is Neil Peart?" by Scott Bullock, *Liberty*, September 1997.

Bob Cook, a contributor to NPR's "All Things Considered" who has written about Jewish issues for that and other media, suggests Peart's Randianism rubbed off a bit on Lee because, as the son of Holocaust survivors, he intuitively understood the risk governments can pose to their own people. "Peart tapped into something in Lee's subconscious that made him a more compelling deliverer of Rand's philosophy than Rand herself," Cook says in "The Spirit of Rand," a 2007 piece he wrote for *Jews Rock*, an Internet publication.[1]

Lee certainly *sounded* like a believer in the band's early years. "I think she's [Rand] brought forth a lot of concepts and philosophies which have confirmed for us a lot of different things," he said during the Miles interview. "I've just found it very positive. I've found a lot of truth in what she writes."[2]

In interviews, the third member of Rush, Alex Lifeson (born Aleksandar Živojinović, his parents were from Serbia), the band's "musical scientist," as his band mates have put it, almost never talks politics or philosophy, leaving that to the more erudite Peart while he limits his remarks to the mechanics of music-making. One of the few times in which Lifeson did dive into politics, in 2012, he cleared up any ambiguity about his views by declaring his fealty to the left. "I'm certainly socially liberal," he says in the June 2012 issue of *High Times*. "Government can play an important role in our lives."[3]

In today's environment, some 30 years after the conservative revolutions of Ronald Reagan in the United States, Margaret Thatcher in the U.K., and Brian Mulroney in Canada in the 1980s, it's nothing new to proselytize the gospel of capitalism. But in the late 1970s, when Rush was running around talking about this stuff, it was seen as oddly out of sync with the times, especially in the U.K., because in that country after World War II, more than in the United States, the consensus was more in favor of creating a robust social safety net through government. Indeed, by many accounts the U.K. really *was* teetering on the brink of socialism, if it hadn't actually crossed the line into it, with even the conservatives after World War II having a hand in the creation of the country's nationalized assets, including its crown gem the National Health Service. Against that background, perhaps Miles' viewpoint can be understood.

But even in the far more capitalist-centric U.S., in the late 1970s the country was in a considerably different place. Until Reagan did what Barry Goldwater in the 1960s failed to do and brought the conservative revolution to Washington, the country was firmly left-of-center, at least in Washington.

---

1 Bob Cook's piece on whether Lee ever shared Peart's Randian dalliance is called "The Spirit of Rand," Jews Rock, October 15, 2007. It's reproduced on *Jewish Toronto*: http://www.jewishtoronto.com/page.aspx?id=75192, retrieved December 2, 2012.
2 A partial transcript of the Barry Miles NME interview with Rush, along with links to the actual article, is at *Rush Vault*: http://rushvault.com/2011/07/27/barry-miles-big-mistake/ retrieved November 19, 2012.
3 "Alex Lifeson: The High Times Interview," by David Bienenstock, *High Times*, June 2012.

Of course, in the 1970s and 1980s there were other popular musical artists that held libertarian or right-of-center views.[1] Frank Zappa and Ted Nugent come quickly to mind. But the lyrics of Zappa, a self-described "devout capitalist" and social libertarian (which would seem to describe Peart pretty well), are mostly inscrutable, certainly to teenagers with mainly sex, drugs, and rock and roll on their minds. And Nugent (who actually recorded on Zappa's label, DiscReet Records, early in his career) was commercially astute enough back in the early days (perhaps not now) to keep whatever his political views were hidden behind his artistic persona, which was summed up by his wearing a loincloth. That, at least, is how it seems to me. Here's a typical Nugent nugget during his mid-1970s heyday. "Dog, dog, dog eat dog / Dog, dog, dog eat dog / Dog, dog, dog eat dog / Dog, dog, dog eat dog / Dog, dog, dog eat dog." ("Dog Eat Dog," from *Free-for-All*, 1976.)

Come to think of it, maybe there *is* a libertarian message in there!

Rush has girls on its mind, too

Of course, before Peart joined the band in the summer of 1974, Rush, too, was very much writing music for hormonal teenagers. Its first album, *Rush*, released on its own Moon label in 1974 with John Rutsey as drummer, talks about nothing more complicated than "Runnin' here / Runnin' there / Lookin' for a girl" and "You're makin' me crazy / The way you roll them eyes / Won't you come and sit with me?"

As we saw, this all changed when Rutsey, nursing health issues and expressing differences with Lifeson and Lee over the band's creative direction, left the band just before the start of their first U.S. tour, as an opening act for Uriah Heep and Manfred Mann. Once Peart took the seat behind the drum kit, the band quickly replaced songs about girls with songs about only one girl: Ayn Rand.

Indeed, the very first song Peart wrote with his new band mates was "Anthem," the opening track on its 1975 *Fly by Night* album, named after Rand's 1938 anti-collectivist novella. That piece declares in no uncertain terms that there's only one way to live your life, and it's not about smiling on your brother and loving one another (as the Youngbloods sang in their 1967 classic, "Get Together,") but rather leaving others to their own success or failure while you steer your own course. "Know your place in life / Is where you want to be / Don't let them tell you that / You owe it all to me / Keep on looking forward / No use in looking round / Hold your head above the crowd / And they won't bring you down / Live for yourself, there's no one else / More worth living for / Begging hands and bleeding hearts / Will only cry out for more."

---

1 At least one list of conservative rock bands and artists is at the *Arkansas Project*: http://www.thearkansasproject.com/republican-rock-stars/ retrieved December 3, 2012. But the real reason to go there is it has an eye-catching picture of Jessica Simpson.

The piece would hardly raise eyebrows today, but coming in the mid-1970s, "Anthem" was a thumb in the eye of the music establishment, which at the time saw rock as an extension of the kind of collectivist values celebrated at Woodstock and enshrined in songs like The Byrds' "Turn! Turn! Turn!" which set to music the lines in Ecclesiastes 3:1 about turning the other cheek.

To this way of thinking, rock wasn't about holding your head above the crowd, as Rush was exhorting us to do, but about getting down in the mud with 500 close friends, washing each others' feet and singing Joan Baez, Phil Ochs, Joni Mitchell, and Bob Dylan in the name of social justice.

In several of its *Fly by Night* tracks, Rush was making clear it was having none of that Woodstockian idealism. In the album's title track, the band enshrines into music the very libertarian idea of the individual as sovereign. In the piece, the narrator gets up in the middle of the night and, seeing the wide eyes of a snowy owl staring at him through the window, says, "I want to be king now, not just one more pawn," and off he goes to make his mark in the world.

I feel bad for the guy's girlfriend. He just leaves her there: "Goodbye my dear / My ship isn't coming and I just can't pretend." That's harsh.

Such a no-nonsense point of view is written into much of the band's early music. The piece "Beneath, Between and Behind," also from *Fly by Night*, might be the first rock song that's structured like a presidential State of the Union address, except with John Galt of *Atlas Shrugged* or Howard Roark of *The Fountainhead* at the podium.

In the piece, the narrator talks about how self-reliant Americans, after rebelling against their kingly foe in 1776, tamed the trackless waste, and then later how shiploads of immigrants arrived, champing at the bit to invent themselves and the material world around them anew. But now this proud heritage of individualism was at risk as the country embarked on ill-conceived grand collectivist projects, none more grand than war-making. But, like any good public address, the piece ends on an optimistic note, with the narrator holding out hope that the country will return to its founding principles and write a good next chapter: "The dream's gone stale, but still, let hope prevail."

Musically, the piece sounds very much like an anthem, with its bold, uplifting power chords during the chorus.

The band followed up that piece with "Bastille Day," the opening track on its third album, *Caress of Steel*, also released in 1975, which looks at another individualism-celebrating revolution, this one the far more ambiguously concluded French Revolution. In a dozen tautly written lines, the piece goes over that historic event in all its stages: the hubris of the aristocracy—"Let them eat cake!"—their subsequent fall at the hands of the peasants—"the guillotine will claim its bloody prize!"—and then the ensuing chaos—"all around us anger burns"—as newly free citizens exchange the moral clarity of the storming of the Bastille with the clouded thinking of power-grabbing and retaliation.

With "Anthem," "Beneath, Between and Behind," and "Bastille Day," the lyrics and the bold, confident music provide a political triptych that any economic free-marketer would want to have on his playlist: disdain for collectivist projects, the heroic overthrowing of undeserving, elitist government; and unstinting praise for self-actualizing individuals who don't need government telling them what to do.

Chris McDonald, in his piece "Enlightened Thoughts, Mystic Words," in *Rush and Philosophy*, calls Rush "perhaps the only band in rock history to have a trilogy of songs devoted to eighteenth-century political movements,"[1] although instead of including "Anthem" in his trilogy, as I've done here, he includes "A Farewell to Kings," from 1977, which talks about the missed opportunities by western liberal societies to capitalize on their success replacing dictatorial monarchies.

It's no wonder the music establishment was left scratching its head when Rush started making a name for itself on the hard-rock circuit as opening act for bands like Kiss and Aerosmith in the late 1970s. While those headline acts were singing about sex, drugs, and rock and roll, Rush was coming in like a classroom nerd, spouting off on this weird individualist rant that seemed completely out of context for the times.

Just awesome rock to me, Dude

In truth, despite all the muttering among critics about the economic libertarianism in the music, much of the band's fan base likely had little or no inkling what the lyrics were about. To them, all this talk about guillotines and trackless wastes was no doubt just a cool way to talk about something other than sex, drugs, and rock and roll, bathing the band in a kind of intellectual aura.

For these listeners, the obscure references were surely part of the attraction, but it was really Rush's pairing of an almost heavy metal-like sound with the musical complexity of progressive rock—varied time signatures, virtuosic musicianship, extended musical concepts—that created the real attraction. As Jeff Wagner in the 2012 heavy metal documentary *Metal Evolution* put it, Rush in the late 1970s was creating a uniquely attractive place to go for people who liked their music hard but also wanted it to be conceptually interesting.

> They were really toying with the new sound of the day, which is this really ultra heavy hard rock that [didn't] have a name yet, and they're also grabbing for prog rock. So, I think it's probably the first real significant bridging of those two worlds.[2]

1 Berti and Bowman, *Rush and Philosophy*, page 243.
2 The *Metal Evolution* episode in which Wagner talks about Rush's place in the development of progressive metal is at *Rush is a Band*: http://www.rushisaband.com/blog/2012/01/29/2978/Rush-featured-in-Progressive-Metal-episode-of-Metal-Evolution retrieved December 4, 2012.

Wagner is the author of *Mean Deviation* (Bazillion Points), which charts the evolution of progressive metal. Wagner says that while progressive rock bands like Yes; Emerson, Lake and Palmer; and Genesis were peaking in the late 1970s, Rush was just starting its climb and was providing a heavier take on what the progressive bands were doing, giving "the people into Zeppelin, the people into Black Sabbath this other place to go."

Classic Rock magazine editor Henry Ewing in *Metal Evolution* calls Rush's 1976 breakout album, *2112*, pivotal for the progressive metal genre, because it showed musicians that they could be as heavy as possible and still explore extended musical concepts and structural complexity. For "metal bands that had an interest in exploring a more progressive side," Ewing says, they saw "what they could do sonically, and because Rush had that hard edge to them, it opened up a whole new world to [them]."[1]

In other words, it was what Rush was doing musically, not in its lyrics, that was in large measure driving its fan base.

But for those who were paying attention to the lyrics, Rush was using its first progressive metal epic piece, "2112," to double down on the ideas Peart had introduced in the band's political triptych "Anthem," "Beneath, Between and Behind," and "Bastille Day."

The storyline of that side-long title piece is by now widely known, even among occasional fans, but, briefly, it's a dystopic science fiction narrative that literally does set Ayn Rand's *Anthem* to music, only it replaces the backward collectivist leadership of the novella with a politburo of priests who rely on computers to keep tabs on their people.

Again, surely for most teens, "2112" was just a 20-minute *tour de force* of musicianship, now widely regarded as one of the first and finest examples of progressive metal, as Wagner and Ewing say. But for critics, "2112" pretty much cast the die that would characterize the band for the rest of its career, even as it expanded into other themes and musical styles starting in the 1980s.

Not only was it setting to music a work of fiction from that kooky Ayn Rand, but it wasn't even trying to hide that fact. Right there in the album liner notes the band credited her as a source of inspiration for the title piece, "With acknowledgement to the genius of Ayn Rand."

To be fair, Peart said in a 1991 *Rockline* interview that he never intended to model "2112" on Rand's novella. Rather, after crafting his story he saw that he had created a parallel narrative to it, so he felt he needed to acknowledge her.

"As the story came together, the parallels became obvious to me and I thought, 'Oh gee, I don't want to be a plagiarist here.' So I did give credit to

1 The *Metal Evolution* episode in which Ewing talks about Rush's place in the development of progressive metal is at *Rush is a Band*: http://www.rushisaband.com/blog/2012/01/29/2978/Rush-featured-in-Progressive-Metal-episode-of-Metal-Evolution retrieved December 4, 2012.

her writings in the liner notes."[1]

This might have been a simple act of Peart covering himself, but to music critics it was the last piece of evidence they needed to validate their suspicions that Rush was a weirdo band that had no place in the rock establishment, at least as that establishment was defined by the self-appointed tastemakers at the time, mainly *Rolling Stone* in the U.S. and NME in the U.K.—although some of the band's harshest critics wrote for other publications that you would have expected to be more sympathetic, like *Creem* and *Circus*.

As far as these tastemakers were concerned, Rush was and always would be a marginalized act, maybe not quite as far removed from relevancy as, say, a Christian rock band, but almost as far off the beaten path.

"They're not a true rock and roll band," Steve Weitzman says in a typical diatribe against the band in a 1981 *Circus* piece, "as their music is all stiffly calculated and pre-planned. Though you wouldn't know it from the crowd's reaction, the band's lyrics are even weaker than the music. . . . The last laugh is had by drummer Neil Peart. He gets to write this caca and doesn't even have to sing it."[2]

As a result, despite the band attracting second-to-none praise for its musicianship in the trade press (*Guitar, Guitar Player, Guitar World, Bass Player, Canadian Musician, Keyboard, Metal Hammer, Modern Drummer, Musician, Sounds,* and the like),[3] with Lifeson, Lee, and Peart consistently taking top or close to top honors in reader polls), the band was virtually non-existent on the radio for its first half dozen albums. Meanwhile, those albums were going gold (and, later, many of them multiple platinum) and the band was developing a following by word of mouth that any mainstream, chart-topping rock band would have loved to have.

A model of moral coherency

In fairness to Ayn Rand, as we talked about briefly before, the prevailing view among academics that her extreme individualist philosophy wasn't worth serious study was probably as much the result of her critics' intellectual standoffishness as any flaws in her reasoning. Again, whatever you think of its merit, her work holds together well and it's not a stretch to say that its ethical component, in which man is considered the measure of all things, is a reasonable point of view, and certainly a completely rational moral position. Indeed, it's really just a robust variant of Aristotle's virtue ethics. Given how frequently Rand comes up in connection with the band, let's take a minute to look at exactly what she's saying in her ethical theory, which up to this point we've only touched upon.

---

1 Peart's comment about not wanting to be seen as plagiarizing Rand is in a Dec 2, 1991, "Rockline" radio interview.
2 "Rush Wrap Up Five-Month Tour," *Circus*, August 31, 1981.
3 The list of musician magazines in which Rush members regularly top reader polls is noted in Chris McDonald's book, *Rush, Rock Music and the Middle Class.* Bloomington: Indiana University Press, 2009, page 120.

Moral goodness in her view is simply to take everything in the world at face value and mold your life accordingly. Since God can't be proven, you can't base your actions on Him. Faith, in her mind, is not a moral position; it's an abdication of moral responsibility. Man, on the other hand, is here. He's concrete. He's real. And he has reason. So, in good Aristotelian fashion, his job is to use his reason to be the best he can be. He can't fall back on unverifiable concepts like God or angels or any kind of supernatural or mystical energy or power.

"Ethics is *not* a mystic fantasy," she says in "The Objectivist Ethics," a paper she delivered at a 1961 University of Wisconsin symposium. "*Ethics is an objective, metaphysical necessity of man's survival*—not by the grace of the supernatural nor of your neighbors nor of your whims, but by the grace of reality and the nature of life." [Rand's emphasis.][1]

It was this atheistic component that made her views so anathema to conservatives in the 1950s, when she first started making a name for herself, and which drove some of the right's intellectual leaders to dismiss her philosophy as cultish and helped marginalize her reputation, despite widespread acknowledgement of her brilliance.

"Keeping Rand at bay was one way religious believers measured their strength within the conservative movement and asserted their dominance over secular libertarians," says Stanford University professor Jennifer Burns, author of *Goddess of the Market: Ayn Rand and the American Right* (Oxford University Press). "William F. Buckley, Jr., himself an avid fan of capitalism, tried to run Rand out of the conservative movement because she was an atheist. He rightly perceived her work as not just a defense of capitalism, but an attack upon Christianity itself."[2]

Fast forward to today, the atheism issue has been largely defanged and her reputation is enjoying a resurgence, led by Rand-admiring conservative politicians like Rand Paul and 2012 Republican vice president nominee Paul Ryan,[3] both of whom are considered serious contenders for the 2016

1 Rand's view that ethics isn't based on a mystic fantasy is in her 1961 University of Wisconsin speech, included in her *The Virtue of Selfishness*. New York: Signet, 1961, page 24.

2 Jennifer Burn's comment about the impact of Rand's atheism on conservative leaders is on her blog: http://www.jenniferburns.org/blog/83-2009-the-year-of-rand retrieved December 4, 2012.

3 We know Rand Paul is an Ayn Rand-admiring politician because he studied her as a youngster (see, for example, "For Paul Family, Libertarian Ethos Began at Home," by Mark Leibovich, *New York Times*, June 5, 2010), and we know Paul Ryan is a Rand admirer by none other than himself. In a 2005 speech to the Atlas Society, an Objectivist group, he said, "[T]he reason I got involved in public service, by and large, if I had to credit one thinker, one person, it would be Ayn Rand. And the fight we are in here, make no mistake about it, is a fight of individualism versus collectivism." An audio recording of the speech, along with transcript excerpts, is at the Atlas Society web site: http://www.atlassociety.org/ele/blog/2012/04/30/paul-ryan-and-ayn-rands-ideas-hot-seat-again retrieved December 5, 2012. You can also read about the speech in "Paul Ryan's Ayn Rand Offense," by Stephen Richer, *Forbes*, August 30, 2012.

Republican presidential nomination in the United States. It's not that conservative politicians are less religious than in the 1950s; that hardly seems to be the case. But they appear willing to separate her atheism from her *laissez-faire* economics and use the latter without the former.

As Burns says, "What's different now is that for the first time, conservatives are willing to overlook Rand's once-controversial atheism."

Burns reinforced this view in an interview she did with Jon Stewart on his Comedy Central show in 2009. "Now you have people like Rush Limbaugh and Glenn Beck recommending her," she told Stewart. "They don't seem to be noticing that she's an atheist. I'm not exactly sure why. That's something I've been wondering about myself."[1]

Stewart's reply was pointed: "Maybe it's just that, they'll conveniently use whoever they want to advance their career? I don't know. I'm just asking. I don't know!"

'What you do is your own glory'

Be that as it may, what this Randian atheism comes down to is an Aristotelian-like self-actualization. For each of us, our highest duty is to ourselves: to take care of ourselves, assume responsibility for our actions, both our successes and our failures, and not "sacrifice" others (in Rand's term) for ourselves—that is, not to treat others with anything but the same respect we expect others to treat us as sovereign individuals with inalienable rights to life, liberty, and the pursuit of happiness. If each of us does this, the world will be the best it can be. That's all her moral views are about.

It's very much Adam Smith's invisible hand of the marketplace applied to the individual as moral beings. Historians and economists will quibble over exactly what Smith meant when he talked about the invisible hand, but sticking to the popular understanding of his phrase, the idea is that everybody benefits collectively when individuals are free to act in their own self-interest. The only restriction, of course, is that our actions not impede the ability of others to act as sovereigns in their own right.

Certainly in the United States, this view is axiomatic, and even those on the far left at a minimum pay lip service to the invisible hand idea. Progressives say the invisible hand needs to be tempered by government, with rules preventing businesses from running roughshod over people and with assistance to people who've been plowed under the capitalist steamroller, but there's little dissent against the basic notion of the invisible hand.

Of course, Smith himself never saw the invisible hand as anything but a principle and in his *Wealth of Nations* he rejects pure *laissez-faire* capitalism in favor of a hybrid model in which private business is conducted in an

---

[1] You can view Jennifer Burn's interview with Jon Stewart on her blog: http://www.jenniferburns.org/blog/73-top-three-questions-about-my-interview-with-jon-stewart-on-the-daily-show retrieved December 5, 2012.

environment that's adequately regulated by government.[1] He was no wild-west capitalist. As he puts it in Book II of his *Wealth*, "[R]egulations may, no doubt, be considered as in some respects a violation of natural liberty. But these exertions of the natural liberty of a few individuals, which might endanger the security of the whole society, are, and ought to be, restrained by the laws of all governments."[2]

Applied to the individual, this invisible hand is at the heart of Rand's moral view, but, in Aristotelian fashion, the key is that we act as *rational* beings. Our lives can't be about finding new and more exciting ways to push our pleasure buttons. Saying we're the measure of all things doesn't mean we measure our lives by how much we indulge ourselves. This gets back to Aristotle's concept of *eudaimonia*, in which we temper our desires so we don't lose our path in pursuit of pleasure. Otherwise, in Rand's view, we become "subhuman" and "drift in a semiconscious daze." Everything we do has to be justifiable in the bright light of day.[3] Only if we can account for our actions as thinking, rational beings does our self-actualization elevate the world. If we make it all about indulgence, then we'll be little more than animals with big brains who devise more and cleverer ways to have fun.

"Desires (or feelings or emotions or wishes or whims) are not tools of cognition," Rand says in her essay "The Objectivist Ethics," compiled in *The Virtue of Selfishness* (Signet). "They are not a valid standard of value, nor a valid criterion of man's interests. The mere fact that a man desires something does not constitute a proof that the object of his desire is good, nor that its achievement is actually to his interest."[4]

Rand saw her ethics as a kind of rational selfishness because, to her, the whole reason to act ethically is to further your well-being, not the well-being of the society, and in her essays, speeches, and books she liked to push the "selfishness" part of her views to the center, aiding and abetting critics who used the word to paint her ethics as, well, selfish.

But really what she means by selfishness is simply self-respect or self-valuing: each of us has intrinsic worth, as an end in himself, and our job is to build value in ourselves—become the best we can be. That means doing what's good for us and avoiding what's bad.[5] But that doesn't equate to

1 You can find a whole list of things Adam Smith says government should regulate without having to read the entire *Wealth of Nations* at *Economist's View*: http://economistsview.typepad.com/economistsview/2010/03/adam-smith-and-the-role-of-government.html retrieved December 6, 2012.
2 The Smith quote on the need for regulations is in his *Wealth of Nations*, Book II, Chapter II, page 94.
3 Rand's quote about our becoming "subhuman" if we spend our days trying to push our pleasure buttons is in her *The Virtue of Selfishness*, page 22.
4 Rand's quote about our desires not being tools of cognition is in her essay "The Objectivist Ethics" in *The Virtue of Selfishness*, page 30.
5 Rand outlines her complete ethics, along with the theory in which she grounds it, in "The Objectivist Ethics," a speech she delivered to the University of Wisconsin Symposium on "Ethics in Our Time" in Madison, Wis., February 9, 1961. A portion of it is included in her compilation of

stepping on others or stealing from others or ignoring the needs of others; it means bettering ourselves while treating others as we expect them to treat us: as people of inherent value.

She identifies three principle values that each of us possess inherently: 1) our reason, 2) our sense of purpose, and 3) our self-esteem. In furtherance of these values, we have three Aristotelian-like virtues that, if we build them into our character over time, can help us achieve our values to their peak form. These are our 1) rationality, 2) productiveness, and 3) pride.

Given these values and virtues, the ideal Randian person is very similar to the ideal Aristotelian person: he's a man of rationality who, out of a sense of his own self worth, strives to perfect himself. He's his own prime mover.

In her view, if each person treats himself as something valuable, then society in a sense largely takes care of itself, because people who value themselves recognize the value of others and always act in good faith. That doesn't mean they always act in a way that make others happy, but they do act in good faith, and that's key.

In a sense, she's building an ethical system in the same way as Aristotle, but she's starting from the individual and moving outward, toward the society, rather than starting from the society and moving inward, toward the individual. The goal is the same, though: people living morally in a moral society.

The only other real difference with Aristotle is simply what each regards as the virtues. For Aristotle, the big four virtues, what we call the cardinal virtues, are temperance, prudence, courage, and justice, while for Rand, they're the three we just listed: rationality, productiveness, and pride.

They're not that different from each other, and in fact, the cardinal virtues in a sense can all be folded into Rand's virtue of rationality, because they all flow from our ability to reason.

It's worth repeating that, whatever you think of her philosophy, it's really not the over-the-top, dog-eat-dog, survival-of-the-fittest moral code that it's so often made out to be. It's as cogent as any other moral philosophy, whether you're talking about a virtue ethics like Aristotle's, a duty-based (deontological) ethics like Immanuel Kant's (actions have moral worth if they're done out of a sense of duty), or a consequentialist ethics like utilitarianism (actions have moral worth if they lead to the greatest happiness for the greatest number of people).

Virtue, deontological, and consequentialist—these are the three main types of normative ethics, each with many variations. Each has its strengths and its flaws. Rand's ethics is a variant of virtue ethics, with its own strengths and weaknesses, but at its core it's perfectly reasonable, and a case can be made that it's surely as reasonable, if not more so, than any deontological or

---

essays, *The Virtue of Selfishness* (Signet: 1961). You can access the address in its entirety at the Ayn rand Institute website: http://www.aynrand.org/site/PageServer?pagename=ari_ayn_rand_the_objectivist_ethics   retrieved December 12, 2012.

consequentialist ethics.

Why might we say this? To act morally under Kant's deontological ethics, you can have no self-interest in acting morally; you can only act morally if your motivating force is a sense of duty to do the right thing.[1] On this basis, if you save a man's life out of a motive to be a hero, you've done a good thing, even a great thing, but is it a moral thing? Depending on how you ask the question, the answer could be no. That's the kind of issue Kant's ethics raises.

Of course, there's a lot more to Kant's ethics than its reliance on duty. You also have to structure your act according to what Kant calls the categorical imperative, which in its primary formulation is to act in a way that can be universalized into a law without creating a rational contradiction. Thus, not only do you have to save the man's life out of a sense of duty, but your action can't create a rational contradiction if it were to be universalized into a law. Depending on how you structure your universalized law, you can open up an infinite number of moral Pandora's boxes. Is Rand's virtue ethics so extreme when looked at in comparison? It's not.

Similarly with utilitarianism, which is most closely associated with nineteenth century British philosophers Jeremy Bentham and John Stewart Mill. Utilitarianism's goal, which is to produce the greatest happiness for the greatest number of people, can be taken any number of different ways, but it remains deeply problematic, because, as Rand herself has pointed out, "fifty-one percent of humanity enslaving the other forty-nine"[62] would be moral under its basic principle. You can twist words, add provisos, tweak meanings, devise scenarios, and so on, but ultimately the axiomatic principle raises as many questions as it answers. Again, is Rand's view so extreme in comparison?

Outliers

To sum up, from a purely conceptual point of view, Rand's moral philosophy is coherent and rational, but her Objectivism has never been treated seriously by scholars, and few would dispute that she has herself partly to blame for that.

First, she wasn't a scholar and she made no effort to build a credible scholarship around her theories, although she no doubt thought she did. Second, her writing, much of which is embedded in her fiction, is corny and strident. That makes it hard to take her work seriously. Third, in her person, she was all angles and no curves: sanctimonious and prickly. And fourth, on a political basis, her philosophy had no unconditional allies on either the left or the right. The left liked her *laissez-faire* approach to people's private lives (leave gays alone, keep church and state separate) but rejected her *laissez-faire* approach to the economy, while the right liked her *laissez-faire* approach to the economy, but rejected her *laissez-faire* approach to people's private

---

1 Immanuel Kant, *Groundwork of the Metaphysic of Morals.* H.J. Paton, trans. New York: Harper Torchbook, 1964, page 65.

lives, not to mention her atheism.

The political movement most closely aligned to her philosophy, libertarianism, Rand herself completely rejected as pretenders to her intellectual achievement. "They are not defenders of capitalism," she said in "Egalitarianism and Inflation," a 1974 lecture she gave at Ford Hall in Boston, "a group of publicity seekers. . . . Most of them are my enemies. . . . I've read nothing by a Libertarian (when I read them, in the early years) that wasn't my ideas badly mishandled—i.e., had the teeth pulled out of them—with no credit given."[1]

In short, despite her high profile in popular culture, she was and has always been an outlier, her work never integrated into academia and attracting no unconditional supporters on either the left or the right. And with her atheism, she won no support among the religious. Even today, with her star rising because of the embrace of conservatives, hers continues to be a brilliant but eccentric legacy.

And for much of Rush's early career, "brilliant but eccentric" probably isn't a bad way to describe how a lot of critics thought of the band, although no doubt many of them would put far more of the weight on the eccentric part than on the brilliant part.

1 John Stewart Mill, *Utilitarianism*. 2nd ed. Indianapolis: Hackett, 2003. page 7.

CHAPTER 3. ARMED WITH SENSE AND LIBERTY

> A vague sensation quickens
> In his young and restless heart
> And a bright and nameless vision
> Has him longing to depart
>   —"The Analog Kid," *Signals*, 1982

On the strength of their breakout album, *2112*, which, with little radio play and no promotion from the band's record company,[1] sold 100,000 copies in its first week and then went on to ship gold shortly after that (and eventually to ship triple platinum),[2] Rush was pretty much given *carte blanche* to follow their bliss in the studio from then on out. "That really bought us our independence from everybody," Lifeson said of the success of *2112* in *Contents Under Pressure* (ECW Press), a 30-year anniversary book on the band released in 2004. "After that, everybody left us alone to do what we thought was right."[3]

What their bliss led them to do was release four studio albums over the next four years (1977–1981) that have come to be the most popular cluster of albums of their career (all four went platinum or multiple platinum) and that define the band in the minds of most listeners: *A Farewell to Kings, Hemispheres, Permanent Waves,* and *Moving Pictures.* In all of these albums we see an expansion of the band's expression of individualism and a deepening of what we might call its Aristotelian-Randian project.

In the title piece of its 1977 *A Farewell to Kings* album, as we saw earlier, there's a pessimism about the West's commitment to the principles underwriting its march to greatness. Instead of the self-reliant individualists we meet in Rand's

---

1 Peart, *Roadshow*, page 17.
2 Telleria, *Merely Players*, page 25, and elsewhere.
3 Popoff, *Contents Under Pressure*, page 43.

novels like John Galt, Henry Reardon, and Howard Roark running the show in our liberal-democratic world, it's nervous connivers like James Taggart, the weak-kneed brother of Dagny Taggart, who are doing so. And in their effort to take the path of least resistance they're hollowing out the West's classic strength. "We turned our gaze / From the castles in the distance / Eyes cast down / On the path of least resistance / Scheming demons dressed in kingly guise / Beating down the multitude and / Scoffing at the wise."

The James Taggart-like scheming demons are the bureaucrats, politicians, and business people who puff themselves up by allocating resources they haven't earned: politicians earmarking taxpayer funds to pet projects, bureaucrats picking economic winners and losers through their regulations and funding formulas, and CEOs who run their enterprises with an eye to short-term shareholder profit at the expense of long-term strength-building.

As Chris McDonald put it in his piece "Enlightened Thoughts, Mystic Words," "A Farewell to Kings" is one big lament over missed opportunity: after throwing off the shackles of kingly oppression and putting in place democracies, the West once again finds itself in shackles, but this time it's not the shackles of monarchy but of scheming hypocrites who strive to leave us all in ignorance so they can work their will with us while paying lip service to our individualist, self-reliant principles.

> [T]he entry of the song's lyrics moves us forward anxiously to the present time. The song asks what future generations will think of us: will they see us as having abandoned the ideals of reason, progress, and humanism which had characterized the Enlightenment? Have we turned away from these "castles in the distance," and returned to our old, pre-Enlightened ways? Peart compares today's "hypocrites" who criticize the humanist-inspired quest for truth and progress with "ancient nobles" who preferred that their subjects lived under their shadow in ignorance[1]

Even the album's radio-friendly song, "Closer to the Heart," which for a while had a vague afterlife as a Christmastime favorite[2] because of its chimes and cozy wish for peace and harmony, keeps the individualism message front and center by locating responsibility for society in the individual, not in the state or a higher power. "Philosophers and ploughmen / Each must know his part / To sow a new mentality / Closer to the heart / You can be the captain / I will draw the chart / Sailing into destiny / Closer to the heart."

You have to look at these and other lines in the piece through a Platonic filter to see exactly what Peart is getting at. The idea that it's both philosophers *and* ploughmen who have a role in sowing a new mentality is to put the two on equal footing, which of course is anathema to Plato's idea of the philosopher as king, whose role alone is it to make decisions about what

1 Berti and Bowman, *Rush and Philosophy*, page 245.
2 Telleria, *Merely Players*, pages 31 and 51.

is best for society. And then to say that both you and I will work together, as captain and navigator ("I will draw the chart") to get us to our destiny is, again, to invest in each of us equally the sovereignty to be a decision-maker.

Do we want peace and harmony? Yes, of course. But peace and harmony come from each of us acting as sovereigns, not from the philosopher-king organizing society in the way he sees fit based on his superior view. Whatever Peart's intention was in writing the line, it works as a great critique of the Platonic point of view.

The band's next album, *Hemispheres*, in which musically it took its biggest leap yet into progressive metal with the side-long title piece, cut the individualism theme into two pieces, one inward looking, the other outward looking.

The inward-looking piece is the title track, which depicts the battle between *akrasia* and *eudaimonia* that each of us wages within ourselves as we strive to become our own prime mover, the autonomous, self-governing sovereign that constitutes a virtuous person in the Aristotelian scheme of things. In the piece, finding ourselves scared and uncomfortable in the wilds, we renounce our autonomy to Apollo, who steps in as a Platonic philosopher-king to organize our world under a collectivist regime that succeeds in taming the wilds around us. But, as can only happen under such a regime, we've bought our stability at the price of our sovereignty, leaving us void of any motivating force to perfect ourselves. "[O]ne day the streets fell silent / Yet they knew not what was wrong / The urge to build these fine things / Seemed not to be so strong."

Then along comes Dionysus, the god of love, to replace the strict rigidity of Apollo, and we gladly throw off our collectivist yoke and plunge head-first into the hedonistic bath of *akrasia*. But, as Aristotle warned, the good life can only last so long. Left unchecked, *akrasia* leads to ruin: the rock star spending his millions on heroin, the globe-strutting playboy plunging his Aston Martin down the side of a cliff. "[T]he winter fell upon them / And it caught them unprepared / Bringing wolves and cold starvation / And the hearts of men despaired."

It's only when we take control of our lives, and neither hand over our autonomy to a philosopher-king nor abandon our reason to live a life of unedited pleasure, *akrasia*, that we can reach a state of balance, or *eudaimonia*, and that's what Cygnus brings at the conclusion of the piece. He steps into the hall of gods and, *voilà*, all becomes right with the world. We achieve Aristotle's Golden Mean, and the two sides of our character unite in a single, perfect sphere. "Let the truth of love be lighted / Let the love of truth shine clear / Sensibility / Armed with sense and liberty / With the heart and mind united in a single / Perfect / Sphere."

Thus, the piece anticipates the key Aristotelian lines we looked at earlier in "Prime Mover," "Rational resistance to an unwise urge" and "Rational responses force a change of plans," which are the necessary actions for overcoming *akrasia* and reaching a state of *eudaimonia*.

And in that last stanza you see what might be Peart's most concise summation of the Aristotelian-Randian project yet: love and respect for one another, love and respect for truth, love and respect for our physical world, the here and now, armed with common sense and the freedom to act as we see fit—it's all there.

The outward-looking piece is "The Trees," the cartoon-like tale that, as we saw earlier, Rand Paul likes so much.

In describing the oaks and maples battling for sunlight in a dense forest, the piece does indeed read like a masterful political critique of collectivism, as Paul said. But it has a whole lot of other things going on in it, too, reading like a masterful critique of trade unions, on the one hand, and, on the other, like a critique of a set of Canadian content regulations from the 1970s that to this day are the subject of withering criticism from both sides of the political spectrum.

Peart in interviews has been emphatic that the piece is just a cartoonish tale about trees—"I saw it as a cartoon, really, and wrote it that way,"[1] he says in a 1980 *Modern Drummer* interview—but it's impossible to look at it closely and not think he's winking as he says that. Durrell Bowman, a musicologist who earned his Ph.D. at UCLA in 2003 studying Rush, makes a compelling case that the piece, both in words and music, is a scarcely veiled stab at regulations the Canadian government passed in 1971 to push back against creeping U.S. cultural hegemony by requiring a minimum amount of Canadian content in Canadian creative works. French-styled cultural protectionism, you might call it.

"One could . . . interpret the eventual narrative solution of the song—legislated equality—as critical of Canadian Content regulations," Bowman says in "How is Rush Canadian?" in *Rush and Philosophy*.[2]

Any fierce individualist would naturally rail against such a governmental move, and "The Trees" seems to be a scarcely disguised attempt to do just that. The Canadian law is known by its acronym MAPL, which stands for "music," "artist," "production," and "lyrics," so when Lee in the song sings about the maples complaining that the oaks take all their light, it's easy to think of the maples as the MAPLs of the law and the oaks as the giant trees so representative of the American landscape.

When in the piece the government steps in and orders all the trees, oak and maple, cut to the same size, "by hatchet, axe and saw," it might well be trying to force equality of outcome on its people, as Paul contends. But, as Bowman is arguing, it also is cutting American cultural hegemony down to size.

Bowman goes beyond lyrical analysis to look at what the song does musically to reinforce his contention. The natural bird sounds in the opening vocal section, for example, speak to the idea that, before the law was enacted, the oaks and maples coexisted in a state of nature. When Geddy a little later

---

1 "Neil Peart," *Modern Drummer*, Vol. 4, No. 2, April/May 1980, Page 12.
2 Berti and Bowman, *Rush and Philosophy*, page 297.

sings "the oaks ignore their pleas," after the maples file their complaint, he shifts his vocal emphasis to the first and third beats from the first and second and also fourth and sixth beats. This suggests the idea of taunting or laughing, Bowman says, or, as he puts it, it's like Geddy saying "nya nya nya."

Bowman covers all sections of the song in this detailed way. In his analysis of the closing section, after the oaks have been cut down to size, he says the fading pitches of G#, C#, and B present an "ominous effect, encouraging us to mock the song's sociopolitical 'accomplishment.'"

Sounds convincing, and Bowman leaves no stone unturned in making his case.

But then again, the piece might also just be a diatribe against unionism, because what do unions do but try to create equality of outcome in the workforce by requiring pay to be based on job type and tenure rather than on merit? That's the view taken by John Hamblett, in his 1979 NME piece with Peart we looked at earlier.

Hamblett accuses Peart of spreading a "definite and resolute dictum against trade unionism and organized labour" with the song, and even asks rhetorically whether Rush should even be given the *right* to play such a piece in public given how impressionable its audience is.[1]

Peart replied that it was simply a look at the "false ideal of equality," not of labor unions specifically. "I simply believe that certain people are better at doing certain things than other people," he said. "Some people are naturally talented—they have a gift or whatever—and some people aren't. This doesn't mean that these people are greater human beings, by virtue of that talent, it merely means they are more talented."

Then, much as Miles had dropped a bomb about fascism, Hamblett, in dutiful Platonic fashion, dropped a bomb about censorship: "Should . . . Neil Peart be allowed to write songs like 'Trees' and play them to who knows how many thousands of young (impressionable?) people . . . ?"

It's hard to imagine such a question being asked today (or even in 1979, for that matter). The idea of squelching an idea simply because it challenges a political belief seems beyond the pale, at least in the liberal West, but perhaps it's not too different than squelching debate in academia in the name of political correctness, which a 2012, *Unlearning Liberty: Campus Censorship and the End of American Debate* (Encounter Books), by Greg Lukianoff, suggests is running rampant today. In a typical example of campus censorship in the book, Keith John Sampson, a middle-aged student at Indiana University–Purdue University Indianapolis, was charged with racial harassment for reading a book within sight of others about how students at Notre Dame defeated the Ku Klux Klan in a 1924 fight. The cover, which shows a picture of a Klan gathering, was deemed racially offensive, and so Sampson was convicted. That happened in the U.S. in 2007.[2] So, against a story like that,

---

1 "Rock Against Right-Wing Rock Being Called Fascist," by John Hamblett, New Musical Express, May 5, 1979, page 7.
2 George Will in a Dec. 2, 2012, *Washington Post* column, "The Closed American

Hamblett's wondering if "The Trees" should be censored doesn't seem so beyond the pale after all.

Be that as it may, whether "The Trees" is taken as a critique of enforced equality, labor unions, or Canadian content quotas, it was nevertheless perceived as a critique against collectivism in the name of individualism, and that didn't sit well with the left at the time.

Now that we have your attention . . .

With Rush now much more on the radar screen of critics,[1] both because of its success building a fan base and because it was developing this reputation as a political outlier, attention to what they were saying was growing more intense, to the point where the band members started to complain about the nature of the criticism they were getting. "A lot of the critics believe they are the resident experts and they make the decision on what's valid and what isn't," Lee said in a *Rolling Stone* interview at the time.[2]

"If people don't like us personally, that's their business," Peart said in a *Hit Parader* interview in that same period. "But it shouldn't affect their attitudes towards the music."[3]

In 1980 and then 1981, the band came out with two of its most commercially popular albums ever, *Permanent Waves* and *Moving Pictures*, both of which carried the individualist theme forward.

In *Permanent Waves*, the band had its first Top 40 hit, "The Spirit of Radio," which reached No. 22, and you couldn't have picked a more unlikely song for them to break into the mainstream music scene with. Not only is it not the usual Top 40 material, with its odd and quickly changing time signatures and multiple musical motifs, but lyrically it was a sharp-tongued critique of the music industry itself as run by the hated caste of business-school CEOs who, musicians complained, were taking the edge off the industry in pursuit of profits. "[G]littering prizes and endless compromises / Shatter the illusion of integrity / . . . / For the words of the profits were written on the studio wall / Concert hall / And echoes with the sounds of salesmen."

The band members over the years have said the piece is something of a tribute to Toronto's CFNY FM, which in the 1970s was a classic free-form station whose slogan was "The Spirit of Radio." Today the station is entirely mainstream, branded as 102.1 The Edge.

"They were totally free-form at a time when all these big programmers

Mind," page A27, summarizes the story of Keith John Sampson getting charged with racial harassment for reading the book on the defeat of the Ku Klux Klan.

1 You can see the increase in media attention on the band in Telleria's *Merely Players*. He tracks the band's interviews in newspapers, magazines, TV, and radio over the course of their career up to about 2001, and the number of interviews beginning around 1980 leap noticeably. See page 358, for example.
2 Telleria, *Merely Players*, page 44.
3 Ibid., page 44.

were coming in and consultants were telling all these station managers how to keep their jobs," Lee says in a 1994 *Up Close* interview. "'Play these records and you'll keep your job.' So there was this one station that was playing anything, and you'd hear very abstract things, very hard things, or classical. It sort of reminded us of what it used to be like when FM just started."[1]

"The Spirit of Radio" also speaks admiringly of the behind-the-scenes engineering ingenuity that brings music into our car or home and that we simply take for granted. "Invisible airwaves crackle with life / Bright antennae bristle with the energy / Emotional feedback on timeless wavelength / Bearing a gift beyond price, almost free / All this machinery making modern music / Can still be open hearted."

It's very much the kind of homage you'd find Rand making in *Atlas Shrugged*, as she does in this passage about the confidence and efficiency of the Taggart Transcontinental building:

> The floor of its hallways were mirrors made of marble. The frosted rectangles of its electric fixtures were chips of solid light. Behind sheets of glass, rows of girls sat at typewriters, the clicking of their keys like the sound of speeding train wheels. And like an answering echo, a faint shudder went through the walls at times, rising from under the building, from the tunnels of the great terminal where trains started out to cross a continent and stopped after crossing it again, as they had started and stopped for generation after generation.[2]

The album contains another piece extolling individualism that did well on radio, "Freewill," which in five minutes provides a remarkably concise critique of metaphysical and moral philosophies that depend on mystical, unverifiable concepts to make sense, like the noumenal world of Immanuel Kant, Plato's Forms, or the Judeo-Christian God. The point of view of the piece is very much in tune with Rand's concept of man as the measure of all things. It rejects the idea of our lives being controlled or "pre-ordained" by "powers we cannot perceive," "stars," "gods," or some "celestial voice," and says instead that we must take ourselves as the measure of all things and act accordingly. "Each of us / A cell of awareness / Imperfect and incomplete / Genetic blends / With uncertain ends / On a fortune hunt that's far too fleet."

In lines like these, the piece is painting a picture of man on the demiurge's spinning top to nowhere ("With uncertain ends"), trying to have the best ride he can ("a fortune hunt"), while knowing the ride is going to come to an end in "far too fleet" a time.

This is life stripped down to the reality we see, with no mystical or supernatural layer waiting for us at the end of the ride, and yet, because of our personal sovereignty, it doesn't follow from this void that we're subject to existential despair. The world might be random, but our life doesn't have

1 Ibid., page 157.
2 Rand, *Atlas Shrugged*, page 14.

to be. As the narrator says, we can still "choose a path that's clear," we can still "choose free will."

Again, it anticipates what Rush later talks about in "Prime Mover," the idea that, although the world is random, just a spinning top to nowhere with no one in control, we ourselves are our own prime mover, and the decisions we make determine the quality of our ride while we're here.

Musically, in *Permanent Waves* the band was coming to perfect what would later be considered a hallmark of its playing: the ability to conjure up images cinematically. The showcase piece on the album for this highly accomplished form of playing is "Jacob's Ladder," a beautifully rendered enactment of the atmospheric condition that goes by that same name. In both the words and the music the band paints a picture of "bruised and sullen" storm clouds gathering like armies before a battle, "looming low and ominous / In twilight premature," and then erupting in a violent thunder storm. The violence stops as quickly as it starts and, when all is calm, the clouds part, and down come the stunning rays of light ("crepuscular rays" in the technical term) that give the atmospheric condition its name.

What's interesting about the piece is it carries on the Randian man-is-the-measure-of-all-things project by giving the piece the same musical and lyrical presence as the biblical story on which the name "Jacob's Ladder" is derived. In the Book of Genesis,[1] the atmospheric condition symbolizes the moment when the clouds part and God, descending to earth upon the rays of light as if they were a flight of stairs, approaches Jacob, the Jewish patriarch, and bequeaths the land beneath the clouds to Jacob for his people.

Rush's trick is to give the piece, in music and lyrics, a big feeling of religiosity—magisterial music, grandiloquent words—but it's all in the service of the natural phenomenon, not the biblical story. It's ingenious.

We'll be talking about this more later, but Rush's usurpation of religious motifs gets at the idea that Chris McDonald talks about in his *Rush and Philosophy* essay, "Enlightened Thoughts, Mystic Words," in which he says the band co-opts religious language and imagery in the service of a very humanistic worldview, thereby giving the same emotional color and power of religion to the rather austere worldview of humanism. If that's the case, than "Jacob's Ladder" is where the band first tries its hand at the practice—and carries it off sublimely.

The album's masterpiece, though, certainly to many fans and critics, is the concluding song, "Natural Science," a progressive metal opus that clocks in at a little more than nine minutes and looks at our place in the world from three vantage points: as tiny biological organisms in a temporary tide pool, as men using science to take what they think is control of the physical world around them, and as men chastened by the knowledge that, despite our advances, we're really no more than those biological organisms in the tide pool, ultimately subject to the overwhelming power of the physical world around us.

---

1 *Genesis* 28:10-19.

Musically, as many of Rush's pieces do, the song dispenses with the typical 32-bar structure of verse, chorus, verse, chorus, bridge, chorus and instead proceeds very much like a story narrative, beginning slowly, with water flowing over a natural bowl in the sand, creating the tide pools. From there we're taken into hyperspace, with all its white-knuckle intensity, and then we return to earth in time to see the tides washing out the pools that were created just a short while previously. "Wave after wave will flow with the tide / And bury the world as it does / Tide after tide will flow and recede / Leaving life to go on as it was."

Even for critics, the piece is sufficient evidence, if more evidence was needed, that the band at this point was simply operating in a place musically that few bands could imagine reaching. Indeed, with *Permanent Waves* as a whole, the band had established beyond any doubt their place as musicians of exceptional ability, characterized by their skill at matching their music to concepts cinematically.

As John Gill of *Sounds* magazine put it with nice concision in a 1981 article on the band, "Rush usually start at a technical . . . level that most bands end with."[1]

Thematically, "Natural Science" is doing very much the same thing as "Jacob's Ladder," deploying sweeping musicality in the service of an ultimately humanist message: we hold the fate of the earth in our hands, yet we remain but microscopic points in a limitless universe. God is nowhere to be found: we are on a spinning top to nowhere, yet it's up to us to live our lives with the dignity and responsibility that comes with being the measure of all things in our part of the universe.

It's also continuing the band's criticism of collectivism with the view that, no matter how smart our leaders get, and no matter how well-intentioned they are in organizing our resources for the betterment of the whole, we simply can't know enough to really control our destiny. "In their own image / Their world is fashioned / No wonder they don't understand."

It's the exact same criticism that the Austrian school economists like Friedrich Hayek had of government intervention in the free market. Steven Horwitz, in his *Rush and Philosophy* essay "Rush's Libertarianism Never Fit the Plan," says the piece is a thinly disguised Hayekian critique of government trying to apply the principles of science to the economy, and it doesn't work. "Our ability to manipulate the natural world has understandably led us to think we can do the same with the social world," Horwitz says, interpreting Hayek. "This 'scientistic' prejudice is at the heart of libertarianism's critique of various forms of social and economic planning."[2]

Rush hit individualism and this collectivist critique equally hard on its next and most commercially successful album, its quadruple-platinum *Moving Pictures*, released in 1981.

Musically, it was moving away from the long pieces that had become a

1 "Permanent Raves," by John Gill, *Sounds*, March 14, 1991.
2 Berti and Bowman, *Rush and Philosophy*, pages 264-266.

mainstay of its progressive metal period (although it still had the longish "Camera Eye," at 11 minutes, on the album), but thematically it was still in the exact same place.

The opening track and arguably its most well-known song of all time, "Tom Sawyer," vaguely associates with the Mark Twain character by describing an independent thinker who, through his reserve, takes command of his place in the world. In the song's key line, "No, his mind is not for rent / To any god or government," you have an unequivocal summation of humanistic individualism and a reprise of the idea in "Freewill" to choose free will rather than to fall back on faith in a supernatural power.

In essence, with the piece, you have Peart's most stripped-down annunciation of individualist principles yet, packaged in music that was radio-friendly enough that it cracked the Top 40, reaching No. 24, and introducing the band to listeners that it otherwise wouldn't have had.

'Tom Sawyer' as libertarian anthem

Whether the band likes it or not, "Tom Sawyer" has become something of a touchstone for libertarians in the United States. The association of the song with Rand Paul and Neel Kashkari is emblematic of that relationship, and its individualist quality surely had something to do with Rush choosing that song to perform when they appeared[1] in 2008 on *The Colbert Report*, Stephen Colbert's Comedy Central show that satirizes conservative American politics.

Given such an individualist, humanist message, it's a curiosity that "Tom Sawyer" ever became so popular on mainstream rock charts. As Lee said in the 2007 book on the band's 30-year anniversary, *Contents Under Pressure*, "The fact that it is so popular still just confuses the hell out of me."[2]

In all likelihood, most listeners don't attend to the words closely enough to form any idea of what the song's about other than that it seems to capture on some level the attractive, plucky character of Twain's *Tom Sawyer*, who, with his friend Huck Finn, lives at the meeting point between civilization and a state of nature.

A good stand-in for our uncertainty over what "Tom Sawyer" really means might be Eric Cartman—the smart but spoiled *South Park* character who seems to always get everyone's goat.

Rush opened its shows in the early 2000s with a *South Park* vignette that was made just for the band by the show's creators Matt Stone and Trey Parker: Cartman and his three friends start to play "Tom Sawyer" on their instruments but they can't agree on what exactly Geddy Lee is saying in the song.

---

1 Rush appeared on *The Colbert Report* on July 16, 2008, a video of which is at *Colbert Nation*: http://www.colbertnation.com/the-colbert-report-videos/176346/july-16-2008/rush-is-here retrieved November 17, 2012.
2 Popoff, *Contents Under Pressure*, page 88.

"A modern day warrior named Tom Sawyer / He floated down a river on a raft with a black guy," Cartman sings.

"That's not Tom Sawyer; that's Huckleberry Finn, stupid!" Kyle Broflovski breaks in.

"I am Geddy Lee," yells Cartman, "and I will sing whatever lyrics I want!"[1]

Even Peart, who wrote the lyrics with Pye Dubois of Canadian hard rock band Max Webster, says he's not sure exactly what he and Dubois are trying to get at with the piece other than that they like the individualist spirit of the character.

"The original lyrics [by Dubois] were of a portrait of a modern day rebel, a free-spirited individualist striding through the world wide-eyed and purposeful," Peart says in a 1985 interview. "There are parts of the song that I don't necessarily understand. But I like the arrogance implied. But it's a mistaken arrogance. There are . . . little games you're expected to play that Tom Sawyer and I don't have time for."[2]

Musically, even though the piece is relatively long for a mainstream chart topper (at about five minutes), it's short for a piece that manages to encapsulate all of the elements of progressive rock in its compact structure. Yet it does that handily by combining virtuosic playing in an asymmetrical 7/4 time signature and a lengthy, very complex instrumental section.[3]

The piece has been listed at Number 19 by VH1 in its list of all-time top rock songs[4] and it was one of the compositions for which Rush was inducted into the Canadian Songwriters Hall of Fame in 2010. ("Limelight," "The Spirit of Radio," "Closer to the Heart," and "Subdivisions" were the others.)[5]

But "Tom Sawyer" is just the first song on an album in which individualism is the dominant theme. The next track, "Red Barchetta," returns to a "2112"-like future with a tale of a young man who rebels against an all-encompassing nanny state by taking his uncle's meticulously preserved sports car out for weekend joy rides. In this world, private car ownership is forbidden, so the young man naturally attracts the attention of a pair of law enforcers in big "alloy air cars" (cars "two lanes wide" that travel on a cushion of air) and he gets into a test of wits with them. They race around the countryside until he

---

1 The video is hosted on YouTube and accessible at *Rush Vault*: http://rushvault.com/2011/01/11/tom-sawyer-background/ retrieved December 30, 2012.

2 Telleria, *Merely Players*, page 160.

3 Bowman includes a detailed analysis of "Tom Sawyer" in his 2003 UCLA Ph.D. dissertation, "Permanent Change: Rush, Musicians' Rock, and the Progressive Post-Counterculture." You can access his paper online at Durrell Bowman.com: http://durrellbowman.com/PDFS/DBowman_dissertation.pdf retrieved December 6, 2012.

4 "Tom Sawyer" as VH1's No.19 top rock song is at http://music.spreadit.org/vh1-top-100-hard-rock-songs/ retrieved December 7, 2012.

5 News on Rush's 2010 induction into the Canadian Songwriters Hall of Fame is at Newswire: http://www.newswire.ca/en/story/716683/rush-robert-charlebois-among-2010-canadian-songwriters-hall-of-fame-inductees-to-be-honoured-at-6th-annual-gala-on-march-28-2010 retrieved December 7, 2012.

makes a winning tactical maneuver: crossing a bridge that's too narrow for the cruisers to cross, leaving them to eat his dust.

As the song fades out, we see him relaxing with his uncle by the fireside. Robert Telleria in his 2002 book *Merely Players* (Quarry Press) says the ending is ambiguous about whether the chase really happened or whether it was just a fireside fantasy. "At the end of the song we realize that the chase may have been imaginary, in the mind of the uncle or nephew reliving a rebellious experience in a fireside chat," Telleria says. But to me the song is pretty clearly depicting an actual chase for two reasons. First, Peart said the lyrics are based on a 1973 short story, "A Nice Morning Drive," in *Car and Driver* magazine, and in that story the chase was an actual, not an imagined, one, and second, the lyrics are clearly presenting the fireside dreaming as coming after, not before, the chase. The dreaming really just seems to be about a yearning for a time when people could just drive their cars around without worrying about the government.

Like "Jacob's Ladder," the song is an example of how the band was perfecting its ability to match sound with content cinematically by evoking images musically. You see this with particular clarity in the middle of the piece when you hear tires squealing and hearts racing as the young man duels with the enforcers.

"The intention of 'Red Barchetta' was to create a song that was very vivid, so that you had a sense of action," Lifeson says in a radio interview on the program called *In the Studio*. "It does become a movie. I think that song really worked with that in mind. It's something that I think we've tried to carry on—become a little more visual with our music. . . . I like the way the parts knit together. I like the changes. I like the melody. I love the dynamics, the way it opens with the harmonics and creates a mood, then gets right into the driving, right up to the middle section where it's really screaming along, where you really feel like you're in the open car, and the music is very vibrant and moving. And then it ends as it began, with that quiet dynamic, and lets you down lightly. So, it picks you up for the whole thing and drops you off at your next spot."

The album's progressive metal showpiece, "The Camera Eye," walks us through a comparison of what looks like New Yorkers and Londoners but is really about the nature of the cities that the people inhabit. We see both New Yorkers and Londoners striding purposefully down the streets of their respective cities, but it's in New York that the city and the buildings are designed with function in mind. Everything about the physical environment, from the high-rise towers to the way the streets channel people through the buildings, is about efficiency. In this sense, the physical infrastructure mirrors the idealized architecture in Rand's *The Fountainhead*. In this conception, physical design is an extension of the people's ambitions to realize the possibilities ahead of them. "The buildings are lost / In their limitless rise / My feet catch the pulse / And the purposeful stride / . . . / I feel the sense of possibilities / I feel the wrench of hard realities / The focus is sharp in the city."

In London, the vibe is very different. The city and its buildings predate the hustle and bustle of people on the go. While the streets of London might teem with the energy of Londoners going about their business, the city itself is calm because, like it's old and venerable buildings, it functions as a repository of history and will be there long after the people you see are dead and gone. The city in this instance is more than a mere extension of the people's ambitions; it is a living record of the always-changing dynamics of life. "Pavements may teem / With intense energy / But the city is calm / In this violent sea."

Structurally, the song takes the same stream-of-consciousness approach that early twentieth century American writer and "Lost Generation" chronicler John Dos Passos uses in "the camera eye" portion of his three most well-known novels, *The 42nd Parallel, 1919,* and *The Big Money.* The novels were packaged together into a single volume, called the *USA Trilogy,* and what binds them together is the increasingly sour look at where the U.S. is heading politically. It's the same theme we saw in "Beneath, Between & Behind," with its look at how the U.S. is failing to live up to its individualist heritage.

Dos Passos will figure into the band's music again, in the mid-1980s, with other pieces inspired by his writing, including "The Big Money" and "Grand Designs," both of which adopt ideas in Dos Passos stories of the same title.

Although lyrically "The Camera Eye" takes a stream-of-consciousness approach, musically the piece is structured in a way similar to "Hemispheres," in the sense that the song is evenly divided between two approaches to life. In "Hemispheres," it's *eudaimonia* vs. *akrasia,* right vs. left, rational vs. irrational, emotional vs. intellectual as people struggle internally to define themselves and externally to define how to organize society, and in "The Camera Eye" it's city as capitalist tool vs. city as something bigger, more rooted than simply being an economic tool. Both songs suggest you need both sides of the equation for people to live balanced lives, but in "Hemispheres" it's about our inner lives and our social organization and in "The Camera Eye" it's about the physical environment around us.

Peart in "The Camera Eye" is tough on New York City, that's clear, but he's not as tough as some have painted him. Carol Selby Price and Robert Price in their 1999 book *Mystic Rhythms: The Philosophical Vision of Rush* (Wildside Press) interpret the depiction of New York as completely spirit-deadening, the streets a maze that entraps rats and the buildings, their tops obscured by dull, gray clouds, a prison for troglodyte-like slaves. "No sky, no hope," they say. London, by contrast, is all misty veiled romanticism of the past, and they draw on poetry of H.P. Lovecraft to show how Peart intended to make a distinction between the two cities.[1]

But I have to disagree with their completely negative interpretation of New York City, because the city, while indeed a hard and unforgiving place,

1 Carol and Robert M. Price, *Mystic Rhythms: The Philosophical Vision of Rush.* Berkeley Heights: Wildside Press, 1999, pages 61-65.

like capitalism itself, is nevertheless a dynamic place of possibility for those tough enough to succeed in it. When Peart writes, "My feet catch the pulse / And the purposeful stride," that's the individual, Tom Sawyer, getting into the rhythm of the city and anticipating the success he will have taming this wild beast. These are the words of a winner who is poised to rise above the crowd. These are not the words of a person cowed by New York's rough edges. You need a tough, heartless place like New York City to provide the dynamic environment in which purpose-driven strivers can succeed. "I feel the sense of possibilities/ I feel the wrench of hard realities / The focus is sharp in the city."

Indeed, it's the very hardness of the reality that concentrates the mind—makes the focus sharp to the limitless possibilities. We'll see this later when we look at *Clockwork Angels* in detail.

The last two songs on the album, "Witch Hunt" and "Vital Signs," give us two very pointed takes on individualism. "Witch Hunt" is an absolutely blistering critique of government, religious, and community leaders who exploit people's fears of "otherness" to gin up mobs of unthinking, brutish vigilantism. And "Vital Signs" returns to the inner struggle of people as they weigh whether to go along with the crowd or assert their independence. It does this by depicting our thinking processes in almost digital terms. "Process information at half speed / Pause, rewind, replay / Worn memory chip / Random sample, hold the one you need."

The song's message is one that recurs throughout the band's work: your life is a long-term project. Don't try to settle or achieve everything now. Be persistent and maintain the courage of your convictions and over time you'll achieve your dreams. "Leave out the fiction / The fact is, this friction / Will only be worn by persistence / Leave out conditions / Courageous convictions / Will drag the dream into existence."

Musically, the two songs couldn't be more different, but they both carry the "moving pictures" project forward by their cinematic execution. "Witch Hunt" is depicted in dark, ominous tones, like heavy chains being dragged and dropped on a stone floor, with the crazed cries of people stirred to a frenzy in the background. You visualize the mob assembling in a patch of dewy grass in the black of night, the only light coming from the moon. You can see the orange glow from their torches casting ghastly shadows on their faces. The music is so much like a series of pictures that it's very much like watching the opening scenes of a movie.

"Vital Signs" is equally evocative but in a completely different way. The piece is built around a digital sequencer, so it conveys the idea of our thinking in digital terms, almost like our brains are chemical computers and if we want our output to be good, we need to be sure our inputs are good. Hence, the song unspools like we're hearing trusted words of advice from HAL, the computer in *2001: A Space Odyssey*, but HAL in this case is our friend and ally, not the HAL in the movie who turns on us in order to preserve the secrecy of the space mission. The good HAL wants to make sure we don't spoil our inputs by succumbing to mediocre group think.

From a popular music standpoint, *Moving Pictures* was the pinnacle for the band. The two remaining songs in the album, "YYZ" and "Limelight," were both huge hits, although in very different ways. "Limelight" was a radio hit, like "Tom Sawyer," reaching No. 18 on the Top 40 chart, and is one of the songs the band is most closely linked to in casual listeners' minds. And yet lyrically it's something of an anomaly not just on the album but among the entire Rush song list, because it dispenses with philosophy and just talks self-referentially about the alienating nature of being in the camera eye: how fans who idealize you think of you as part of their life, like a friend, while to you they remain strangers who are invading your privacy.

"YYZ" (pronounced "YY *Zed*") is arguably the most interesting song on the album from a strictly musical perspective. As an instrumental, all of its meaning and emotion is conveyed musically, and while it was never a popular radio hit in the way "Tom Sawyer" and "Limelight" were, it was a smash with musicians and the broader community of progressive metal aficionados. Indeed, it's easily one of the band's most important songs in all its 40 years from the perspective of this critical group of listeners. It's power lies in how it translates its content, which is about traveling to different parts of the world, into purely musical form.

The piece starts with a musical rendition of the letters "YYZ," the alphabetic code for Toronto's airport, Pearson International Airport, translated in the dots and dashes of Morse code. Thus, you hear Peart tapping out "— . —— — . —— —— . ." on a set of bells on his drum kit. ("Y" is dash, dot, dash, dash, and "Z "is dash, dash, dot, dot.) Lifeson on guitar and Lee on bass then come in and pound out the same code, with Peart now beating on his drums. After repeating the phrase a number of times, the band pauses for a moment and then they're off on their musical journey.

As Peart describes it in an interview he gave for a 1988 biography on the band, *Rush: Visions* (Omnibus Press), by Bill Banasiewicz: "There are parts of the song that are semi-evocative of the feelings that are engendered when you are going to the airport to leave. You are sort of feeling edgy and tense because you are having to leave home and go to work, and you are thinking that you are half at home and half away. It's a very transitional period, and you always have a sense of infinite possibilities at the airport. You can change your mind and fly anywhere in the world, and all of a sudden you are not in Toronto anymore; you are in the world."

On YouTube, where there's a big subculture of amateur musicians posting videos of themselves covering songs for comment by other musicians, no fewer than 150 *drummers* have posted their version of the piece. (I stopped counting after 150; the number of videos was just too daunting to count). There are similar numbers of guitar and bass covers and by full ensembles, so when you add in all of the "YYZ" covers, you're looking at something approaching 600 or 700 videos by amateur musicians trying to play that one piece.

John Reuland of Princeton University has taken a close look at the community of musicians for whom these YouTube videos are serious business and says the attraction of Rush's songs, like "YYZ," is their intricately composed complexity. Because the band's pieces are so precisely structured, it's possible for musicians to aspire to replicate them note for note, despite their complexity. The songs thus take on a kind of mathematical challenge: they're complex, yet because they're so precise, they can be mastered if you apply enough blood, sweat, and tears. Reuland calls this aspect of the band's music an "aesthetic of replicability." It's an aesthetic on which the individual performances of each song "are constructed as artifacts that, importantly, are meant to sound as if they can be reproduced exactly."[1]

Contrast this aesthetic of replicabilty with the aesthetic of, say, jam bands. For players who cover the songs of jam bands, like the Grateful Dead or Phish, the goal isn't precise replication; it's reinventing the song each time you play it, infusing it with moods based on how you're feeling that day. A similar point can be made of musicians covering songs of bands that aren't jam bands *per se* but that compose and perform with a much looser style, like Led Zeppelin. The quality of the musicianship of Led Zeppelin is unquestioned, but that quality is different than what you hear coming out of Rush. Led Zeppelin's musical ancestry is rhythm and blues, emotional and improvisational; Rush's musical ancestry, Reuland suggests, is European classical music, precise and replicable.

For this reason, while "Tom Sawyer" and "Limelight" are the songs most popularly associated with Rush's biggest selling album, it's the songs, like "YYZ" and "Witch Hunt," which showcase the band's cinematic playing style, that arguably have served as the main driver of the band's success as a cult band. Thus, while *Rolling Stone* magazine and the rest of the mainstream music establishment were skewering Rush, in significant part for its counter-left individualist message, musicians in a big subculture of Rush admirers were trying to play these songs as precisely as classical musicians try to play Bach or Corelli.

Following *Moving Pictures*, in 1982, the band released its last album with its long-time producer, Terry Brown.

With *Signals*, not only was it embarking on a very different musical style (which was in large measure why Rush and Brown parted company after 10 successful albums together over eight years), Peart was very much broadening his lyrical themes. To be sure, the band continued to hit individualism hard, especially in the album's big radio hit, "New World Man," which is both a celebration of individualism and a matter-of-fact look at the contradictory forces that push and pull a person as he tries to maintain command of his life. But aside from that song, the theme of individualism goes subterranean. Gone are the kind of lines in the band's early pieces, like "Something for Nothing," from the bands 1976 *2112* album, where individualist principles are

1 Berti and Bowman, *Rush and Philosophy*, page 60.

front and center. "What you own is your own kingdom / What you do is your own glory / What you love is your own power / What you live is your own story."

Instead, the band looked at individualism in the broader context of the human condition. In the album's other big popular hit, "Subdivisions," for example, the lyrics paint a picture of the individual rising above the crowd, but the piece puts the focus on the stultifying rigidity of the suburbs, both in its physical layout as a grid and in the behavioral norms that suburban kids expect of one another as uncompromisingly as do the priests in "2112."

In the way it's structured, the song isn't a political or even philosophical song at all; it's a sociological song. Unlike in "The Camera Eye," where the piece looks at the tall buildings of New York City as an extension of man, almost as if the buildings are tools to be used to help man be the most productive he can be, and the buildings of London as separate from man, something more rooted in history, the grid-like layout of the suburbs is seen from the opposite direction: the impact that this grid is having *on* man. In other words, it takes the position of Marshall McLuhan in his landmark 1964 work, *The Extensions of Man*, that we mold our tools (in this case, the suburbs) and they in turn mold us. So, what we're seeing is how our suburbs, which we created to increase efficiency and accommodate our growing reliance on private car ownership after World War II, turned the tables on us and are now molding us—and not in a good way.

The song points to the fact that many young people, some more self-aware than others, light out for the city, but many of them lack the fortitude to succeed. They end up selling "their dreams for small desires / Or lose the race to rats / Get caught in ticking traps." For many of these suburbanites who try but fail to conquer the city, they "start to dream of somewhere / To relax their restless flight / Somewhere out of a memory of lighted streets on quiet nights." In other words, they return to the suburbs and melt back into the crowd, defeated.

Not so the New World Man. In Rush's other big radio hit from the album "New World Man," which was the band's one and only No. 1 song, in 1982, the title character is very much a suburbanite who lit out for the city and is now striding across the landscape a winner. "He's a rebel and a runner / He's a signal turning green / He's a restless young romantic / Wants to run the big machine."

But that doesn't mean he can let his guard down and relax. The piece is about the recurring battle to maintain one's integrity and one's values in the face of unrelenting forces working against any one of us who holds himself up as his own beacon of light. And these forces aren't just external forces; they're the conflicting values we hold within ourselves that, "Hemispheres"-like, are constantly sparring for supremacy. "He's old enough to know what's right / But young enough not to choose it / He's noble enough to win the world / But weak enough to lose it."

Of course, in a twist that Ayn Rand would surely agree with, the piece can also be taken as a cautionary note for the West in general and North America in particular. Substitute "country" for "man" and you have a perfect description of the tightrope that the United States or Canada or the two together, or all the West in general, walk as each country tries, or all of them together try, to be both leader and self-interested participant on the world stage.

Rand was constantly railing against the weakening of the United States' commitment to the individualist principles on which the country was founded. At the time she was peaking, in the 1950s and 1960s, she saw evidence all around her that the United States was inching toward the same collectivist mentality that had already (in her mind) ruined the U.K. and the continental European countries. The U.S. Congress kept disappointing her with laws that smelled way too much like the leftist do-goodism that she saw as a threat to the country's integrity.

"What we need today is to erect a corresponding philosophical structure, without which the material greatness [of the United States] cannot survive," she says in one of her last essays, "Don't Let It Go," compiled in *Philosophy: Who Needs It?* (Signet Books). "A skyscraper cannot stand on cracker barrels, nor on wall mottoes, nor on full-page ads, nor on prayers, nor on meta-language. The new wilderness to reclaim is philosophy, now all but deserted, with the weeds of prehistoric doctrines rising again to swallow the ruins. To support a culture, nothing less than a new philosophical foundation will do."[1]

Although there's no reason to suppose Peart shares any of Rand's extremism on this issue, his writing, particularly in his first book, The Masked Rider (ECW Press), about a 1988 bicycle ride he took over the entire length of Cameroon in western Africa, makes clear he nevertheless saw his native Canada and the other country he spends so much of his life in (and now lives in), the United States, as constantly being pushed and pulled in conflicting directions. And thus you can take the song as a cautionary tale for North America.

It's North America that's an eager young runner that wants to run the big machine (the world order); it's North America that has a problem with its poisons (pollution, nuclear waste), but that also has the structure and the optimistic, educated population that will find a way to address it. It's North America that's cleaning up its system (the Clean Water and Clean Air acts in the U.S.) to keep its nature pure. It's North America that's learning to match the beat of the Old World Man (assume the world leadership role that was Europe's for so long) and that's learning to catch the heat of the Third World Man (not to treat the countries of Africa and other developing parts of the world as colonial dumping grounds the way Europe did).

On through the song you can go, substituting North America or the West for the individual: North America is young enough to make mistakes but it's also mature enough to mend the mistakes it makes. It's old enough to

---

1 Ayn Rand, *Philosophy: Who Needs It?* New York: Signet, 1984, page 213.

know what's right (foster developing countries) but young enough not to choose it (exploiting them instead for their natural resources, working with the dictators that it knows are keeping their own people down), and so on.

Thus, the song can be taken at both these levels, capturing the pressure individuals are under to maintain their integrity and capturing the pressure western democracies are under to balance their short-term self-interest with their long-term interest in doing what's right for the world.

The other tracks on the album maintain the individualist theme in a similar undercurrent fashion.

In "Analog Kid," we see one of those suburban kids in "Subdivisions" at the precise moment when he hears the siren song of the big city and the universal yearning to make his mark on the world ("a bright and nameless vision / Has him longing to depart).

In "Digital Man," we see the same kid, now grown up and deeply embedded in the hustle and bustle of the city, so absorbed in his life on the cutting edge of what's new, that he is at risk of losing touch with himself, if he hasn't already done so. He's completely made the break from his "analog," or pastoral, past, and is now fully vested in his "digital," or urban, present. The question that hangs over the song is whether his digitalized present has hollowed him out or whether he will, like the New World Man, find a way to balance the internal conflict that life in the modern world forces all of us to confront.

In a sense, we see the outcome of the digital man's life in "Losing It," a piece in which Ben Mink, a long-time collaborator of k.d. lang and a good friend of Geddy Lee's, plays a hauntingly beautiful electric violin in one of the few Rush pieces (prior to *Clockwork Angels*) to use an outside collaborator (not counting Hugh Syme, who periodically plays keyboards on recordings in addition to providing the band's cover art). The piece is organized into two vignettes, the first about an elderly woman who in her prime was a star dancer but is now too stiff to do much more than shuffle around in her living room with the curtains closed to keep out the light, and the second about an elderly man who, in his prime, was a dashing and celebrated writer in the mold of Ernest Hemingway but who now can barely string two sentences together. Both in their own way, when they were young, lit out for the city and conquered it, but now they are faced with their quickly diminishing relevance, and it's frankly sad. So, here we get to the downside of living our life on a spinning top to nowhere: what does it mean in the end? Are we all just doomed to fade from relevance, our shades drawn to keep out a present that's leaving us behind?

From the point of view of the faded stars, the end is indeed sad, but from the point of view of the rest of us, with the legacy they leave behind, the end is a good one. They might die sad and lonely, and that's a shame, but the one consolation is that the world is clearly enriched by their accomplishments. That, at least, is something they can take to the grave with them.

The darkest piece on the album, "The Weapon," revisits "Witch Hunt" and its blistering critique of leaders who exploit people's fear and ignorance to gin up vigilante mobs, but this time the aim is to dig deeper into the psychology of how these leaders do what they do. Hence we see how religious leaders, who themselves are scared and paranoid about life, hold out their hand to help people at vulnerable moments but rather than help the vulnerable solve their problems, they bring them down to their own level and exploit them for their own purposes. "Like a steely blade in a silken sheath / We don't see what they're made of / They shout about love, but when push comes to shove / They live for the things they're afraid of." We'll be talking more about this piece later.

The outlier on the album is "Chemistry," an interesting piece in which the band steps back from examining the world around them and instead examines, in autobiographical form, their own relationship with one another. I say "autobiographical" form, but really the piece conducts its exploration at the chemical level, and concludes that the three members of the band (who collaborated on the lyrics) share a chemical bond with one another, a bond that's too valuable to tinker with, because for reasons even they don't understand, they can communicate with one another at a level that goes much deeper than words. "Oh, but how / Do they make contact / With one another? / Electricity? Biology? / Seems to me it's Chemistry / . . . / Emotion transmitted / Emotion received / Music in the abstract / Positively / . . . / Elemental empathy / A change of synergy / Music making contact / Naturally."

In a sense, the band has become self-aware of this special bond between them and has come to value it explicitly. It's worth noting that it was starting around this time, 1982, as they were champing at the bit to go down different musical paths (different from what long-time producer Terry Brown wanted to do), that they considered adding another member to the band. They later rejected that idea on the grounds that bringing in a new personality risked upsetting the chemistry they had going on between them. As Peart says later, in his 2007 book *Roadshow*, "We were still apprehensive about the chemistry thing and, certainly, proud of what we could do with just the three of us. So we decided to carry on ourselves."[1]

Timothy Smolko, one of the essayists in *Rush and Philosophy*, puts the chemical connection in the song in a broader perspective, saying it refers to the connection between musicians as they play together and also in the relationship musicians have with their listeners. "With words such as 'signals,' 'energy,' 'reaction,' 'telepathy,' and 'synergy,' the lyrics describe the body language, eye contact, the symbiotic connection between musicians and the connection between musicians and their audience," he says in "What Can This Strange Device Be?"[2]

That's a fair interpretation, and the song does indeed work at that level. But I think the song is really just about the band members, because in the

1 Peart, *Roadshow*, pages 75-76.
2 Berti and Bowman, page 233.

lyrics (which, again, all three members collaborated on), the number three is emphasized: "Two to one" in one instance and then "One, two, three / Add without subtraction / Sound on sound / Multiplied reaction."

These references are revealing, because the number three at the time was becoming a recurring motif in the band's music and in the imagery on its album covers as a stand-in for the three of them: the three arches at the Toronto City Hall on *Moving Pictures*, the three red spheres and balls of fire on *Hold Your Fire*, the three TVs on *Power Windows*, the three climbers on *Test for Echo*, the "rock, paper, scissors" imagery on *Presto*, the three tinker toy pieces on *Different Stages*, one of their compilation albums, and so on down the line, until you get to *Clockwork Angels*, the band's latest album, released in 2012. There, the number three isn't highlighted but we see the "U" in "Rush" depicted as the ancient runic symbol for amalgamation—yet another way of saying the same thing about chemistry: the whole is better than the sum of its parts.

No end to the thread

Rush is celebrated for its nose-to-the-grindstone work habits, and you can certainly see that in its output. By 1982, with *Signals*, its ninth studio album, the band had cut and released 80 original compositions, and in one way or another three quarters of them address the idea of individualism. By 2012, when they released *Clockwork Angels*, their nineteenth original studio album (their 2004 EP *Feedback* doesn't count because it's a collection of covers), they had cut and released another 85 original songs, more than a third of which touch on individualism as well. In "The Body Electric," on the 1984 *Grace Under Pressure* album, for example, we see a humanoid, after he acquires a sense of self-awareness, try to deprogram himself (an interesting take on Ayn Rand's *Anthem*, which involves people being treated like humanoids), and in "Grand Designs," on the 1985 *Power Windows* album, we see individualists who swim against the stream. In "Dreamline," on the 1991 *Roll the Bones* album, we see a return to the universal impulse of kids to leave their comfort zones and light out for adventure in the city, in this case armed with nothing more than a "radar-fix on the stars" and a "liquid-crystal compass."

We don't need to look at all of the pieces here to see the continuing thread of individualism in the band's music throughout its career. It's sufficient to say that, in his lyric writing, Peart continued to ground his philosophical views on an individualist foundation. Yet in the band's later albums, Peart's lyrical canvas was much broader. He began to look at a linked set of issues: the worsening state of the planet, the continuing inequalities among people, and the excesses of vulture capitalism.

All three of these themes go to the heart of the band's classical liberal orientation, in contradistinction to its reputation as a libertarian rock band. What these all have in common is their "bleeding heart" character: just as

Peart in later years down-played his libertarianism by describing himself as a bleeding-heart libertarian, these recurring themes in the band's music show Rush very much sees a place for government in softening the edges of capitalism. And that's what we're going to take a look at now.

CHAPTER 4. INDIVIDUALISM: IT'S NOT JUST ABOUT YOU, YOU KNOW

> Hand over hand
> Doesn't seem so much
> Hand over hand
> Is the strength of the common touch.
> —"Hand Over Fist," *Presto, 1989*

The 1985 *Power Windows* album marks a clean line of demarcation for the band in its sound and in what it writes about. For a significant share of fans, the change was not a good one. *Power Windows, Hold Your Fire, Presto* . . . these later 1980s albums are all troubling for the band's classic progressive metal purists, and in interviews the band acknowledged it lost some long-time listeners over them. But Lifeson, Lee, and Peart in many interviews made it clear the changes were necessary to grow as artists rather than stagnate by doing the same thing over and over again. Lee said the band needed to do things differently to avoid succumbing to cliché, and if that meant losing some fans, that was the price the band had to pay. "There are lots of reasons why fans have turned away from us at certain points in our career," he says in the 2011 documentary *Metal Evolution.* "There's nothing we can do about that."[1]

Sonically, the music became more pop-sounding, characterized by a wiry guitar, the addition of electronic drums, and a new focus on compositional bombasticity, for lack of a better term. Gone were the meaty, Zeppelin-like

---

1 Lee's *Metal Evolution* quote about Rush losing audience members as it moved away from its long and hard progressive metal concept pieces to shorter pop sounding pieces is at the beginning of the last episode, near the 15 minute mark, and can be accessed at *Rush is a Band*: http://www.rushisaband.com/blog/2012/01/29/2978/Rush-featured-in-Progressive-Metal-episode-of-Metal-Evolution   retrieved December 4, 2012.

guitar work and screechy vocals from the earlier albums that the band's earliest fans liked so much.

Lyrically, and most importantly for our purposes, the band's message seemed to blur as well. As opposed to its output between 1975 and 1982, when it focused like a laser beam on the power of the individual to take matters into his own hands and drive change, a staple of capitalist myth-making, starting with *Power Windows* the band seemed to turn critical of *laissez-faire* capitalism and its excesses: suddenly it was writing about the need to rein in greedy business people before they ran roughshod over helpless people and destroyed the environment. What was going on?

In truth, the band had been sending cautionary signals about unbridled capitalism all along, particularly in its 1977 album *A Farewell to Kings*. The title track, as we saw earlier, talks about the way scheming demons are beating down the multitudes and scoffing at the wise and hypocrites are slandering the sacred halls of truth. Who are these scheming demons and hypocrites? Among others, they're the same professional CEOs and moneymen that Rush complained about in "The Spirit of Radio," that is, arrogant profiteers for whom only the almighty dollar is a lodestar.

On that same album Rush took a stab at what's needed to change this dollar-first mentality. On "Closer to the Heart," the band asks our leaders to reorient their thinking away from a single-minded pursuit of what's best for themselves to take a broader perspective. "And the men who hold high places / Must be the ones who start / To mold a new reality / Closer to the heart."

"Cinderella Man," with lyrics written by Lee based on the 1952 Jimmy Stewart Christmastime favorite *Mr. Smith Goes to Washington*, goes down this same road, portraying a man who made his wealth and now wants to use it to help the needy. "Because he was human / Because he had goodness / Because he was moral."

Helping the needy in this context is an extraordinary sentiment, considering how purple with rage Ayn Rand would become every time she talked about altruism of any kind. So, even at the height of their Randian period (this was 1977), there was no shortage of pieces critical of go-it-alone capitalism.

But now it was 1985 and the band seemed to be criticizing private enterprise straight on. Indeed, almost in its entirety, *Power Windows* is an explicit critique of power, much of it exercised by capitalists but the critique is directed at all forms of power. But, as we'll see, there's a method behind this madness.

Opening track "The Big Money," which references John Dos Passos' story of the same name about the corrupting power of American capitalism, portrays big business as a game show in which the deck is stacked in favor of the host, with the contestants mere pieces to be used as needed. "Sometimes pushing people around / Sometimes pulling out the rug / Sometimes pushing all the buttons/ Sometimes pulling out the plug."

In Dos Passos' story, published in 1936 and later packaged as part of his *USA Trilogy*, we get portraits of businessmen who climb their way to the top and, very much like we see in Rush's "Digital Man" on *Signals*, they lose their souls along the way and end up caricatures of bloodless capitalists who can only measure their lives by the success of their bank accounts.

Stylistically, in the same way that Dos Passos deployed experimental literary techniques in his trilogy (such as "camera eye"-styled stream of consciousness and "newsreel"-styled excerpts of headlines and articles), Rush's piece also uses an experimental stylistic motif: the TV game show.

Thus, the opening of the song sounds like the opening of a game show: with a flourish of big, round notes that give way to a carnivalesque jingle and the kind of upbeat patter you hear when the game show host bounds out, waving to the studio audience.

The next song on the album, "Grand Designs," which also references Dos Passos, describes our overly commercialized world as a scheme by business leaders to simplify the world into one big profit-making machine by paring down all complexity to two dimensions: producers and consumers. Everything else is beside the point. "A world in two dimensions is a mass production scheme" is the way the song captures this idea.

In the Dos Passos story, the title "The Grand Design" references the grand design of Franklin Delano Roosevelt's New Deal as he tries to pull the U.S. out of the Great Depression. In his story, Dos Passos is very much channeling the libertarian critique that such all-encompassing, government-led efforts to solve problems are doomed to fail. No matter how elaborate or well thought-out these schemes are, the people who run them are simply unable to anticipate everything that's needed for them to work; indeed, only freely acting people, organized in markets, can grow an economy out of its problems. This is exactly the critique of government intervention in the economy of Austrian School academics Ludwig von Mises and Friedrich Hayek that made them so quotable by libertarians.

In "Territories," we see the same two-dimensional mindset we see in "Grand Designs," but in this case it's from the point of view of nationalism. Instead of motivating us to act on our better angels, Rush says, our leaders bait us to turn people and cultures elsewhere into "others," and to "shoot without shame / In the name of a piece of dirt / For a change of accent / Or the color of your shirt."

The band's next album, *Hold Your Fire*, goes further down this road, devoting several tracks to our need to rein in capitalist excess lest our leaders exploit all of our natural resources and the whole game is up. "Second Nature," as we saw in the Introduction, is structured like an open letter to business and government leaders asking them, with the health of the earth hanging in the balance, to get out of their two-dimensional mindset and start thinking about the world holistically. "Something's got to give," the band says in the piece. "It ought to be second nature / I mean, the places where we live / Let's talk about this sensibly."

And "High Water," a piece that celebrates the life-giving and life-preserving nature of water, takes the form of a meditation. "We still feel that elation / When the water takes us home / In a driving rain of redemption / The water takes me home."

Hold Your Fire also has the song "Tai' Shan" on it, the "error," as Lee called it, because of its earnestness. Lyrically and musically the piece might not represent the band's best work, but thematically, it fits seamlessly into the album. Like "High Water," it takes the form of a meditation but in this case the meditation is about that other necessary element of life: earth. We harvest our food from earth, we anchor ourselves to earth, we dance in celebration upon earth, and we use earth as our stairway to heaven, so to speak, by climbing as high as we can go to bring us closer to spirituality. "The clouds surrounded the summit / The wind blew strong and cold / Among the silent temples / And the writing carved in gold."

Elsewhere on the album the band looks at time, creativity, and our primitive instincts. No where do we see characters like Tom Sawyer or the rebel in "Red Barchetta." There's nothing about making a grand exit in the middle of the night with the ambition to be one's own king, no ode to Ayn Randian self-assertion, no call to get off the couch and make your mark. Indeed, in tone, the pieces seem to have more in common with Joan Baez, Phil Ochs, and Joni Mitchell and washing the feet of our 500 closest friends than early Rush.

Other later albums at first glance seem to eschew the whole individualism thing as well. *Presto*, released in 1989, focuses on connections, to one another, to the environment, and to culture; *Roll the Bones*, released in 1991, focuses on chance; *Counterparts*, in 1993, on relationships; and *Test for Echo*, in 1996, on communications.

Are we even talking about the same band?

Respecting the sovereignty of others

But Rush has hardly moved on from individualism; the concept remains firmly in place. What's different is that the band has swung individualism around and is looking at it from the other side of the equation.

It's worth remembering that individualism comes with two sides. The first is about exercising the dignity that's inherent in each and every one of us as an individual sovereign. The other is to respect the sovereignty of others by not violating their dignity as individuals.

Rush has simply moved on from a preoccupation with the first perspective and turned its attention to the second perspective.

Thus, when Rush criticizes capitalist excess in "The Big Money," it's simply calling out our professional CEO class for misinterpreting its financial power as a license to view people only as consumers. We are consumers, yes, but we aren't just a faceless mob of people to be advertised to so we'll buy things; we remain, each of us, sovereign individuals to whom dignity must always be accorded. Once you forget that as you amass financial power, you start to treat us as something other than individuals, as something other than as ends in ourselves, and at that point you've violated the code of individualism. You are now acting immorally.

Even Ayn Rand would agree with Rush on this critique, because she was always consistent in her view that the morality of amassing wealth and power through trade is tied to our mutual respect of one another. "When one speaks of man's right to exist for his own sake, for his own rational self-interest, most people assume automatically that this means his right to sacrifice others," she says in the introduction to her 1961 compilation of essays, *The Virtue of Selfishness* (Signet). "Such an assumption is a confession of their own belief that to injure, enslave, rob or murder others is in man's self-interest—which he must selflessly renounce. The idea that man's self-interest can be served only by a non-sacrificial relationship with others has never occurred to those humanitarian apostles of unselfishness, who proclaim their desire to achieve the brotherhood of men."[1]

Rush returned to this theme again and again on pieces in its later albums. In "Superconductor," on its *Presto* album, it revisits its criticism of the music industry we first saw in "The Spirit of Radio" by pulling back the curtain on the manufacture of pop stars. With the professional CEO class in control, artist and repertoire (A&R) executives develop pop acts on the basis of target marketing so they can slot different acts into different market segments. "Orchestrate illusions," "designing to deceive"—it's just like finding a formula for a new beer. But we're not just a mob of consumers, and to manipulate people's emotions by manufacturing pop acts that know how to push the right emotional buttons is to violate the cardinal rule of individualism.

That's why, in "Heresy," the band's piece about the fall of the Berlin Wall, on its next album, *Roll the Bones*, which was released a year after the wall came down in 1990, the last thing you hear is the question of who will pay for the decades of Cold War hell that communist and Western Bloc leaders thrust all of us into. With the Cold War, countries were merely part of a game board as the United States and its allies and the Soviet Union and its satellite states used the globe as a battlefield for proxy wars. All for what? An ideology that leaders tried to push on a bewildered public. "All those wasted years / All those precious wasted years / Who will pay?"

Again, completely Randian in its viewpoint. From Rand's perspective, communism, to the extent it seeks to control all aspects of public and private life through a totalitarian form of government, cannot treat an individual as a sovereign to whom dignity is accorded. Totalitarianism can only treat people as instruments of the state, because only the state possesses the sovereignty to make decisions. Even if people in such a state have some degree of autonomy, the size and shape of that autonomous sphere is determined

---

1 Ayn Rand, *The Virtue of Selfishness*. New York: Signet, 1961, page 85.

by the state and revocable at any time. "The degree of socialization [in a totalitarian government] may be total, as in Russia," says Rand in her essay "The Monument Builders" in The Virtue of Selfishness, "or partial, as in England. Theoretically, the differences are superficial; practically, they are only a matter of time. The basic principle, in all cases, is the same.""[1]

It's because totalitarian regimes in the very nature of their organization trample on individual sovereignty that the song is very clear that it's the totalitarian side of the Cold War, the "dull grey world of ideology," not the Western democratic side, for all its faults, that ultimately must pay for the decades of wasted lives. As Peart says in an essay he wrote in 2014 on the topic, "It seemed—and seems—outrageous that the entire planet endured decades of anxiety, not to mention all the stunted lives in these Shadowlands [Eastern Europe], under the totalitarian boot-heel, for the sake of some misguided ideology."[2]

To be sure, there is plenty of blame to go around. To its critics on the left, the United States has never lived up to its high-minded rhetoric of liberty and justice for all. Instead, throughout the Cold War and into today, the country whose Constitution enshrines the idea of individual sovereignty has consistently leveraged its dollar hegemony to maintain a global financial dominance and create an elite of ultra-wealthy capitalists at the expense of the labor class. The effects of that have never been more plain to see than today, with the wealth of global business executives and investors rising into the stratosphere while the income of labor barely budges, even though the pace of technological innovation has exploded. Michael Hudson, research professor of economics at the University of Missouri in Kansas City, has written extensively on the disconnect between the values of the United States and the ruthless way it has leveraged its global financial power since the end of World War II and the beginning of the Cold War to thwart genuine free-market reform in other countries, including its allies. "U.S. diplomats pressed foreign governments to regulate their nations' trade and investment to serve U.S. national objectives," Hudson writes in *Super Imperialism* (Pluto Press: 2003) about the self-dealing way the United States structured its trade agreements with other countries at the height of the Cold War. "Foreign economies were to serve as residual markets for U.S. output."[3]

1 Ibid., page 86.
2 From Peart's June 2013 blog post "Shunpikers in the Shadowlands," at neilpeart.net. Accessed June 1, 2014.
3 *Super Imperialism: The Origins and Fundamentals of U.S. World Dominance* (London: Pluto Press, 2003, by Michael Hudson. Hudson's point is that the United States, by substituting the dollar for gold in 1971 as the global value standard, effectively forced other countries to invest their reserves in U.S. Treasuries and other government-backed instruments, like Fannie Mae and Freddie Mac mortgage-backed securities, thereby tying their economies to U.S. debt. In a perversion of economics, as the U.S. grows its debt, other countries become more, not less, reliant on the U.S. economy, because its dollar is the global reserve currency. The effect has been a wealth transfer that favors

In short, critics like Hudson suggest, far from being an exemplar of individualist values, the U.S. has been no better than its communist adversaries in running roughshod over individual sovereignty.

Of course, the irony of the song is that no one will pay in the end. Despite the decades of living in hell on both sides of the divide, all on account of an ideology that can only treat people as means, never as ends, there is really no action to take to make reparations for all of those wasted years. So, we must simply move on. "Do we have to be forgiving at last? / What else can we do? / Do we have to say goodbye to the past? / Yes, I guess we do."

Rush will take up this theme again. "Wish Them Well" on *Clockwork Angels* is about turning the other cheek, and that's all we can do here.

The band's focus on environmentalism, which starting with *Power Windows* makes an occasional appearance in Rush's repertoire, is all about the consequences of our leaders, business and government alike, not respecting our sovereignty as individuals. Surely clean water, clean air, and livable cities are prerequisites for any person to exercise his or her sovereignty. I can't maintain control over my life if a company or an industry or a government is making my water unfit to drink or my air unfit to breathe. The conundrum is that businesses can't produce products and create wealth without tapping into the world's resources, and tapping into those resources is rarely a clean process. But that's where government is supposed to come in. It's not supposed to control every aspect of our lives like a communist regime might try to do; it's supposed to set ground rules by which businesses operate so that we can have wealth-creating products without destroying the fabric on which we all depend for life. It's not an either–or proposition. We can tap our resources in a way that looks to the health of the environment, now and in the future, but doing so requires a thoughtful response by government. And although costs will go up, that's only because prices are set to reflect the true cost of producing the product, not the cost as subsidized by the destruction of our environment.

During the *Clockwork Angels* tour, Peart talked about the fracking boom in North Dakota as a great example of this tension between creating wealth and harming the environment. While riding his motorcycle on the backroads along the Canadian and U.S. border and then down into the Midwest to play some dates during the 2012 tour, he ran right into the middle of the inflection point of the fracking boom: unbelievable traffic for such a rural state as North Dakota, roads torn up, new ones going in with little thought, convoys of huge trucks and land-moving equipment, wells being dug in sensitive ecosystems. "Each new well means another drill rig, well pad, pumpjack, debris pit, flare pit, storage tanks, and access road on the landscape," he says on his blog in a September 2012 entry. "Each new well requires 2,000 'trucking events' to complete its setup and to begin pumping oil. . . . Groundwater is poisoned,

global capital at the expense of production, inhibiting true free-market reform in countries that, since the Cold War, have tried to develop along the same lines as the West.

often permanently, farmland is destroyed, often for decades, by leaks of the poisonous 'brine' used in the process (and, unbelievably, the oil companies alone are responsible for reporting their own spills, with almost no oversight). Surface water from the prairie wetlands that serve as migration oases for millions of birds is pumped away to dampen the dusty roads. Tens of thousands of workers—not to mention tens of thousands of semis—have a far-reaching effect on the environment. Just for one small example, those encampments of house trailers—where does their sewage go?

"And yet . . ." he continues, "in a few brief years North Dakota has shot from being a state in population decline, in a time of economic recession, to having the lowest unemployment rate in the United States, workers flocking in from everywhere, and a billion-dollar state surplus. All of a sudden, North Dakota is the second-largest oil producer in the United States, after Texas. This is indeed a boom."[1]

Is there tension? Yes. Does economic growth have to be either–or? Not if ground rules are set. Even libertarian hero Friedrich Hayek makes it clear in his classic 1944 work *The Road to Serfdom*, there will be instances in which the price mechanism alone is insufficient to deal with harmful externalities like environmental destruction.

> Nor can certain harmful effects of deforestation, or of some methods of farming, or of the smoke and noise of factories, be confined to the owner of the property in question or to those who are willing to submit to the damage for an agreed compensation. In such instances we must find some substitute for the regulation by the price mechanism. But the fact that we have to resort to the substitution of direct regulation by authority where the conditions for the proper working of competition cannot be created, does not prove that we should suppress competition where it can be made to function.[2]

Thus, "Second Nature," "Tai' Shan," and "High Water" on *Hold Your Fire* and "Red Tide" on *Presto* aren't a turnabout on individualism, even though they entreat us to think beyond ourselves on the environment. Rather, they're an expression of what it means to treat one another with the respect due to our sovereign nature.

From standing alone to walking together

The piece most emblematic of this change in perspective is "Hand Over Fist" on the band's 1989 *Presto* album. In a sense, the piece creates a visual metaphor for this focus on our responsibility to treat others with the dignity

1 Neil Peart, "The Better Angels," *News, Weather and Sports*, October 2012, www.neilpeart.net.
2 Friedrich Hayek, *The Road to Serfdom*. Chicago: University of Chicago Press, 2007., page 87.

that's due to each of us as sovereigns. In the piece, we're given as our set piece the rock, scissors, paper game we're all familiar with from when we were growing up. When the piece begins, we see the hand position of the game in two of the three competitive relationships with one another: paper covering stone and scissors cutting paper. Stone, which crushes scissors, is separated out. "Hand over fist / Paper around the stone / Scissors cut the paper / Cut the paper to the bone / Hand over fist/ Paper around the stone / Scissors cut the paper / And the rock must stand alone."

As the song evolves, the point of view switches from the competitive (paper covers stone, scissors cut paper, stone crushes scissors) to the cooperative. We see stone (the fist) opening up to greet a passing stranger, and although we can feel the strength in the stranger's hand, we don't find this threatening because our hand and the stranger's hand are both open. When they come together, we create an image of cooperation: hand over hand. "Hand over hand / Doesn't seem so much / Hand over hand / Is the strength of the common touch."

It's a neat piece of lyric-writing and fits in well with the other tracks on *Presto*, which focus heavily on how people relate to one another. But by showing that the rock does *not* stand alone, that even in an individualistic context it can only function in cooperation with others, we get this vivid metaphor for the idea of dignity that's at the heart of individualism. And it shows that individualism isn't synonymous with going it alone. There's no reason to think individualists can't work cooperatively with one another. It's not about *whether* we work with others but *how* we work with others.

We see this quite a bit in the band's later output. In *Test for Echo*, the 2006 album that to some extent looks at communications in our digital age, we get a sense of how much of our relationships today are of an unhealthy, exploitative, even voyeuristic-exhibitionistic kind.

In a voyeuristic-exhibitionistic relationship, people don't treat each others as an ends in themselves but rather as means. As a voyeur, I treat you as a means to whatever it is I'm after, and as an exhibitionist you do the same. Nowhere in the voyeuristic-exhibitionistic equation is dignity, unless we see mutual dependency as a kind of dignity, and I don't see any psychology that would support that idea. We see this especially clearly in the album's title piece, in which our news and reality TV programs are portrayed as tools that exhibitionists deploy to get exposure and which voyeurs—TV viewers—deploy to ogle others' exposure. "Some kind of trouble on the sensory screen / Camera curves over caved-in cop cars / Bleacher-creatures, would-be desperadoes / Clutch at plausible deniability / Don't touch that dial / We're in denial / Until the showcase trial on TV."

Peart wrote the lyrics with Pye Dubois, his collaborator on "Tom Sawyer," and he describes this voyeuristic-exhibitionistic relationship in contemporary media as simply wacky. "'Excuse me, does anybody else think this is weird?'" he says in a 1996 *Canadian Musician* interview. "'Am I weird?' While the answer to those questions might be 'Yes!' It's good to know that you're not the only one."

Lee calls the relationship a form of exploitative, out-of-control media madness. "It's like a view of things that are happening in our culture through the eyes of the instant media that we get and the things that we see that are not right," he says in *Contents Under Pressure*. "And yet it's still going on, still exploited."

The voyeuristic-exhibitionistic relationship shows up later on the album in "Virtuality," a piece about online relationships. At the time the album came out, 1996, social media had yet to take off (Myspace was launched in 2003, Facebook in 2004) but chat rooms, online matching services, and other types of Internet communications were in full bloom. The piece focuses on the alienating nature of spending hours a day cultivating relationships with others whose nature we know only through what they share with us online and through what we can glean from their *virtual* persona. "Clinging to the wreckage of the lost ship Fantasy / I'm a castaway, stranded in a desolate land / I can see the footprints in the virtual sand."

The big criticism of the piece at the time of the album's release was that it would be dismissed as a period piece. As Martin Popoff, the biographer of the band who wrote the 2004 book *Contents Under Pressure*, says, "'Virtuality' is bound to sound dated, given its Internet theme." But lo and behold, a few years later Facebook and the whole social media phenomenon took off, completely transforming how we relate to one another online and making the piece prescient rather than dated.

In both "Test for Echo" and "Virtuality," the idea is that we're using our media in ways that violate people's dignity, and that's not only unethical, from a Kantian perspective, but anti-individualistic.

Although it's not intended to be a serious song, "Dog Years," on the same album, actually provides an antidote to the type of exploitative communications we see in the other songs. The piece uses a comparison between dog years and people years to talk about how we trudge through life and then, before we know it, we're running out of time. In the piece, dogs are portrayed as not particularly smart—"In a dog's brain / A constant buzz of low level static"—but one thing you can say for them is their communications are pure, not tainted as ours are: The moon comes out and they howl at it. They come across a fire hydrant and they leave their calling card. It's all very natural. As the piece says, "One sniff at the hydrant / And the answer is automatic." Pure communications. No second-guessing. No ulterior motives. If only our communications were that honest.

Instead, what we get, as people rather than as dogs, are other people pushing their agenda out to us, whether or not we want what they're offering. In "Totem," we hear about "Media messiahs preying on my fears/ Pop culture prophets playing in my ears," and in "Time and Motion" we hear about lives connecting in "webs of gold and razor wire," meaning people use carrots and sticks, or bribes and threats, to get people to do what they want rather than simply connecting with people on the basis of mutual respect.

"Half the World," another song on the album, brings together all of these ideas about using people as means rather than as ends by painting a picture of the world cut in two pieces. On one side are self-actualizing individuals—what you might call Randian individualists who take their lives into their own hands and pursue their goals, treating others with the respect they're due—and on the other side, non-self-actualizing individuals who look to others for validation. "Half the world lives / Half the world makes/ Half the world gives/ While the other half takes / Half the world cares / While half the world is wasting the day / Half the world shares / While half the world is stealing away."

In this piece we see Rush's early individualist anthem "Something for Nothing" all over again, except from a global rather than from an individual perspective. The people in "Something for Nothing" who got off the couch and took control of their lives rather than passing their days "waiting for the winds of change / To sweep the clouds away," are the ones who comprise the half of the world that gets on with the business of living: making, learning, trying, and caring about things. Those who stay on the couch, including those who are kept on the couch by a state in which individual sovereignty isn't recognized, are the ones who can only hate what the other half does, because they themselves are too self-loathing to find any good anywhere. To hate someone, you have to objectify them, turn them into something other than a sovereign individual worthy of respect.

Allegories of cooperation

The last piece on *Test for Echo*, "Carve Away the Stone," moves inward to the level of psychology and presents a character rolling a stone up a hill, as Sisyphus was condemned to do for eternity in Hades. The point of view of the song isn't the Sisyphean character, though; it's a person off to the side giving the burdened character advice. So, while the burdened character is laboring to get the stone up the hill—in one stanza he has a ball and chain around his ankle—there's another person suggesting he "chip away the stone" or "carve away the stone" to make it lighter. It's actually pretty good advice. If you have to keep pushing the stone up the hill, why not chip or carve parts of it away to make it less of a burden? Nowhere is it written that you can't do that. Then the person off to the side suggests rolling away the stone—just roll it off the hill.

The interesting point is that the person off to the side giving advice wants the Sisyphus character to reduce the size of the stone or roll it away altogether because he has his *own* boulder to roll up the hill. "If you could just move yours / I could get working on my own." In other words, we're all faced with a Sisyphean task in this world of ours. The song has kind of a trick ending.

The first way to take the ending is ironically. The person off to the side has plenty to say to the Sisyphean character, yet he leaves his own burden untended. It's a little like an alcoholic dispensing advice about how to stay sober. But I don't think this is how Rush intended us to take the piece. Among other things, the line "I could get working on my own" has a genuine wistfulness about it. Instead, the piece advances the individualistic idea about self-interest: it's in my interest to get you off the hill so I can start rolling my own boulder up it. So, on that basis, here is my advice.

It's very much like the allegory of the long spoons,[1] which you might be familiar with as a tale popular in church and temple about the difference between Heaven and Hell that's been passed along over the centuries in one form or another in virtually all cultures.

In the allegory, we're escorted into Hell, where we see a table heavy with pots of mouth-watering stew and yet the people sitting around the table, each with their own spoon, are starving. The problem is that their wrists are tied to slats which prevent them from bending their arms at the elbow. So, although they can fill their spoon with stew, they can't get their spoon to their mouth. The result is misery and torture as they stare at and smell the food but can't eat it. They are truly damned.

We're next escorted into Heaven, where we see once again the table laden with pots of delicious smelling stew, and once again it's surrounded by people with wooden spoons in their hands and also with their wrists tied to slats. But here everyone is content and talking, obviously well fed. The difference is that instead of trying to feed themselves, they feed their neighbors, which doesn't require them to bend their arms at the elbow. Thus, by caring for each other, rather than thinking only of themselves, they're able to keep themselves fed despite the limitations they face.

What this suggests is, once more, it's all about *how* we work together, not *whether* we work together. The damned and the blessed are presented with the same conditions, but the damned make their own Hell while the blessed make their own Heaven. In Hell, the damned might seem to be acting individualistically, but they're actually violating the cardinal rule of individualism, which is to treat others as worthy of respect and not to do anything that would prevent others from exercising their sovereign powers. Thus, they in fact are not acting individualistically, just individually. In Heaven, the blessed are the ones acting individualistically, even though they're acting cooperatively, because they're dignifying one another as sovereigns, worthy of respect.

So, with "Carve Away the Stone," we're getting "Hand Over Fist" from *Presto* all over again. Yes, we can crush scissors with stone or we can cut paper with scissors or we can cover stone with paper, but that's just acting as individuals in a dog-eat-dog world, where no one wins. Maybe that's what Ted Nugent was singing about in his 1976 piece. What we want to do is

[1] To learn more about the "Allegory of the Long Spoons," see for instance the web site of the Unitarian Universalist Association of Congregations: http://www.uua.org/re/tapestry/children/toolbox/session1/sessionplan/stories/109416.shtml retrieved December 7, 2012.

greet the stranger with an open hand, no matter what he presents us with, because in that way, no matter what cards we've been dealt, we can all win.

Playing what we're dealt

The idea that it's up to us to decide how we live our lives and treat others with respect no matter the hand of cards we've been dealt is a recurring theme in Rush's music. We see it in "2112," "Something for Nothing," and "The Trees," among others in the early years, and we see it in "Prime Mover," where we're on our spinning top to nowhere and we can choose to 1) despair, 2) have a bacchanalian free-for-all, or 3) provide our own point to life. (Of course, we know what the answer is: to provide our own point to life. And then we see this idea acted out, in epic narrative form, in *Clockwork Angels*.)

What's interesting is that Rush explores the different options of chance— the idea that we have no say in the hand we're dealt—in two very different ways. The first is in the band's 1991 album *Roll the Bones*, and the second is in its 2007 album *Vapor Trails*. And yet in both cases the band comes back to the same conclusion: create your own Garden of Eden by acting on your own value set.

In *Roll the Bones*, we're presented with an existentially absurd world in which at any time everything that confers meaning on one's life can fall apart, making the very act of living a gamble. The album's title track lays out the playing field nicely, by saying without equivocation that the world is absurd. "Why are we here? / Because we're here. / Roll the bones! / Why does it happen?/ Because it happens. / Roll the bones!"

Thus, in a completely absurd world like this, you go with the flow. If the dice are hot you take a shot, and if they're not, you don't.

The problem is, by the time you recognize you're on a winning streak, the streak might have already ended and without knowing it you're about to start heading down, or *vice versa*. As the band says in another piece on the album, "Face Up," "I'm on a roll now / Or is it a slide? / Can't be too careful / With that dangerous pride / I'm in a groove now / Or is it a rut? / I need some feedback / But all the lines are cut."

That's a great way of articulating what any businessperson knows: so much of success or failure is the product of happenstance. In 2004 MySpace was on a rocket-ship ride up the growth curve—only it wasn't. That's the year Facebook launched and, by the time News Corporation bought the ground-breaking social networking site, a year later, its users were abandoning it for Facebook and now the site is practically a ghost town. The trajectories of AOL, Yahoo!, de.lic.ious, Digg, and so many other once-hot Web properties were exactly the same: Just when everybody thought they were going up, the momentum had already turned and they were on an unstoppable drop to the bottom.

What we have with the two pieces, "Roll the Bones" and "Face Up," in essence, is the same set-up we've seen many times before, most notably in

"Prime Mover," where, through no choice of our own, we're on a spinning top to nowhere, a context which forces us to live in existentially absurd conditions.

Other pieces on *Roll the Bones* take the idea out of the abstract and put it in the flesh-and-blood world by showing us, first, how we deal with this absurdity when we're young and champing at the bit for excitement, like the young man in *Clockwork Angels*, and then second, how we deal with it after we've been knocked around a bit and matured.

In "Dreamline" and again in "The Big Wheel," we see the young and the restless throwing caution to the wind. In "Dreamline," two young lovers, armed with only a "radar-fix on the stars" and a "liquid-crystal compass," leave their dull lives in the heartland for the bright lights of Hollywood and Las Vegas. Everything is good as long as they're moving. Their past is a "flickering light" and the future is a "long-range filter." The only thing that matters is the present. In "The Big Wheel," a young man enters the rough-and-tumble fray of life. His values aren't set yet. All he wants is to get to the top, even though he's not even sure what that means. So he's ready to trade whatever he can find in himself that's of value. And he wants to play the game as long as he can, with the hope that at some point the "odd number" will come up to make him a winner.

In effect, the two pieces are telling the same story, although in "Dreamline" the focus is on a young couple using pop culture ideas as their point of navigation and in "The Big Wheel" it's on a young man who has only his goal to reach the top as his guide-point. In both cases, we have no idea what becomes of them. It's an open question whether they will survive and come up with their own set of values, as the young man in *Clockwork Angels* does, or whether they will end up in the gutter by the time they're 25, or whether they'll succumb to existential despair.

But we get a clue to what happens, because two other pieces on *Roll the Bones* give us a picture of people who've survived being knocked about in life and have made their peace with the world. In "Bravado," we find peace in the world no matter how badly fortune treats us, as long as we have our dreams, take pride in what we do, and have love in our heart. Those are the value-points that provide an antidote to absurdity. If we have those, then "we will pay the price"—that is, get knocked about—but we "will not count the cost." The price we pay won't seem like much of a cost to us, because we will have so much more: our dreams, our pride, and our love.

In "Ghost of a Chance," once more we're given love as our value-point. Throughout life, we go through a "million little doorways," "a million little crossroads," and so does everybody else. And yet it's possible that out million little doorways and our million little crossroads will intersect at some point with someone else's, and that someone might well be a person we can love and stay in love with over time. So, it's the belief that we will one day find love, our value point, "through all that masquerade" and find sustenance in our existentially absurd world.

Rush's 2007 album *Vapor Trails*, released after the band's longest career hiatus, a five-year period in which it produced no new work as group, presents us with the same absurd conditions but in a much darker tone than what we see in *Roll the Bones*. But are the band's value-points the same? The answer is yes.

Close, but not succumbing, to despair

Vapor Trails is an important album in the band's career, because the five-year hiatus represented a retrenchment after it endured its own tragic ride on the wheel of fortune, with Peart losing his daughter in a highway accident in 2008 and his wife to cancer the following year. (And, as if to add insult to injury, he also lost his dog in 2008 to disease and his best friend, Brutus, was holed up in a New York jail on marijuana charges.)

From a thematic standpoint, the album is a remarkable testament to the enduring strength of the band's philosophy, because the dark tone notwithstanding, the value-points articulated in the pieces are unchanged. Two pieces on the album, "Sweet Miracle" and "Out of the Cradle," are celebrations of optimism amidst darkness, with love the value that triggers light.

In "Sweet Miracle," we're given allusions to religious miracles—walking on water, talking to angels, and praying for magic—but in each case what we see are illusions. Instead of walking on water we're standing on a reef (about to be swept under by the tide), instead of talking to angels we're just talking to ourselves, and instead of praying for magic (with the goal of disappearing), we're just hiding in plain sight. It's all very down to earth and real, and it's only when we discover love that our prayers are answered and we leave the darkness and fly up to the light.

"Out of the Cradle," the last song on the album, uses an almost riddle-like device to take us to the same place. You start with the question, What's a power with a hundred names? And then you quickly get some hints. "It's not a place, it's a yearning / It's not a race, it's a journey / It's not an act, it's attraction / It's not a style, it's an action."

You then get some more hints, masked in enigmatic imagery: "It's a dream for the waking / It's a flower touched by flame / It's a gift for the giving / It's a power with a hundred names."

Then, the answer to the riddle is set up for us with a flourish. "Surge of energy, spark of inspiration / The breath of love is electricity."

So, the answer is love, as it was in "Sweet Miracle," just as it was in all of the earlier songs.

The main literary device of the piece is the line, "Here we come out of the cradle, endlessly rocking," which you might recognize from the poetry you learned in high school, because it's taken from Walt Whitman's autobiographical poem, written in 1859, "Out of the Cradle, Endlessly Rocking."[1]

Whitman's poem is about death and rebirth. The idea is that you have to die first before you can come back as the person you were meant to be. At the point your old ego dies, your new one is born and comes "out of the cradle, endlessly rocking."

In Peart's own life, after spending the first year after the deaths in his family in a stupor and the second year wandering around Canada, the United States, and Mexico on his motorcycle "trying to soothe his baby soul," as he says in his 2009 book *Ghost Rider*, he finds love again, giving him a surge of energy to start his life anew. Thus, for him, love brought him back to life in a surge of energy, giving him (and the band, by extension) the power to rock on endlessly. And they have. Since *Vapor Trails* released in 2002, the band has produced a whirlwind of work that includes three studio albums and three world tours. And Peart has put out three books and collaborated on two novels.

But *Vapor Trails* also gives us plenty of the dark side of our absurd world as well, with pieces like "How It Is" and "The Stars Look Down" reminding us about that spinning top we're on. In both pieces we stand at the precipice of despair and look down into its darkest depths.

In "The Stars Look Down," we're presented with a world in which the stars watch passively as terrible things happen to us, even though we've tried to lead a morally good life. What makes it worse is that, like the boy in *Clockwork Angels* who was brought up to believe the world has a plan, we walk around believing there's a purpose for us. But in reality, we're like a fly on a wheel who's going around and around and who looks proudly at all the dust he's kicking up, but in fact he's not going anywhere except in circles, or we're like a rat in a maze who thinks he's choosing his own direction, but of course his choices are dictated by the environment he's in. It's all very Kafkaesque. "How It Is" gives us much the same attitude. "Foot upon the stair / Shoulder to the wheel / You can't tell yourself not to care / You can't tell yourself how to feel / That's how it is / Another cloudy day."

We're given the Sisyphus character all over again, but this time there's no person off to the side offering us helpful advice. Instead, it's just us, all alone, faced with the weight of having to move on when we have no will to do so.

The darkest piece of all is the album's title song, "Vapor Trail," which describes the transitory character of our lives by comparing the legacy we leave to the kind of vapor trail, or contrails, that jets leave behind in their wake. At first the contrails are crisp with clear, sharp lines, making them seem solid and substantive, but they very soon start dispersing in the atmosphere and before you know it they're just insubstantial whiffs of vapor, hardly distinguishable from a naturally occurring whispy cloud, and then they're

---

1 "Out of the Cradle, Endlessly Rocking" was written in 1859 and included in Walt Whitman's 1860 compilation *Leaves of Grass*. E. Sculley Bradley and Harold W. Blodgett, eds. New York: W. W. Norton & Co., 1985.

gone entirely. It makes you think of the aging writer or the aging dancer in "Losing It," the piece from the *Signals* album we looked at earlier. Their careers, once celebrated, are over and they spend their final days wondering whether their accomplishments ultimately will matter and whether they'll be remembered at all.

There are other dark songs on the album. "Ceiling Unlimited" borrows its title from an aeronautical term that refers to the lowest layer of clouds that obscures vision. When pilots are able to fly under the "ceiling," they can operate using visual flight rules. When the ceiling is too low to fly under it, they have to fly using their instruments, which isn't as enjoyable. When the ceiling is unlimited, it's an inspiring sight and the world stretches out before you. Sadly, even when we have the world stretched out before us, we often tend to restrict our gaze to what's immediately before us. What we concentrate on are the viciousness on the street, the slack-jawed gaze—but these are just the limiting vision of what we get when we hold a mirror up to our world. If, on the other hand, we could just move beyond the limited world immediately before us, we can find inspiration in how great our world can be. But, unfortunately, we often can't.

"Earthshine," as with "Ceiling Unlimited," is a piece named for a technical term, in this case referring to a fairly rare phenomenon in which reflected earthlight is visible on the moon's night side, giving a ghostly glow to the portion of the moon bathed in earthshine. In a typical situation in which we see earthshine, we see a regular crescent moon, but with the rest of the moon, which is normally obscured, visible in a ghostly light. It's eerie and beautiful at the same time. In the piece, "earthshine" is used as a metaphor for how one feels after suffering a grievous loss. One no longer feels a part of the world but rather a pale facsimile of a person whose light isn't his own but only a reflection off the light of another.

"Secret Touch" is almost a companion song to "Earthshine," because it evokes the idea that once you're scarred by life, you become out of sync with the rhythms of the world around you, and your scar remains with you, like a secret touch on the heart. "Out of touch / With the weather and the wind direction / With the sunrise / And the phases of the moon / Out of touch / With life in the land of the loving / Out of sync / With the rhythm of my own reactions / With the things that last / And the things that come apart / Out of sync / With love in the land of the living."

As a collection of songs, the *Vapor Trails* album is not an uplifting story, but it has the virtue of giving us a reality check. When the band said in its piece "Prime Mover" that we live our lives on a spinning top to nowhere, it wasn't kidding. This is what existential despair looks like, and it's not pretty. But the album starts and ends on an uplifting note. The opening song, "One Little Victory," is a song that could be used in a motivation seminar to knock people out of their stupor and get on with the business of living. It exhorts you to rise above and achieve one little victory, because that can give you encouragement to go out and achieve one more after that, and then another, and so on. "Celebrate the moment / As it turns into one more / Another chance at victory / Another chance to score."

In essence, you're thumbing your nose at despair and saying, at the end of the day, we can be stronger than the dark forces we meet with in life. Then, at the end of the album, we get "Out of the Cradle," the piece that leaves us with the imagery of us endlessly rocking into the future after our death-rebirth experience.

In a narrow sense, the album is about the band: it came face to face with despair, but ultimately it chose to create its own meaning in the world, and the lodestar it used as its driver is the idea of love. In a broad sense, the album is a vindication of the band's philosophy and helps explain where the band was going in the mid-1980s, when it dropped its almost obsessive focus on the me-first side of individualism and started focusing on the you-too side of it.

As we saw, this change in orientation doesn't have to be seen as a repudiation of individualism but a reaffirmation of it, by reminding us that individualism comes with two responsibilities. The first is to yourself—get off the couch, make your mark—and the second is to others—let others make their mark, too, by treating them as sovereign individuals. Why is treating others with respect so important? Because all of us are fellow travelers on this spinning top to nowhere, so what one does impacts others, regardless of our intentions. Peart is fond of quoting an old Chinese saying that one should be gentle with passing strangers because we can't know what sorrows the person has endured.[1] That's what we have here.

Thus, whether I choose despair or a free-for-all, ultimately I pull everyone down with me. Only if I choose the third way, which is to create my own meaning and live my life in accordance with that does the world have a chance to be the best it can be. It all starts with me.

And in creating our own meaning, what value points do we use? Well, we know what Rush's value-points are: love and respect. The two are inseparable. In our interactions with the world, we confer respect and we seek it in return. But of course respect by itself isn't enough. It's a necessary but not a sufficient condition, because it doesn't touch your need for intimacy. So, you also need love. When you have love and respect together, you have the necessary and sufficient conditions for achieving happiness—even on this existentially absurd life on a spinning top to nowhere that we call home.

---

1 Peart likes to quotes the Chinese saying about treating passing strangers gently because you never know the hardships they enduring. One place where he quotes it is in "The Prize" in his *Far and Away: A Prize Every Time.* Toronto: ECW Press, 2011, page 293. The actual line is "Be kind, for everyone you meet is fighting a hard battle."

Chapter 5. The Voice of Gawd

> Christians have their hymns and pages.
> Hava Nagila's for the Jews.
> Baptists have the rock of ages.
> Atheists just sing the blues.
>
> Romantics play Claire de Lune.
> Born agains sing "He is risen."
> But no one ever wrote a tune
> For godless existentialism.
> —"Atheists Don't Have No Songs," *Steve Martin*

If we picture our world as a spinning top to nowhere, with no one in control, we are indeed faced with three choices: sink into despair, go wild, or create our own meaning. This is what existential absurdity is all about and, from the perspective of what we've been exploring up to this point, it's up to each of us to muster the strength of mind to take control of our lives if we're to live in a good way.

Of course, it goes without saying that many of us, perhaps most if us, don't see the world as absurd in this way, or if we do, we try not to think about it too much. Instead, we take the view that the world is very much a planned enterprise and what we see is only the tip of the iceberg: the here and now. It's not that the world is absurd; it's that the great mass of what it means to be living is beyond our knowledge, because God is the creator of the world and His work is inscrutable to us, mere mortals.

We'll leave it to others to decide whether it's existential absurdity or a planned enterprise that correctly expresses the nature of the world, but what we can take away from the creative work of Rush over the past 40 years is that it represents an impressive lexiconic project of humanistic values, and, as Chris McDonald has pointed out in his 2011 paper on the topic, it's given humanism quite an impressive set of tools to express its values in an inspirational way.

There are many different understandings of humanism, including some historical and even modern ones in which some deistic notions of God are part of the mix, but in general it's the view that the world is what you see. There's nothing mystical or mythical about anything, and so to live morally in this world we're to act in a way that respects each person as an individual, because by doing that, we create the conditions for each of us to thrive as much as possible. As articulated by the American Humanist Association's manifesto, which provides us with a good template of what the perspective is all about, humanists are "committed to treating each person as having inherent worth and dignity, and to making informed choices in a context of freedom consonant with responsibility."[1]

It would be hard to find a clearer expression of everything we've been talking about up to this point. You have the idea that each of us is a sovereign individual with inherent dignity, worthy of respect by others and responsible for treating others with respect. You thus have the Aristotelian idea of each of us striving to achieve the highest aim of our nature, the classical liberal idea of sovereigns coming together in a spirit of mutual respect to create a governing structure that works for everyone, and the Randian Objectivist idea of pursuing our highest aims, allowing others to do so as well, and all in a context of the here and now.

All very nice and beautiful, you might say, except that humanism's rejection of the mystical or mythological leaves us with—well, a fairly sterile landscape. Absent are the beautiful and emotional church hymns, the meditative chanting, the gorgeous and soaring cathedrals, the mesmerizing paintings, the stories that fire the imagination.

In his look at Rush and humanism, McDonald quotes anthropologist Edward Bruner on the challenge the humanist worldview faces as it seeks to inspire people: "[T]he problem facing the humanist is not so much one of replacing the gods but finding a language to replace the Word with new sacred words that will allow us to celebrate the survival of the human spirit."[2]

In the rest of his quote, which McDonald doesn't include, Bruner says humanism has in fact inspiring words at its disposal—"civilization," "progress," and "culture," among them[3]—but these are so commonplace that whatever power they might have had at one point is now lost in their ordinariness.

Well, this is really too bad. Because the basic axiom of humanism—to

1 The quote from the American Humanism Association manifesto is at its web site: http://www.americanhumanist.org/Humanism/Humanist_Manifesto_III retrieved December 8, 2012.
2 Berti and Bowman, *Rush and Philosophy*, page 251.
3 The rest of Bruner's quote is in his (with Victor Witter Turner) *The Anthropology of Experience*. Chicago: University of Illinois Press, 1986, page 47.

treat others with the dignity they're due and to expect others to do the same for you—is cut from the same cloth as the axiomatic principles of the Judeo-Christian moral view. That might sound odd at first, given how we tend to imagine humanists sitting around dismissing believers' notions of God, and believers sitting around dismissing humanists as amoral hedonists.

But at least in the basics—that is, the fundamental axiomatic principles out of which the rules for living flow—humanistic morality is arguably little different than the Judeo-Christian view. If we look at just two foundational aspects of Judaism and Christianity, the Golden Rule and the Ten Commandments, you'll see why someone might say this.

The Golden Rule, in which we're to treat others as we would have them treat us, is the same type of moral rule based on universalizability as Kant's categorical imperative. They're not exactly the same, because the Golden Rule puts the moral agent at the center of the question ("Do I want people to treat *me* in this same way?") while Kant's rule replaces the *me* with *rational contradiction* ("Would it create a rational contradiction if everyone did this?"). But they're very similar and they both get at the same idea, which is to treat others as ends in themselves, never as means.

The same is true of the Ten Commandments. If you remove the first four rules, which relate to worship, the six remaining rules are consistent with the principles of any humanistic philosophy:

Honor your father and mother.

Do not murder.

Remain faithful to your spouse.

Do not steal.

Do not lie.

Do not covet.

Each of these six Commandments flows out of the idea that each person is a sovereign individual to whom respect is due by virtue of inherent dignity. There is no daylight between this Judeo-Christian morality and humanistic moralities in an axiomatic way. (Of course, the devil is in the details, and how these rules get translated and implemented in different religious and in different secular contexts is surely infinitely variable, but we're keeping things on a foundational level.)

Where humanistic morality and religious morality part company is really just in the source, or genesis, of the moral rules. For humanists, the rules are products of our nature or intellect. Going back to the American Humanist Association, moral living derives from "a philosophy of reason . . . . [W]hen it comes to the question of the most valid means for acquiring knowledge of the world, Humanists reject arbitrary faith, authority, revelation, and altered states of consciousness."[1]

For those coming out of a Judeo-Christian context, rules for moral living

---

1 The American Humanist Association quote on the rejection of arbitrary faith, revelation, and so on, is at its web site: http://www.americanhumanist.org/Humanism/What_is_Humanism retrieved December 7, 2012.

are handed down to us from God. Thus, for religion, moral rules come with an additional set of instructions pertaining to the role of worship, and we see those in the first four dictates of the Ten Commandments:

There is only one God.

Do not worship idols.

Do not speak God's name in vain.

Keep the Sabbath (dedicated day of worship).

In a nutshell, it might be obvious and trivial to say, but once you remove the element of worship from the mix, humanism and Judeo-Christian belief seek the same moral ends and in the same way. Only in the genesis of their rules do they differ. And yet, while trivial, it can also be helpful to remind ourselves of this once in a while.

So, duly reminded, let's think about the problem facing humanism and it's this: humanism is b-o-r-i-n-g.

As Steve Martin sings in "Atheists Don't Have No Songs," quoted at the start of this chapter, "Atheists just sing the blues."

Not only are atheists singing the blues, they're looking at boring paintings, building boring buildings, and, maybe worst of all, they're talking "progress," "culture," and "civilization" while Jews and Christians are talking skies opening up, seas parting, arks floating, tablets descending, wounds healing, water turning into wine and the dead coming back to life.

Is it any wonder the moral view of humanism looks monochromatic against the blast of color of church and temple?

As essayist Alain de Botton says in his book *Religion for Atheists*, which received quite a bit of attention in the press when it was released in 2012, "Secular society has been unfairly impoverished by the loss of an array of practices and themes . . . because they seem too closely associated with, to quote Nietzsche's useful phrase, 'the bad odours of religion.'"[1]

De Botton's point is that secularists have robbed themselves of the power religion enjoys by stripping their views of everything except concrete reality. "We flee from the idea that art should be uplifting or have an ethical mission," he says in his book. "We don't go on pilgrimages. We can't build temples . . . strangers rarely sing together. We are presented with an unpleasant choice between either committing to peculiar concepts about immaterial deities or letting go entirely of a host of consoling, subtle or just charming rituals for which we struggle to find equivalents in secular society."

De Botton goes on to spend considerable time talking about ways secular society would benefit by appropriating aspects of the religious infrastructure—art, architecture, and music, among them—and putting them to work in the cause of secularism. After all, he says, much of what we think of as religious (at least in a Christian context) such as Christmas, monasticism, and praying in temples, had their origins in pagan uses and were themselves appropriated by the Church.

---

1 Alain de Botton, *Religion for Atheists*. New York: Pantheon, 2012, page 14.

Christianity, he says, "took over celebrations of midwinter and repackaged them as Christmas. It absorbed the Epicurean ideal of living together in a philosophical community and turned it into what we now know as monasticism. And in the ruined cities of the old Roman Empire, it blithely inserted itself into the empty shells of temples once devoted to pagan heroes and themes."[1]

Rush is on the job

After he makes the same point in his essay, McDonald takes the next step, which is to say, in effect, "Worry no more, humanists. Rush has been on the job and essentially appropriating the language and power of religion already and deploying it in the service of humanism. So, we don't have to think of humanism as a sterile gathering in the cold light of a grey community building. With Rush's example, we can turn it into something magisterial and sublime, like religion."

Rush, McDonald says, "transposes humanism into timeless, imaginary and mythical domains where they appear, not as historically contingent arguments or sites of intellectual disagreement, but as universal, ever-consistent principles that become almost like tenets of faith."[2]

Rush's treatment of "Jacob's Ladder," which we touched on earlier, is a case in point with its use of the magisterial and the sublime to describe not the biblical tale of the same name but the natural weather phenomenon. "Witch Hunt" is another example, with its use of iconic images of witch-hunting vigilantism to shine the spotlight on anti-intellectualism.

What Rush does in these and other pieces is to take the tropes of religion, like evocative music and ecumenical phrases, and deploy them as arrows to pierce the protective armor of religion. We see this early on, in one of the band's most Randian pieces, "Something for Nothing," when it plays off the Lord's Prayer. "What you own is your own kingdom / What you do is your own glory / What you love is your own power / What you live is your own story."

In that passage, the relationship of these words to their original intention is turned on its head, because it says the kingdom, the power, and the glory belong not to God, as they do in the Lord's Prayer, but to us: it's our kingdom, our glory, our power, and, in a fourth line that Rush adds, our story. We're told to look to ourselves, not to a supernatural being, for the answer to what we're looking for. "In your head is the answer / Let it guide you along / Let your heart be the anchor / And the beat of your own song."

A few years later, in 1982 in "The Weapon" on the *Signals* album, which we looked at briefly earlier, Rush goes further, and says not only are we to find the answers for ourselves, but that the last place we want to look for spiritual guidance is in a house of worship, because all we'll get in a

---

1 Ibid., page 15.
2 Berti and Bowman, *Rush and Philosophy*, page 252.

house of worship is a passive-aggressive effort at indoctrination by the very people we're looking to for help. "With an iron fist in a velvet glove / We are sheltered under the gun / In the glory game on the power train / Thy kingdom's will be done."

In the passage, the velvet glove of the clergy will shelter us, but in exchange we have to accept the iron fist that lurks inside it. There's a gun in its hand, and it's holding it to our head. All the church or temple can offer us is another imperfect human being who has buried his own problems inside his belief system and is looking to turn the tables on our neediness by making us believers, too. Our needs are beside the point. It's more important that we validate his belief system. If we don't, then his beliefs are at risk of being dismissed as imaginary. Since we can't touch, taste, hear, feel, or smell God, but can only believe in Him, he can have validation for his belief only if other people believe in Him, too. Because if he's the only believer, than how does he know his beliefs aren't just in his imagination? Can a religion exist if it has no believers? Is a religion any different from a fantasy if it has only a single believer?

Carol Selby Price and Robert Price in their 1999 book *Mystic Rhythms* (Wildside Press) say Peart's view of religion is very much like Nietzsche's condemnation of Christianity as a "'slave morality,' the creed of the cringing cowardly herd, for whom 'faith' can be defined as not wanting to know the truth, whose real fear is the fear of their own freedom."[1]

Knowledge is the one thing that can pierce the armor of religion, the Prices say, because it exposes belief as a "core of fear." It's for that reason that any person who refuses to share in a religious belief has the potential to expose that belief as imaginary. And that's a threat to the identity of the religious. Hence extremism. And that's what we walk into when we walk into a house of worship looking for spiritual guidance.

Peart brought this topic up himself in a 2012 post on his blog during the *Clockwork Angels* tour. He had just read *The Better Angels of Our Nature* in which Harvard cognitive scientist Steven Pinker argues that people have become less violent over time because of improving education, victories of reason over superstition, and the strengthening of the democratic ideal. What's missing in Pinker's account, Peart notes, is any impact on non-violence from religion. Indeed, he says, often the most violent are those who profess religious faith the loudest, because in their loud professions of faith they're masking their own skepticism that the whole thing isn't just some big fantasy.

"We all know that people who are pretending something get very angry if mocked," Peart says, "because they are embarrassed, a tiny step from resentful rage—and as for guilty doubters of a faith, they may well be the fiercest voices in the choir."[2]

The idea that religion is the last place you ought to look to foster peace

1 Carol and Robert M. Price, *Mystic Rhythms*, page 18.
2 Neil Peart, "The Better Angels," *News, Weather and Sports*, October 2012, www.neilpeart.net.

and harmony in the world is captured in a number of Rush's songs, but probably most emblematically in "Closer to the Heart," which appropriates Christmas-sounding bells and the message of brotherly love, but it does so in the service of an entirely secular viewpoint. In that piece, various categories of people are earnestly entreated to take the goal of peace and harmony into their own hands and bring it about. But notable for its absence is any appeal to religious leaders. Rather, we get appeals to blacksmiths and artists, philosophers and ploughmen, and we're urged to be our own captains so we can sow a new destiny closer to the heart. But nowhere do we find any appeal to religious leaders, which seems like an odd omission unless we understand religious leaders to be the "iron fist in a velvet glove" Peart talks about in "The Weapon."

Indeed, from Rush's perspective, the different types of religion are just so many choices among countless choices we have at our disposal— some serious, some not so serious—with which we can try to impose a philosophical frame around our life. We see this in "You Bet Your Life," the closing song on *Roll the Bones*. The piece takes Catholicism and other religious variations, including some Eastern belief systems, and throws them into a big mixing bowl of random beliefs and cultural tropes and says they're all just so many products on a shelf that we can try out and discard at will. Catholicism won't work? Why don't we try anarchy? Anarchy won't work? Let's try existentialism. Existentialism won't work? Why don't we make it "Arm chair rocket scientist graffiti" existentialism?

The point is that, no matter what belief or philosophy we pull off the shelf, we're still on this randomly spinning top, and, in the end, our religious beliefs are interchangeable with any other identity marker that we try out for a time. "Anarchist reactionary running dog revisionist / Hindu Muslim catholic creation evolutionist / Rational romantic mystic cynical idealist / Minimal expressionist post-modern neo-symbolist / Arm chair rocket scientist graffiti existentialist / Deconstruction primitive performance photo realist / Be-bop or a one drop or a hip hop lite pop metallist / Gold adult contemporary urban country capitalist."

"Totem," from the band's 1996 *Test for Echo* album, goes down the same road. It ticks off a list of any number of belief systems we can try on for a while—Christianity, Buddhism, Hinduism, Catholicism, paganism—they're all represented on the totem pole we dance around over the course of our life. But ultimately, all of these belief systems are beside the point, because it's not any one system that determines how we fare in the world; it's us, our psychology, our mood that does. That's the only thing that matters. If we're feeling good, the world comes across as a lovely place; if we're not, it doesn't. You can almost call "Totem" a song about cognitive behavioral therapy, because it essentially articulates the basic precepts of that school of psychology. "I believe in what I see / I believe in what I hear / I believe that what I'm feeling / Changes how the world appears."

You can think of cognitive behavioral psychology as the opposite of the classic Freudian view in which you make people feel better by having them surface and explore their problems. To the cognitive behavioral therapist, that's the *last* thing you want to do. Rather, you want to have people surface and explore their joys. So, instead of sitting someone down on your couch and inviting them to wallow in their agony, you suggest they identify what they like the most and then have them build their life around that. And that's what "Totem" is saying: how you feel changes how the world appears, so why not surface what you like and spend your life in *that* world?

Religion is beside the point, and in fact it's often the source of the problem, because it creates the kind of dichotomous thinking—good–bad, black–white, right–wrong—that puts you in a behavioral box and punishes you psychologically for sinning, something that no one but a perfect being can avoid because of the material nature of our biology.

Mitch Earleywine, professor of clinical psychology at SUNY Albany in New York, whose work we touched on earlier, says Rush over the years has created music that serves as a kind of delivery system of cognitive behavioral therapy. In his essay, "Rush's Revolutionary Psychology," in *Rush and Philosophy*, he says the band has been telling people for years to avoid getting entrapped in dichotomous, either–or thinking, lest they spend their lives beating themselves up for their inevitable failures. Instead, he says, Rush exhorts its listeners to find the joy.

That's what Rush's flipping The Lord's Prayer on its head is all about: You build your kingdom, find your glory, exercise your power, and write your story.

"Rather than leaving us all spinning in thought," Earleywine says, "both cognitive behavioral therapists and Rush recommend concerted action. . . . The key to improved moods is a dynamic life filled with behaviors consistent with your values."[1]

Of course, building your kingdom, writing your story, and so on, have to be done in concert with others—consistent with other people's inherent dignity—as we saw; otherwise you cross the line, like the business leaders in "The Big Money" who forget that people are more than just the sum total of what they consume. So, in this humanistic world there are rules, but they're based on rationality like those that govern cognitive behavioral therapy or even Kant's categorical imperative. These rules produce a guide for action based on context, as opposed to religion, which imposes universal either-or rules that keep us in an artificial psychological box.

With this context as background, where Rush's humanistic ideal really comes out in full force is on the band's most recent two albums, *Snakes and Arrows* in 2007 and *Clockwork Angels* in 2012. With these works, the band dispenses with subtlety and tackles the differences between humanism and religion head on, openly criticizing the maladaptive effect of religion in *Snakes and Arrows* and articulating a humanistic belief system that competes

1 Berti and Bowman, *Rush and Philosophy*, page 99.

head-on with a belief in God in *Clockwork Angels.* We're going to look at these two albums now.

'Faith is a higher faculty than reason'

Peart became an avid motorcyclist in 1994, when his first wife, Jackie, bought him a BMW R1100GS touring bike as a birthday present.[1] It took him a while to get the hang of it (he says he had to do a riding test three times before he passed), but once he did, he became a touring nut, and since the band's 1996 *Test for Echo* tour he's preferred the rigors of traveling by motorcycle over the comfort of traveling by jet to get from one tour date to the next.[2] Thus, over the course of four North American tours since then, plus his 1998 trans-country ride "to soothe his baby soul" after the loss of Jackie and his daughter, he's covered hundreds of thousands of miles of the United States, much of it over old state highways and backroads rather than the country's gleaming interstates, what he and his riding partners call "mileage disposal units."

Of course, even these hundreds of thousands of miles are a drop in the bucket for a musician who's been touring the country by car, bus, bicycle, and now motorcycle dozens of times since Rush first set out as an opening act for Uriah Heep and Manfred Mann in 1974.

What all this travel has given him is a familiarity with the backroads of America and its cultural changes that few Americans themselves have. And few changes are bigger than the rise of religious fundamentalism in the country. "Pariah dogs and wandering madmen / Barking at strangers and speaking in tongues," he writes in "Far Cry," the opening track on *Snakes and Arrows.* "It's a far cry from the world we thought we'd inherit / It's a far cry from the way we thought we'd share it."

Peart writes in his book *Traveling Music* that when he was growing up in small-town Canada, not far from Niagara Falls, Americans just seemed a bit cooler than Canadians,[3] and all those fabled roads yet to be traveled south of the border—Route 66, Sunset Strip, Highway 1—were all part of his "book of dreams" (his North American road atlas).[4]

He indeed ended up traveling those roads, and in his many travel memoirs he recounts some pretty good times. But now the environment has changed, and what he sees today are the bumper stickers and the church signs in every part of the country that possess all the coolness of an old scold bent on

---

1 Peart describes his introduction to and subsequent enchantment with motorcycling in all of his books, and in several of them he calls the road atlas his "book of dreams," most recently in his essay "A Little Yellow Cabin on Yellowstone Lake" in *Far and Away: A Prize Every Time.* Toronto: ECW Press, 2011, page 168.

2 Neil Peart, *Traveling Music: The Soundtrack to My Life and Times.* Toronto: ECW Press, 2004, page 118.

3 Ibid., page 74.

4 Peart, *Far and Away,* page 168.

draining the life from the living to make room for an afterlife for the dead. "If you take Satan for a ride, pretty soon he'll want to drive," "What's missing from CHURCH? 'UR,'" "RSVP for Eternity."[1]

Are these religious slogans really where we thought the country was heading in the 1960s and 1970s? After the stifling conformity of the 1950s, when intolerance for anyone who was different was the rule, the 1960s and the 1970s seemed like a breath of fresh air. Culture seemed to be moving in a forward direction, with ignorance and intolerance going the way of hair grease and grey flannel suits. But it wasn't permanent change at all; we're right back where we started, only with ignorance and intolerance now playing in a new key. As the band says in "The Way the Wind Blows," from *Snakes and Arrows*, "It's like we're back in the Dark Ages / From the Middle East to the Middle West / It's a world of superstition / . . . / Now it's come to this / Wide-eyed armies of the faithful / From the Middle East to the Middle West / Pray, and pass the ammunition."

Peart says in his 2010 book *Roadshow*, about touring the country on motorcycle for the band's 30-year anniversary tour in 2007, he initially intended to keep his thoughts to himself on the rise of fundamentalism in the United States, but there was one church sign that got his goat: "Faith is a higher faculty than reason."[2]

Even for people of faith, he says, the sentiment in that statement is so backward that it screams out for a rejoinder. "At this point in recounting my American travels," he says, "I begin to think that even if the voice of reason is increasingly drowned out by the evangelical crowd, that is all the more reason to speak up. Spiritual yearnings are natural to many people and may give them solace or hope, but extremists of any kind are not content with faith as armor, they must forge it into a sword."[3]

In "Armor and Sword," the second track on *Snake and Arrows*, we see the battering we all endure as we grow up—the snide and bullying remarks, the backstabbing, the criticism of our parents—and our response is to build a wall around ourselves as a "consolation / A way to take us out of ourselves." It's a wall that has the effect of keeping others out but it also has the unintended effect of keeping us locked inside our own armor. "The snakes and arrows a child is heir to / Are enough to leave a thousand cuts / We build our defenses, a place of safety / And leave the darker places unexplored."

Our need to validate our retreat is commensurate with how effectively we've cut ourselves off from everything outside the wall. The more embedded we are in the belief system we've adopted, the more we need to bring others inside the wall—and the more extreme we become against those who refuse to validate our choice. As Rush says in the piece, "What should have been our armor / Becomes a sharp and angry sword."

So, here we are, so invested in our belief system that we can neither

1 Peart, *Roadshow*, pages 116, 117, and 127.
2 Ibid., page 131.
3 Ibid., beginning on page 132.

acknowledge the reality outside us nor go down deep within ourselves to see what really lies there, lest we expose our commitment to our belief system as a mistake. The more force we're required to draw upon to keep our own questioning thoughts from surfacing, the more defensive we become against those who would reinforce our own doubts. We lash out, in other words, and wield our shield as a sword: "Confused alarms of struggle and flight / Blood is drained of color By the flashes of artillery light . . . The battle flags are flown / At the feet of a god unknown."

For many people, having grown up in and been surrounded by a belief system all of their lives, it might be asking too much for them to get far enough outside what they're familiar with to even ask whether they should revisit their beliefs. They've grown "the way the wind blows," as Rush says, and that's that. But they're not the ones lashing out at those who would question their beliefs. As Peart says in a video the band produced to go with the *Snakes and Arrows* album, there are "two kinds of faith: a good kind that could be protective and help people, and a bad kind that is militant and you want to kill people."

Most people, of course, have the good kind of faith, where their faith is simply a shield from the snakes and arrows of life. It's the others, the "preaching voices—empty vessels of dreams so loud"—who wield their swards "in the temple and marketplace"—that are out there demanding that everyone validate their beliefs. For those who might be the target of their wrath, the best thing to do, Peart says in "Faithless," is to simply keep your head down. Be a stone in the river, the willow in the wind, or the desert flower that only blooms at night. Let the anger flow past you without it disrupting your own quiet resistance to the madness.

Blowing people up because they're apostates? Mutilating women because they can't love the person their parents selected for them? Destroying carvings thousands of years old because they don't represent your beliefs? Bombing health clinics because they allow abortions? Denying rights to men and women because of their same-sex orientation? Cordoning off an entire people in the name of national security? Steer clear of the madness.

Taken as a whole, *Snakes and Arrows* shines a light on the maladaptive nature of religion to the extent it spawns extremists who use their faith to force the world to conform to the tenets of their beliefs rather than conform the tenets of their beliefs to the world. The album takes the form of an extended essay, or commentary. There is no storytelling going on.

Parable over commentary

The band takes a completely different approach in its follow-up album, *Clockwork Angels*, in which it keeps its focus on religion but leaves the commentary to others. Instead, taking an approach many of us would be familiar with from Sunday school, it gives us a parable of a young man, Owen Hardy, who, like the protagonist in Ayn Rand's *Anthem*, Equality 7-2521, isn't ready to fall into his pre-assigned role in life. But the parable has something of a twist ending, because although he ends up finding his Garden of Eden, it's not quite the Garden of Eden we learn about on those Sunday mornings.

The tale is told over the album's 12 tracks and, like the band's early foray into progressive rock, "The Fountain of Lamneth" from *Caress of Steel* in 1975 and "2112" in 1976, among others, each track is a distinct piece that can be understood and listened to on its own but also advances the story in the larger narrative. Peart says the narrative is based loosely on Voltaire's *Candide*, a story about a man born into unfortunate circumstances (he was illegitimate) who uses his native wit to chart a successful, if adventurous, course through life, even becoming quite wealthy for a time, but who ultimately eschews the drama for a quiet, contemplative life with his loved ones.

At the beginning of Rush's version we're introduced to Hardy, who grows up happily enough on a farm and takes comfort in what he had been taught about the world and his role in it. From his earliest memories, he was brought up to believe the world has a plan and is the best of all possible worlds. But at the time we meet him, he's questioning all that and champing at the bit to embark on a different chapter of his life. "For a boy, life on the farm was idyllic, but for the young man I became, that very peace and predictability were stifling, unbearable," he says in the prose introduction to the opening track, "Caravan."

This is a rather clever set-up to the story, because in one fell swoop we're presented with a confrontation with two of the great historical belief systems of the world, one religious and the other philosophical. The religious system is the idea that we have to live in the best of all possible worlds because God is omniscient and omnipotent, and so He can only create the best of all possible worlds. On the philosophical side, it's the Platonic view that the world is created by the demiurge in the model of eternity but ultimately not under the control of him or any deity. This is a deistic view, the idea that god started the world spinning but now it's on its own. We also hear about the benevolent watchmaker, a Platonic philosopher-king character who governs society but ultimately cannot bend it to his will. In his wisdom he decides what your lot in life is going to be, and your job is to ask no questions, thank you very much. "It's not ours to understand."

What we come to see in the course of the story is that neither view is correct. Instead, what's correct is the Aristotelian view of the Prime Mover— that everything in the world, by seeking its own perfection, helps bring order and meaning to where there is none.

Reason and faith must be reconciled

As we have seen, the idea that ours must be the best of all possible worlds comes from Gottfried Leibniz, who, like many rationalists during the Enlightenment, sought to show how faith can exist in a world that is governed by hard and fast laws. Leibniz posited in his *Theodicy* that an all-knowing and all-powerful being could not create a world He knew to be inferior to any other conceivable world, so the world we're given by definition has to be the best possible. As for why evil and other bad things exist, Leibniz's view is that bad things are necessary to bring out the best in us: without danger there can be no courage, without dishonesty we can't weigh the value of honesty, and so on. As he puts it,

> [O]ne has no cause to complain of the fact that usually one attains salvation only through many sufferings, and by bearing the cross of Jesus Christ. These evils serve to make the elect imitators of their master and increase their happiness.[1]

Not everyone took to this idea, mainly because it's so easy to imagine a more perfect world than ours simply by postulating one additional person whose goodness makes him an "elect imitator" of Jesus.

One person who most decidedly didn't take to this idea is Voltaire, who, coming up a generation after Leibniz, lambasts it without mercy in *Candide*, his greatest work and a work that has endured far longer in the public imagination than Leibniz's *Theodicy*. (To give Leibniz his due, his more important work is *Monadology*, in which he lays out a metaphysics based on an infinite number of atom-like units that form the building blocks of the world we live in and perceive. Monads get around the vexing mind–body problem in philosophy (how something without physical presence can interact with something material) by existing in a pre-established harmony, so rather than interacting in a causal sense with one another, they act in synchronization with one another.)

In *Candide*, the title character is the bastard nephew of a wealthy baron who has the Leibnizian philosophy of optimism in the *Theodicy* instilled in him by his tutor, Pangloss. Candide and the baron's daughter, Lady Cunégonde, love each other, but the baron will have none of that and after the two kiss for the first time Candide is thrown out of the house. A lifetime of raucous adventure ensues, including adventures that get their own treatment in *Clockwork Angels*: a dramatic shipwreck at sea, a journey to El Dorado (one of the "Seven Cities of Gold"), and, in the end, a retreat from the drama of the world to a peaceful spot where one can focus on the simple act of tending a garden.

Threaded throughout the narrative is a mind-numbing cascade of natural disasters, confrontations with nasty, brutish people, and horrible strokes of misfortune.

The story thus takes on the form of a wicked satire of Leibniz's idea and we're left with the feeling that, if this is the best of all possible worlds, then, as Woody Allen once said, God is an underachiever at best. Our best of all

---

1 Leibniz's passage on the need for bad things in the world to help us achieve good things is in his *Theodicy: Essays on the Goodness of God, the Freedom of Man and the Origin of Evil*, E.M. Huggard, trans. Project Gutenberg, 2005, page 122 VII.

possible worlds doesn't just contain evil; it's practically built on evil, and the only way to get away from it is to seal yourself off in your own Garden of Eden, because you're never going to find the Garden of Eden out in the world at large.

In *Clockwork Angels*, the adventure is presented as a flirtation with the chaos of *akrasia* as a prerequisite to, or necessary condition of, reaching a state of *eudaimonia*. Women, gambling, drinking, fighting, making your mark in the big city—it's the lure of Sodom and Gomorrah. For a young man, staying content on the farm is hardly natural; the desire to conquer the world is the much more natural path and that path isn't complete until one comes out on the other side a survivor, having met evil head on and overcome it. That's how we learn about life and come to our own conclusions about what life ultimately is all about. And so in "Caravan," Owen hops onto a steamship and descends into hell. "On a road lit only by fire / Going where I want, instead of where I should / I peer out at the passing shadows / Carried through the night into the city."

In setting out in this way, Owen is taking on Leibniz and Plato at the same time, on the one hand testing the notion that this is the best of all possible worlds, and on the other challenging the idea that he has to stay on the farm lest he disrupt the carefully calibrated order of the republic.

For the watchmaker, who fills the role of Plato's philosopher-king, Owen's independence is an existential threat to the harmonious functioning of society, because it's critical that each member of society buy into the established order. In the same way that the religious depend on others buying into their narrative to give their beliefs validation, since no validation can be found in the natural world, the Platonic republic depends on the people buying into the roles assigned to them, because there's hardly anything natural about suppressing your identity in the name of social harmony.

To Plato, the idea that everyone buy into his republic's rigid hierarchy is so important that he says it's okay for the philosopher-king to tell a creationist-like myth to keep people from questioning their lot. In this "noble lie," as it's come to be called, the leaders are born with gold in their blood, the warriors with silver, and the producers with iron and brass. Therefore, if you're unhappy with being born a worker, there's nothing you can do about it—it's just your lot in life. Of course, sometimes a leader will give birth to a son that has iron or brass in his blood, and in these cases, the leader will have to suck it up and send his son down to grow up with the other worker children. So, he is not suggesting that it's all good, even for the leaders.

"They shall by no means give way to pity in their treatment of them, but shall assign to each the status due to his nature and thrust them out among the artisans or the farmers,"[1] Plato says in the *Republic*.

---

[1] Plato's point that leaders have to send their sons down a notch on the social hierarchy because they have "brass or iron," instead of "silver or gold," in their blood is in his *Republic*, 3.414e–15c. Conversely, if a worker has a talented son, then leaders can elevate him on the idea that he has "gold or silver" in his

And sometimes a worker will have a son that's born with some gold in his blood. In these cases, the leaders will elevate him to become a leader. So, there is some social mobility, but it's the leaders who say who has what in their veins and who can be elevated to a different social status.

"If from [workers] there is born a son with unexpected gold or silver in his composition they shall honor such and bid them go up higher, some to the office of guardian, some to the assistanceship."

Plato is quite frank that this is all just a big "contrivance," a noble lie, but it's justified on the grounds that it will make the people "more inclined to care for the state and one another."[1]

Against this background, a farm boy like Owen Hardy thumbing his nose at this pseudo-cosmic order is tantamount to a crime against the state. He's challenging the basic organizational premise of the republic and exposing, like Dorothy does the Wizard of Oz, that behind the curtain we find just a regular man with his hands on an impressive array of levers.

And so we see in "Brought Up to Believe," the second track on the album, the young man in what amounts to a soliloquy talking about the very thing he's not to talk about: whether the cosmic order he was taught is really cosmic in nature or whether it's all just a big line. "I was brought up to believe / The universe has a plan / We are only human / It's not ours to understand / . . . / The universe has a plan / All is for the best / Some will be rewarded / And the devil take the rest."

At what end of the debate does the young man's mind come out on? Well, we know from "Caravan" that he's decided the farm can't contain his big thoughts, so, like the boy in "Analog Kid" and the couple in "Dreamline," he's lighting out for the city. He has in effect made himself the most dangerous man in the republic, because in his action he has delegitimized the governing order of his society.

This isn't to say he's wiser than the leadership class or the philosopher-king. He's no more certain about the true order of the world than they are, but like Socrates, he knows what he doesn't know and doesn't pretend otherwise. In his mind, the world isn't pre-ordained to unfold a certain way, but neither does he know what the true order is. He's agnostic, you might say, and ready to experience life in full so he can decide for himself what is right.

So, his journey begins in earnest in the album's title track, "Clockwork Angels," after he hops off the steamship that carries him to where all the action is, Crown City (with "crown" having a connotation to the philosopher as king).

Owen's first destination is the central square, called Chronos Square, at the center of which is a tall clock tower. There, circling above and around the tower and bathed in light are the clockwork angels, mechanical icons

blood: 3. 414e–15c.
1 Plato, *Republic*, 3. 415c–d.

whose graceful, synchronized movement can be likened to the moving images of a Chinese lantern and that inspire in the people below a belief in the graceful, synchronized order of the world. "Celestial machinery—move through your commands / Goddesses of mystery, so delicate and so grand / Moved to worship, we bow and close our eyes / Clockwork angels, promise every prize."

The clockwork angels are the human-crafted icons that put a concrete face on the abstract idea that the world is governed by a cosmic order. They are very much equivalent to the giant, awe-inspiring face of the Wizard of Oz, only instead of inspiring through fear they inspire through their loveliness. "Clockwork angels, spread their arms and sing / Synchronized and graceful, they move like living things / Goddesses of Light, of Sea and Sky and Land / Clockwork angels, the people raise their hands—as if to fly."

The term "Chronos," in Chronos Square, relates to time, as in "chronology," "chronicle," and so on. Chronos was the Greek god of time, who, depending on the culture, is depicted in different ways. The Greeks depicted him as a kind of serpent with three heads, the Romans as a naked man in front of the Zodiac wheel, and, in later Western cultures, he was portrayed as a bearded timekeeper, the benevolent Father Time.

The angels, representing light, sea, sky, and land, are the offspring of Chronos and a goddess, Ananke, who represents inevitability—as in the inevitable march of time.

There are two key images in the piece. The first are the icons, bathed in light and circling the clock tower in the same way that images circle in a Chinese lantern, and the second are the people in the square below, bowing their heads in prayer to the angels.

In the first image, it's not an accident that the angels are depicted like images in a Chinese lantern, because we're being asked to think of Plato's allegory of the cave, in which the prisoners shackled in place by chains live out their lives believing the shadows flickering in the firelight against the cave wall in front of them are gods moving about. To the prisoners, who have known no other reality, the images are the most real and comforting thing in their lives, which is why, when one of them suddenly finds himself free and experiences life outside of the cave, he's denounced as a heretic when he tries to tell them the images on the wall are just shadows.

In the second image, the people below are very much prisoners in the same way as the cave inhabitants as they worship the floating angels and look to them as a devout believer might look to a statute of Mary to reassure them that all is right in the universe. "Lean not upon your own understanding," we hear in the piece (in a passage from Proverbs 3:5). "Ignorance is well and truly blessed / Trust in love and perfect planning / Everything will turn out for the best."

Thus, in single blow, we see the stunning contradiction at the heart of Plato's central idea about his republic. On the one hand, he calls out the worship of gods for what it is, an ignorant belief in mere shadows, yet on the other hand he seeks to maintain order in his own republic by casting shadows of his own, the noble lie, to keep his own people in ignorance. It's a neat piece of lyric-writing by Peart, to be sure.

And to see just how fragile this sense of order is, we're next introduced to the title character of the fourth track, "The Anarchist," who is a fellow we all know: a man who looks back at all the snakes and arrows he endured as a child and has organized his life around one pursuit: revenge. Like the child who prefers negative attention from his parents to no attention at all, he will ensure he gets the whole society paying attention to him by destroying it. "Oh—they'll never forget me," he says.

At first glance the anarchist looks very much like the foil to the philosopher-king—the very embodiment of the disorder that the philosopher-king's carefully constructed icons and noble lie are intended to defend against—but in fact the anarchist is the foil to the independent thinker, the Owen Hardy character, who is the real threat to the republic.

For a command society like the republic of the philosopher-king, where all power is undemocratically invested in one person or one group of people, a character like the anarchist is actually a godsend, because now the leader has an enemy to point to as he tightens the strings around the republic. As the leader might say, "the world is a dangerous place, with people who are ready to throw everything into chaos at any moment, so you understand why we have to keep such a tight rein on things."

A cat and mouse game ensues, as the anarchist looks for the time and place to make his mark and the leader of the republic dispatches his warriors to try to root him out. In a way, the game creates its own sense of order. If the anarchist succeeds and unleashes his chaos, the damage will necessarily be limited in scope because the anarchist's real intention is only to draw attention to himself; he couldn't care less how the society is organized, and whatever damage the anarchist inflicts will be quickly dealt with, most likely by tightening even further the society's coercive instruments of order.

But an independent thinker like Owen Hardy is a fundamental threat to a command society, because in his very person he delegitimizes the philosopher-king's whole enterprise.

The dynamic between the anarchist and the independent thinker comes to a head in the fifth track, "Carnies," when the two enter each other's orbit. The anarchist immediately pegs Owen Hardy (who's now working as a carnival hand in the central square) for an innocent and tosses him a bomb detonator. Hardy's intentions are to alert everyone to the presence of the anarchist, but when he sees the detonator flying his way he catches it on reflex, and all at once the tables are turned against him in spectacular *Candide* fashion: the carnival-goers mistake him for the anarchist and raise a hue and cry for his capture. So, the one person who poses a moral challenge to the society is suddenly on the defensive for posing a physical challenge to the society, even though he's the one person who can actually save the society from itself. He is, in fact, the prisoner who had escaped Plato's cave and returned to tell the other prisoners they've been looking at shadows on the wall all this time. And just like the reception given the enlightened prisoner in the cave, Hardy is being condemned as a threat to their way of life. "Accusations ringing loud / A ticking box, in the hand of the innocent / The angry crowd moves toward him with bad intent."

And of course he is a threat to their way of life—all under the watchful eyes of the clockwork angels, who are supposed to be looking after the people's interests. But of course they aren't; they're looking out for the state's interests.

As we saw in the album's title track, the people look up to the angels as their guardians: as long as the angels are circling the clock tower, the people know they're protected and everything is right in the world, so they don't have to bother themselves with understanding what their lives are really about. But in Plato's republic, the interests of the people are defined as those interests which are in the interest of the state. So there really are no individual interests separate from the state. So, "justice" in Plato's republic doesn't mean justice for individuals; it means justice for the state alone. Anyone accused of acting unjustly—that is, acting against the interests of the state—has no individual rights with which to defend himself against his accusers.

As Karl Popper, the British Plato critic we looked at in the first chapter, says, Plato saw "justice" as a synonym for "'that which is in the interest of the best state'. And what is in the interest of this best state? To arrest all change, by the maintenance of a rigid class division and class rule."[1]

That means that the angels circling above, and to which the people look as their protectors, are simply agents of the state whose vigilance is on behalf of the state and not the people who are worshipping them. Which is why it's perfectly right that the angels do nothing to protect the people against the anarchist but allow the people to become a vigilante mob that runs the individual thinker out of town—which they do. With "Carnies," then, we see the allegory of the cave in Plato's *Republic* enacted right before our eyes.

The sixth album track, "Halo Effect," appears as an interlude, with Owen Hardy reflecting on a woman, Francesca, with whom he had fallen in love during his stint as a carnival hand. She was one of the performers, beautiful, and "with wings on her heels," but he now realizes she wasn't anything at all what he thought she was. Rather, everything he thought about her was his own fantasies projected onto her. "The ideal, that I wanted to see," he says in another soliloquy on the album.

This disillusionment with the beautiful, winged woman is very much the same disillusionment he has with the beautiful, winged women circling overhead, the clockwork angels. They certainly were nothing that he thought they were. They did nothing to protect him and, as he knows now, are simply creations of the state. The idea that they are up there as our protectors is just

---

1 Karl R. Popper, *The Open Society and Its Enemies: The Spell of Plato*. Princeton: Princeton University Press, 1962, page 89.

a fantasy that we're projecting on what, in the end, are mere idols.

But, there's little time to think about that. Owen Hardy is a man on the run. He's run out of town by the vigilante mob (think of the imagery in the opening of "Witch Hunt") and so he hops onto a streamliner that makes a regular run along an established trade route to the wild frontier towns. His goal is to escape his past in one of the famed "seven cities of gold" that are reputed to lie somewhere just beyond civilization's border. It's the Wild West, where one has to take law and order into one's own hands, but as a man on the run, he has nothing to lose.

The notion of "seven cities of gold," with a town called Cibola the most notorious of them, is derived from the tales of the Spanish explorer Coronado and the search for El Dorado. Peart says he had Cormac McCarthy's novel *No Country for Old Men* in mind when he wrote the lyrics to the piece, "Seven Cities of Gold," the seventh track on the album. In it, we get a glimpse of life completely de-linked from the overly rigid, clockwork precision of society in a philosopher-king's republic. In a country like this, "A man can lose his life," he says, just the thing that someone with nothing left to lose is prepared to lose.

In effect, we have anarchy, which makes it clear, if more clarity was needed, that the anarchist really doesn't want anarchy; he wants validation. If the anarchist really wanted anarchy, he would have been the one to hop on the steamship and live his life out in the rough and tumble of Cibola or one of the other cities of gold. But in fact he stays in the clockwork-rigid republic and plays cat and mouse with the warriors. Again, he's the sulking boy who will take negative attention if he can't get positive attention. He has no intention of blowing up the society that validates his anti-social behavior.

But our independent thinker, who is genuinely searching for an understanding of how the world is ordered, is the one who finds himself in a state of anarchy. He was always willing to put himself before the world's chaos, and now he's arrived in chaos central. "The nights grow longer, the farther I go / Wake to aching cold, and a deep Sahara of snow."

Like the pioneers and explorers of the Wild West, for Owen it's a journey across the frontier in search of El Dorado. "A man can lose his past, in a country like this / Wandering aimless / Parched and nameless / A man could lose his way, in a country like this / Canyons and cactus / Endless and trackless." (Note the meter of the lines is the same meter used in "Double Agent" on Rush's 1993 *Counterparts* album, which is also about wandering in an environment without order, although in "Double Agent," the environment is the warped state of mind of the narrator, a double agent.)

Like others for generations before him, our traveler never finds Cibola or any of the other cites of gold and barely escapes the frozen desert with his life. But he makes it back to the port city where he earlier hopped on the steamship, so he hops on another ship and, in the eighth track of the album, "The Wreckers," heads back to civilization. But then nature intervenes. The ship is tossed about in a terrible nighttime storm. The captain steers the ship toward a beacon of light on the shore only to discover, too late, that the light was set as a trap for just the kind of storm-tossed travelers Owen's ship represents. The ship crashes on the jagged edges of unseen reefs and everyone but Owen Hardy perishes. The remains of the ship are picked over by the desperate and completely amoral shore-dwellers who set the trap, and Owen once more ekes out a narrow escape. But now he's left to ponder the astounding lack of humanity he just witnessed. "All I know is that sometimes the truth is contrary / Everything in life you thought you knew / All I know is that sometimes you have to be wary / 'Cause sometimes the target is you."

Peart says he based the lyrics on *Jamaica Inn*, a novel by Daphne du Maurier in which a tribe of English people off the coast of Cornwall in the early 1800s set traps just like the one depicted in the piece, for the purpose of ransacking ships. "It's just a shocking example of inhumanity," Peart says in a June 12 interview with *Rolling Stone.* "I wove all of that into the story of this album."[1] To put du Maurier in context, she wrote *The Birds* and *Rebecca*, two of Alfred Hitchcock's most memorable movies, so you might think of her as one of Hitchcock's favorite writers.

The story of "The Wreckers" is the climax of the narrative arc of *Clockwork Angels.* In the piece, Owen Hardy confronts not pure evil, which is represented by the anarchist, but complete amorality. Here there's no point to the evil except survival, with people acting no different than animals—or acting no different than the wind and the rain that tossed the ship about. The wreckers, in other words, are people whose desperation for survival has led them to return to a state of nature. That means Owen Hardy has gone from his boyhood farm as the Garden of Eden—the idealized state of nature—to the state of nature in Thomas Hobbes' *Leviathan*, in which the life of man, outside of society, is "solitary, poor, nasty, brutish and short."

Everything after "The Wreckers" we might call the denouement of the narrative arc, starting with the ninth track, "Headlong Flight," which was released as a single just before the release of the album in mid-2012. The piece shows Owen Hardy hightailing it back to the Garden of Eden that he left behind, but he's not returning to the life he left behind; he's returning to a sanctuary of his own creation, one in which he'll be surrounded by those who are the polar opposite of the wreckers, those whose love and respect he cultivates and gives love and respect back in return.

The key idea in "Headlong Flight" is the necessity of experience to understand the context of your life. Although Owen's returning to a simple life, the garden will have a different meaning to him because he's a different person, thanks to the experiences he's had over the course of his adventurous life. "I have stoked the fire on the big steel wheels / Steer the airship right across the stars / I learned to fight, I learned to love and learned to feel."

In the piece, Owen Hardy says he wishes he could live it all again, but

---

1 "Q&A: Neil Peart On Rush's New LP and Being a 'Bleeding Heart Libertarian'," by Andy Greene, Rolling Stone, June 12, 2012.

of course he can't, and that's less important than the fact that he lived the experiences once. You need to have the experiences once—that's absolutely necessary—otherwise you'll never understand life. And Owen Hardy achieved that by having his life lesson. The fact that he wishes he could do it all again seems more like a bit of whimsy thrown into the piece rather than something that carries any philosophical weight. Peart says he wanted to use the line to honor his friend and mentor, Freddie Gruber, the longtime jazz drummer and teacher who passed away in 2011. Gruber, who in the early part of his career played with Charlie Parker and other be-bop acts, always lamented that he couldn't live his life over again. "That is not a feeling I have ever shared about the past," Peart said in a write-up he released when "Headlong Flight" came out as a single. "I remain glad that I don't have to do it all again." But those words nevertheless "inspired the chorus 'I wish that I could live it all again,'" he said.[1]

The remaining three pieces of Clockwork Angels wrap up the narrative. "Brought Up to Believe 2 (BU2B2)," at not quite 90 seconds long, is a device to bring to a conclusion the uncertainty raised in the original "Brought Up to Believe." In that first piece, Owen Hardy is questioning the order of the universe as he was taught it; in the second piece, he's concluded that the order he was taught is false—a noble lie. Even so, we learn in BU2B2, he chooses to live, and not succumb to despair, because the world still has love and laughter as value points worth cultivating. "I still choose to live / Find a measure of love and laughter / And another measure to give / I still choose to live / And give, even while I grieve / Though the balance tilts against me."

In effect, love and laughter (and we can add in respect) are the value-points that make life worth living, even in a world of existential despair, and our ability to experience love and respect (and have love and respect returned to us) is what constitutes a good or happy life. If you have these, then everything else that seems important in life—the ambition to make your mark, for example, or to bend society to your designs—become beside the point.

Indeed, it's the lack of these value points in their lives that drives the philosopher-king to create his rigid, totalitarian society and the anarchist to spend his days on the periphery of society threatening its destruction and the wreckers to spend their nights plundering the ships of their victims.

To bring this back to where we started with Aristotle, the value points they're pursuing are the wrong ones because they can only be achieved at the expense of other people—that is to say, by treating others as objects or as means rather than as sovereigns in their own right worthy of respect. The philosopher-king decides what strata of society each person will occupy without regard to what the individual wants, the anarchist will

---

1 Peart's comment about his old drum instructor, Eddie Gruber, is in an April 19, 2012, press release, "Rush Announces 2012 *Clockwork Angels* Tour," from Live Nation.

blow up anyone who happens to be present when he sets off his bomb, and the wreckers will murder you and plunder your possessions without even knowing who you are.

These actions are anathema to a person who has, and gives, love and respect, because for people who are rich in these value-points, the world is a place of happiness. Not only is there no reason to try to bend society to your will, there's no desire to try to bend another individual to your will or to even wish ill of another person, even those who would do you harm. For people who would do you harm, in fact, all you can do is forgive and forget.

And that's what Hardy does in the penultimate piece on the album, "Wish Them Well." The piece has the feel of an anthem to pacifism with its injunction to just "wish them well" when people do bad things to you. "Anger and grudges are burning embers in the heart not worth carrying through life," Hardy says in the prose introduction to the piece. "The best response to those who wound me is to get away from them—and wish them well."

Peart has said in interviews that allowing yourself to smolder in anger over the ill way people behave, to you and to others, is to rob yourself of vital energy that could be put to better, more positive uses. "That's a really important realization in life," Peart told Jim Ladd in a June 2012 interview on the SiriusXM classic rock show *Deep Tracks*. "All you can do with [negative] people is turn your back and walk away, be glad you're not that way, and wish them well."[1]

Although it sounds like a lesson of Jesus Christ—turning the other cheek, meeting aggression with forgiveness—for Owen Hardy, allowing aggression to go unmet is a psychological, not a religious, response. As Peart says in his interview with Jim Ladd, "You can learn healthier ways to respond to negativity and to toxic people."

> If you can't avoid them [he continues], you say, "Okay, bye-bye. I'm glad I'm not like you. I'm gone." Don't waste your energy on returning grudges and hatred and the negative feelings that only poison you. That's one thing I've always hated about the feeling of anger. It leaves me with such a hangover. If I get mad at someone, like if someone cuts me off gratuitously in traffic, that anger that you can carry isn't good for you and it doesn't help the situation one bit, so [it's better] to just say, "Okay, you're a jerk. Bye. You're not in my life."[2]

Since Peart is using the language of psychology in the context of forgiving and forgetting—"negativity," "toxic people," "energy," "poison"—he brings us back to Earleywine's idea of Rush as a kind of cognitive behavioral therapist. To be aggressive, you must feel inside yourself anger and rage and other

[1] Peart's comment about turning the other cheek is in a June 13, 2012, radio interview with Jim Ladd on SiriusXM Deep Tracks, channel 27.
[2] June 13, 2012, radio interview with Jim Ladd on SiriusXM Deep Tracks, channel 27.

anti-social, non-productive states of mind. But by refusing to personalize someone's negativity toward you, you keep yourself from absorbing that negative energy, enabling you to keep your energy focused on the positive.

We thus have in a key concluding part of *Clockwork Angels* a continuation of Voltaire's criticism of Leibniz's religious proposition. Peart is taking one of the most well known injunctions of Christian teaching—turn the other cheek—and locating its source in our psychology rather than the bible. To McDonald's point in his essay about humanism, it's yet another example of Rush using the language and imagery of religion in the service of humanism. (You can also add in the fact that the 12 chapters of *Clockwork Angels* are organized under a set of Pagan runes, each one telegraphing the essence of the action.)[1] *See Appendix II.*

We see this device of using religious motifs in a secular context again, with equal clarity, in the last piece of the album, "The Garden," with its explicit allusion to the Garden of Eden. But what we see is that, this isn't the bible's Garden of Eden, it's Aristotle's.

In this Garden of Eden, we're not in a world of virgin innocence, before man has eaten from the tree of knowledge of good and evil, which is the garden of Owen Hardy's childhood; rather, we're in a Garden of Eden of our own making, based on the knowledge of good and evil that we've acquired over our lifetime.

This garden, we can say, is the place at which we arrive when, having acted as our own prime mover over the course of our life, we have actually reached our destination and fully realized Aristotle's notion of *eudaimonia*, or state of true happiness. On this view, the bible's Garden of Eden is only a starting point for achieving the good life, and rather than Adam and Eve being kicked out of the garden for eating from the tree of knowledge of good and evil, taking the bite of that apple is the necessary first step to becoming a happy person.

What's central to Aristotle's view is the idea that it takes the course of a lifetime to reach a state of *eudaimonia*. It makes no sense to size up how a person conducts himself when he's still in the thick of living, confronting temptation, and looking for opportunity. That determination is something we can make only after a person has lived his life and now, as he settles down into his twilight years, is it appropriate to take stock of where this person has been and how he's conducted himself. In Aristotle's language, "for as it is not one swallow or one fine day that makes a spring, so it is not one day or a short time that makes a man blessed and happy."[2]

---

1 The meaning of the 12 *Clockwork Angels* runes is derived from my own research, which I posted on *Rush Vault* in May 2012. The post went on to become my most heavily accessed page on the site, with some 10,000 views in six months, which is a lot for the site. You can access it at http://rushvault. com/2012/05/03/meaning-of-rushs-clockwork-angels-runes/ Also, see Appendix II, "The Meaning of the *Clockwork Angels* Runes."

2 Aristotle's idea that we judge a person's character over the course of a life is in his *Nicomachean Ethics*,1098a18.

And even in our twilight years you can't really tell whether one is happy, because even the most tested among us hasn't faced everything we could possibly face in life. There's always the chance we could do something out of character as our life is winding down. But this isn't an all or nothing matter: it's just that we can tell more about a person's life the more he's lived it, so are we more able to say a person has indeed led a good life the more he has managed his life in an admirable way. In other words, we can keep a running tally, but until the person's life comes to a close, it's always just a snapshot in time.

Does this mean if Owen Hardy had stayed on the farm his whole life and was now in his twilight years, we couldn't know whether he's led a good life? Well, we could know his potential for living a good life, for sure. But whether he has reached a state of *eudaimonia* is another matter. Because *eudaimonia* is about living a full life—developing your potential in the face of temptation and opportunity—so it becomes a legitimate question to ask whether one can be said to develop his full potential if he never takes that bite from the apple.

We can't assume, and in fact it's hardly likely, that all those workers in a Platonic republic who are consigned to their position by the needs of the society and at the direction of the philosopher-king are realizing their full potential. Of course we can't know what their full potential is unless they themselves go out in the world, experience it to the fullest, and let their nature unfold before them. Without that confrontation with the world, in all its temptation and opportunity, we can't know who we are. And without knowing that, we can't realize ourselves in full and reach that *eudaimonic* state.

So an Owen Hardy who stays on the farm, carrying out his assigned role in life, might have all the qualities we like in a person—friendliness, trustworthiness, honesty—but until he's taken himself out of that assigned context and managed his life at the point of friction with the world and tested himself (as Rush says in "Vital Signs," "The fact is, this friction / Will only be worn by persistence"), can we say who this person really is and whether he's reached a state of *eudaimonia* and become in the broadest sense a happy person. At the end of the day, we have to act as our own prime mover and be the decision-maker of our life. We have to leave the farm. Only then can we return later in life and make it our *eudaimonic* Garden of Eden, which is what Owen Hardy does at the end of *Clockwork Angels*.

When looked at through this Aristotelian lens, what we see in "The Garden" are two strands of thought coming together in a neat package. On the ethics side, it's the *eudaimonic* idea of having to confront the world in all its temptation and opportunity before we can see whether we're a good person or not. On the metaphysical side, it's the idea that we must act as our own prime mover before we can say we've realized our true nature. Being a good person and realizing our true nature are one and the same thing, and equate to happiness. And this state of *eudaimonia* is fleshed out in substantive terms as love and respect. These are the only value-points we can pursue in harmony with, rather than at the expense of, other people.

This idea is summed up in one of the concluding lines of the piece. "The treasure of a life is a measure of love and respect / The way you live, the gifts that you give / In the fullness of time / It's the only return that you expect."

CHAPTER 6. THE CASK OF '43

> Leave out conditions
> Courageous convictions
> Will drag the dream into existence
> —"Vital Signs," *Moving Pictures, 1981*

The *Wall Street Journal* in August 2012 ran a short news item in its financial section about a $300 million security that a company was shopping around for investors.[1] It's the kind of news blurb you find in the *Journal* on any given day, except that this security wasn't collateralized by home mortgages or derivatives, as you would expect; it was collateralized by Bob Dylan, Neil Diamond, jazz singer Cassandra Wilson, and Rush. The company, SESAC, manages the royalty income of artists' public performances and was telling global investors that Rush and the others are bankable acts, that together over the next five years they're going to produce $300 million in fees to the company, and that they're so confident in the demand for the bands that they're willing to bet 5.25 percent interest that they'll get every penny of that $300 million.

Risky business? Given how easy it is for people to copy and download music on the Internet, maybe even a popular act like Rush can't bring in the promised amount of revenue. But Goldman Sachs clearly saw a risk worth taking. As the underwriter of the security, it was basically saying to investors, if SESAC doesn't collect its projected $300 million in fees, we'll make you whole. Don't worry about it. We know SESAC's acts are surefire winners, each one an icon in its own way: Bob Dylan as the conscience of the 1960s, Neil Diamond as the hit maker beloved by millions, Cassandra Wilson as the jazz singer whose unique timbre is on more than four dozen albums and film scores, and Rush as . . . the world's

---

1 The news of Rush being included in the bond issue by SESAC is in "The Bonds, They are A-Changin'," *The Wall Street Journal*, August 8, 2012.

largest cult band.

The SESAC security is interesting for a number of reasons, first among them is what it says about how far Rush has come since the mid-1970s when it was dismissed by critics, ignored by *Rolling Stone*, and misread by NME. Today, it's arguably one of the few music acts so secure in its reputation and bankability that it can help collateralize a $300-million bond offering.

But it also validates what Lee said in the band's 1978 interview with *Maclean's*, when their success seemed so out of phase with the "turn on, tune in, drop out" times they were living in. "For us, capitalism is a way of life."[1]

It's a cliché to say that the times have caught up with the band, but that is indeed what has arguably happened. Now treated as elder statesmen of rock, Lifeson, Lee, and Peart have essentially received every accolade they possibly can, even finally getting their long-overdue induction into the Rock and Roll Hall of Fame in 2013—this despite *Rolling Stone* founder Jenn Wenner having once likened Geddy Lee's voice to Donald Duck's[2] and the magazine's senior editor David Wild saying in 1999, "It ain't ever going to happen."[3] (Wenner is the founder of the Rock and Roll Hall of Fame.)

So it is that the band that has been putting the power and majesty of religion to the cause of humanism for the last 40 years has done more than part the Red Sea; it's caused Hell to freeze over. What has changed?

---

1 "To Hell with Bob Dylan," by Roy MacGregor, *Maclean's*, January 23, 1978, pages. 26-30. Available at *Rush is a Band* http://www.rushisaband.com/display.php?id=2213 retrieved December 15, 2012.
2 Wenner's comment about Geddy Lee sounding like Donald Duck is one of the most passed-around tropes about Rush. One place you can read it is in "Rush vindicated: a Rock Hall of Fame berth for Canadian band," *Omaha World-Herald*, October 5, 2012.
3 Wild has since wished the band well. The week before their Rock hall induction, he said on Twitter "#GodBlessRush. Many people never thought their day would come. I know because I was one of them. I was wrong. #RockHall." (You can access that tweet at https://twitter.com/Wildaboutmusic/status/325098749217095681.)
In any case, the original Wild quote is from a 1999 talk show appearance and is a favorite among Rush fans for showing the bias against the band. Here's how the quote is portrayed on various Rush fan sites:

> "David Wild, an editor for Rolling Stone magazine and one of the individuals who casts votes to induct artists into the Rock and Roll Hall of Fame, said that as far as the induction of Rush was concerned 'it ain't ever gonna happen. Regardless of their success, Rush has never achieved critical acclaim and no one will ever vote for them.' He also said, 'with the exception of "Tom Sawyer," most of it gives me a headache.' He later added that technical proficiency is not considered a valid reason to induct an artist and that 'Rush really hasn't done anything unique.'"

See for example *The Rush Forum* http://www.therushforum.com/index.php?/topic/65232-boycott-rolling-stone-magazine/ and *Erik and Danna* http://www.erikandanna.com/rush/hall_of_fame.htm both retrieved December 23, 2012.

Mythmakers of a generation

Although the band got its start in the 1960s and hit its stride in the late 1970s, it was never really playing to its baby boomer peers; it was always playing to Generation X, the boomers' younger brothers and sisters.

The boomers' younger siblings grew up on videogames and were far more vested in 1980s entrepreneurialism than in 1960s social consciousness, says the musicologist we met earlier, Durrell Bowman. For them, Peart's larger-than-life, videogame-like mythmaking, with his lyrical narratives about adventure with a purpose, blended with the epic music of Lifeson and Lee to give Gen Xers a cultural narrative they could call their own. And it wasn't a narrative about fairness and equality, as Joan Baez sang in "We Shall Overcome" at Woodstock; it was about man, machine, and self-actualization. To speak in a gross generalization (which can sometimes be true), that's a story the boomers simply didn't get.

"The people in positions of power today are in their 40s now and they grew up with the band and they're finding that it resonates more with them than bands that rock critics have talked about in the past," says Bowman. These 40-somethings are a "post-counter-cultural, progressive, entrepreneurial culture, and they see something similar in the music of Rush."[1]

And now these Gen Xers, as they move into leadership positions in business, science, government, art, education, and entertainment, are simply giving *their* band, the conscience of *their* generation, its day in the sun. Hence all the awards and accolades that have rained down on the band in the last decade or so. (In addition to its Rock Hall induction, the band was inducted into the Canadian Music Hall of Fame in 1994, recognized with Canada's highest civilian award, the Order of Canada, in 1996, inducted into the Canadian Songwriter's Hall of Fame in 2010, and given its own spot on the Hollywood Walk of Fame, also in 2010. And maybe best of all, back in 1993 they were named Honorary Members of the Harvard Lampoon, founded in 1876, the first musicians to be inducted into the legendary—and world's longest continuously published—humor magazine. Their prize: a large pizza.)

Chris McDonald in his 2009 book *Rush, Rock Music and the Middle Class* (Indiana University Press) sees the delayed embrace of Rush not so much as a generational matter but as a class matter. In his analysis, Rush is an avatar of middle class values and he sources much of critics' antipathy toward the band in the 1970s and 1980s to a kind of class warfare, with music critics, characterized by those who write for *Rolling Stone* in the U.S. in the role of the elites—educated, intellectually detached, and searching for the authentic—on the one side, and Rush and its fans in the role of the middle class, on the other.

1 Bowman's point about Rush speaking to Gen X and not baby boomers is in an interview he gave for my web site, *Rush Vault*: http://rushvault.com/2011/06/30/40-years-later-has-rush-won-out-over-rock-critics/

The value-set of the middle class, as McDonald relates it, is self-improvement: take responsibility for yourself, work hard, better your position. This is very different from elites, for whom such studied self-improvement is gauche and who instead value authenticity, charity, and intellectual distance. These ideals, as translated into rock criticism, means that elites are always looking for the natural, on the one hand, and the ironic—the vehicle of their detachment—on the other.

Or, put another way, McDonald says, music critics were coming at rock with a kind of "hip intellectuality," embracing "grass-roots, black, and working-class popular culture" on one side, and "the educated, critical register of twentieth-century American high culture *literati*" on the other.[1]

Thus "authentic" artists like The Ramones and the Kinks, that channeled the black roots and rebelliousness of rock, and those with ironic intellectuality like David Bowie and the Talking Heads, were the "canonical" types of bands that critics loved to love, while a band like Rush, neither authentic nor ironic, was simply outside the conversation.

Its music was too self-serious, and thus it lacked that intellectual distance that critics love, and it was "too white," neither channeling the blues roots of rock nor authentically capturing the rebellion against conformist American society. Indeed, with its embrace of middle-class values, it was moving in the opposite direction of the elites by rebelling against their ideas of charity and *noblesse oblige*.

Although he doesn't single him out, Creem writer John Kordosh channels just the kind of elitism McDonald is talking about. Kordosh, who by his own admission disliked the band's music and couldn't keep that fact out of his writing, clashed with Lee and Peart more than once in the early 1980s. In an interview that's almost as infamous among Rush fans as Miles' NME interview, Kordosh, who had just covered Rush's 1981 Detroit show during their *Moving Pictures* tour, pronounced Rush's music completely humorless and intolerably pedantic.

> The best that can be said about these musicians-by-innuendo is that Alex Lifeson is a competent post-Page guitarist. Geddy Lee, who played—excuse me, strapped on—a double-necked bass during one song, plays with all the gusto of a teen-aged girl who's thinking about giving up ballet lessons for punk rock. And Neil Peart can hide behind every triangle, gong, bell, empty paint can, and any other percussion instrument he can think of—adults will prefer one good wallop from Charlie Watts from now until 2112. Wait a minute, I forgot that Geddy Lee is also the group's vocalist. At least, I wanted to."[2]

1 McDonald, *Rush, Rock Music and the Middle Class*, page 187.
2 Kordosh's criticism of Rush is summarized in Telleria, *Merely Players*, page 45. Also, in an interview for *Rock Critics*, he discusses his spat with Rush and why he likes The Kinks: http://rockcriticsarchives.com/interviews/johnkordosh/johnkordosh.html retrieved December 8, 2012.

It's a good guess that for Kordosh, the bands that really set the standard for rock are the Rolling Stones and the Kinks, with their blues roots, rollicking attitude, and even hint of danger in both their music and in the approach to their career. I don't want to speak for him, but it appeared to bother him to no end that in Rush there was none of that. "This miasma of moronism," as he called their music, "is about as dangerous as getting shampoo in your eyes. In other words, it has nothing to do with rock 'n' roll."[1]

John Reuland of Princeton University makes the same point as McDonald about the band's anti-elitism, but he comes at it from a different direction. In an essay he wrote for *Rush and Philosophy* called "Nailed It!" He draws on scholarship about the nature of elitism to show how Rush's music, because of its self-conscious complexity and pedantry, stands in violation of elitist values. What elites value is a kind of naturalness, or looseness, in which people do a difficult thing without betraying the effort that goes into it, almost as if their talent or skill is a birthright. That's why it's cool for someone to pick up the guitar and make playing look effortless, but it's nerdy to show how long and how hard and how carefully one has been practicing.

For the cool person, it's the naturalness of playing the instrument that's the point; for the nerd, it's nailing "Mary Had a Little Lamb."

That's why for elites, a John Coltrane is the coolest thing there can be. For him, you never know what his saxophone will become in his hands. It will reflect whatever his emotions are at that moment. There's no separation between what he's feeling and what he's playing. With Rush, there's too much of the nerd getting up on stage and showing how precisely he can play. That's why some critics have disparagingly labeled their work baroque: their pieces are like big, ungainly musical compositions that have all the spontaneity of a Corelli *concerto grosso*.

"Refusing to pass itself off as natural, Rush's presentation of virtuosity does not attempt to conceal the labor behind it," Reuland says. "Explicitly presented as available for emulation, Rush's music has no pretenses about being anything other than a fiction [that is, not authentic] in the etymological sense of the word, anything more than a made object, an artifact."[2]

These two different takes on the class divide between music critics and Rush make a lot of sense, and of course McDonald crafted an entire book out of his thesis, but they don't entirely answer the question of why, after all these years of making music, the band is suddenly being treated with a kind of reverence that the critical community never would have bestowed on them before. What has changed? And the answer to that, arguably, is the generational shift we're seeing, with baby boomers and their ideas of elitism heading into retirement and Gen Xers, with their very different ideas of what's important, taking their place in positions of leadership.

We see this same shift taking place in our politics, certainly in the United States, with our battles today over the amount of government we want and

1 Telleria, *Merely Players*, page 45.
2 Berti and Bowman, *Rush and Philosophy*, page 65.

how much debt our government should carry. The government ideal of the 1960s and 1970s, aside from whatever you think about the proper role of government today, was, in its essence, elitist and collectivist at that time.

Within the span of just 15 years, from 1964 to 1979, a period that included Republican as well as Democratic administrations, we had in the U.S. in addition to the enactment of Medicaid and Medicare (both created in 1965), the creation of a whole alphabet soup of departments and agencies, including CPB, DOE, DOT, ED, EPA, HUD, NEA, and NEH. (Respectively, these are the Corporation for Public Broadcasting (CPB), 1967; the Department of Energy (DOE), 1977; the Department of Transportation (DOT), 1966; and the Department of Education (ED), 1979; The Environmental Protection Agency (EPA), 1970; the Department of Housing and Urban Development (HUD), 1965; and the National Endowments for the Arts (NEA) and for the Humanities (NEH), both created in 1965.)

Looked at from today's perspective, when all the talk is about cutting programs, to see the extensiveness of that list of departments and agencies that came out of just that 15-year period is to see just how much the environment has shifted from the late 1970s to today. You really did have in the 1960s and 1970s the flowering of a Platonic model of society in which people looked to government to deploy public resources for tackling social problems.

Of course, this activism was never labeled collectivism; it was labeled the New Frontier during the administration of John F. Kennedy and the Great Society during the Lyndon B. Johnson years, but by any name it was a collectivist-leaning approach. And it wasn't just happening in the United States. During that same period, in Canada, you had Pierre Trudeau and his "Just Society," the hallmark of which was implementation of Canada's universal health care system and a large expansion of the country's welfare programs. And in the United Kingdom, where progressive politics (under the "post-war consensus") had been a part of the cultural landscape since the end of World War II, you had nationalization of heavy industries like coal mining, evolution of the country's massive welfare state, and the flowering of the country's National Health Service.

Of course, that Platonic approach began to unravel in the 1980s, reflected in the elections of Ronald Reagan in the United States, Margaret Thatcher in the U.K., and Brian Mulroney in Canada. Since that wave of conservative victories, the cultural vibe has been all about rolling back this kind of heavy public involvement in society. Even with Democratic leaders such as Bill Clinton in the 1990s in the U.S. and Tony Blair in the U.K. in the 2000s, whose policies from the beginning played progressivism in a moderate key, the days of creating programs, departments, and bureaus to direct public resources into social problems are really very much over, at least for the time being.

Rhetorically, even the West's longtime collectivist nemeses, Russia and China, have stopped talking Plato. Today, you can hear them reciting all the buzzwords, if not putting in place all the practices, of capitalism. In a word, it's a flowering of Aristotelianism, at least in rhetoric and aspiration.

It's outside the scope of what we're talking about here to show that our loud and vitriolic battles today over the role and size of government are the result of the generational shift between baby boomers and Gen Xers. It's easy to say Gen Xers are bringing into positions of power their individualist entrepreneurial consciousness while baby boomers are trying to protect as much of their collectivist achievements from rollback as they can.

Nothing is that simple, of course, especially since so much of the agitation on the right these days is coming from none other than the baby boomer themselves. But as Kate Zernike has shown in her book on the Tea Party, *Boiling Mad*, although older, retiring baby boomers are the face of the small-government movement, so much of the energy, organization, and power of the movement is being driven by their Gen X and younger partners who look to famously Randian politicians like Rand Paul and 2012 Republican vice presidential nominee Paul Ryan as their political models.

"The contrast was striking" Zernike writes. "The [Tea Party] panelists on stage were baby-faced despite their suits and stylized stubble, while the people in the audience were 'seasoned,' as one young panelist gently put it— twice their age or more. . . . But this was how the movement had grown, this mash-up of young and old. . . . It was what made it so contradictory, so combustible."[1]

So, are our politics going through a hairy generational shift, just as they did in the 1960s and 1970s, when the baby boomers were coming of age? At least on the surface, you can make a case that they are.

Not yet ready to exit the lighted stage

Against this changing of the guard, the music of Rush has found its moment, which is why the band's recent tours, including its 2007 *Snakes and Arrows* and 2012 *Clockwork Angels* tours, have been anything but nostalgia acts. Unlike other bands of Rush's vintage that have been hitting the concert circuit in recent years, Rush's shows are not trips down memory lane but, in the eyes of critics, fresh and vital moments. As Ron Hubbard put it in his September 2012 *Pioneer Press* review of the band's *Clockwork Angels* show in Minneapolis, the new music "stole the show" and represented "the beginning of a fascinating new chapter in this band's admirably lengthy history."[2]

Chad Hobbs, in his Columbus, Ohio, *Clockwork Angels* concert review for Examiner.com, said very much the same thing. "Not many classic rock bands can get away with playing virtually their entire new album. Rush, however, can do it for a couple of reasons. The first and foremost reason being that the

---

1 The mix of young and old in the Tea Party movement is in Zernike, *Boiling Mad*, page 4.
2 "Nearly four decades later, Rush is still proving it matters," Ron Hubbard, *Pioneer Press*, September 25, 2012.

quality of the songs hasn't waned in recent years."[1]

These are very different reviews from what we saw in the press for other 70s and 80s acts that were on the road at the same time as Rush in 2012, biggest among them Kiss and Mötley Crüe, which toured together to promote Kiss's new album, *Monster*.

In critics' eyes, *Monster* and the accompanying concert tour were all about yesterday, with the music "formulaic," "unremarkable," and "lyrical nonsense,"[2] and the tour a bombastic exercise in over-produced theatrics around the two bands' old hits that included dancing girls hanging on scaffolding above the stage in Mötley Crüe's part of the show and the kit for Kiss drummer Eric Singer moving on a roller coaster-like track during his solo.

Likewise for Def Leppard and Poison, who also joined up for a tour in 2012. They met the same kind of reception as Kiss and Mötley Crüe. "In front of a half-capacity crowd at Quicken Loans Arena last night," Jeff Niesel says in his review for *Cleveland Scene*, "both groups resorted to arena rock clichés (sing-a-longs, hand-slapping, acoustic segments) during their respective sets that, while entertaining, ultimately rang hollow."[3]

"Def Leppard quickly dove into the material most of the fans in the packed 20,000 seat amphitheatre came to see," says Pat Reavy of the *Deseret News*. "The set list focused primarily on the *Hysteria* and *Pyromania* albums. This year marks the 25th anniversary of the massively successful *Hysteria* album, prompting the band to give it special attention. Eight of the 12 tracks were played."[4]

This isn't to disparage Kiss, Mötley Crüe, Def Leppard, or Poison, from whom you expect, and would be disappointed not to get, the old hits and classic theatrics they offered up in 2012. It's just to show the different trajectories the bands are on, with critics who for decades dismissed Rush as outside the mainstream now praising the band for remaining fresh and vital while giving other rock acts from Rush's vintage a thanks-for-the-memories nod of appreciation.

So, Rush has very much come full circle: A band for so long outside the conversation now being put directly in the middle of the conversation by a new generation of politicians, music critics, and others in positions of leadership who've internalized the band's stories.

1 "Rush delights fans old and new," Chad Hobbs, *Examiner.com*, September 21, 2012.
2 "Kiss, Monster," Scott McLennan, *Boston Globe*, October 9, 2012.
3 Jeff Niesel's review is in "Concert Review: Def Leppard and Poison at Quicken Loans Arena," *Scene Magazine*, July 7, 2012. "[T]hese two bands (they also toured together last summer) do have one thing in common—they know how to please their fans. In front of a half-capacity crowd at Quicken Loans Arena last night, both groups resorted to arena rock clichés (sing-a-longs, hand-slapping, acoustic segments) during their respective sets that, while entertaining, ultimately rang hollow."
4 "Concert Review: Def Leppard/Poison USANA 6/20," Pat Reavy, *Deseret News*, June 21, 2012.

As it happens, this evolution is captured in two of the band's most ambitious concept pieces, "The Fountain of Lamneth," the 20-minute-long musical tale from 1975 that draws on the heroic atmospherics of *The Odyssey*, and *Clockwork Angels*, which taken together provide a neat pair of bookends to the band's career arc. What we see is that *Clockwork Angels* completes the individualist circle introduced by "The Fountain of Lamneth" by fleshing out what Aristotelian success looks like.

A band's evolutionary arc

In a story that sounds remarkably similar to *Clockwork Angels*, the boy in "The Fountain of Lamneth" grows up in relative comfort but very soon decides that the stay-at-home life is not for him. "My way of life is easy / And as simple are my needs / Yet my eyes are drawn toward / The mountain in the east."

But to leave home the boy first needs to break away from the authority figures in his life for whom adventures are more than a waste of time; they're a violation of the rules and expectations that members of the society are expected to honor. The boy does indeed rebel, after a conflict with his authority figures—"Stay! Go! Work! No!"—and embarks on his journey, and things are bad right from the start: he's knocked unconscious in a sea storm and awakens to find his ship bobbing aimlessly and the crew gone. His predicament is a tough metaphor for his life: outside his home and against the raw currents of the world, he is alone and adrift. But he eventually washes ashore and there, as he slowly comes to, he's met by Panacea, the pale and ambergris-scented beauty who takes him in and nurses him back to health.

Under her care, he succumbs to a haze of pleasure-seeking, his days and nights a blur of love and libation. Amidst such pleasure, his body despairs of ever returning to his journey. But ours is no weak-willed wanderer; with the inner strength of Ulysses, he frees himself from Panacea's spell and completes his journey—only to find the end anticlimactic: nothing is at the Fountain of Lamneth except disappointment. But then he realizes, as in "Prime Mover," that it's not the end that makes the journey worth taking; it's the journey itself. By throwing himself into the wide world with just his wits to guide him, he's become a different, more complete person, one who knows what he's all about.

"The Fountain of Lamneth" is based loosely on *The Odyssey*, as *Clockwork Angels* is based loosely on *Candide*, but the central narrative of the two tales is almost identical and, more broadly, the two share the classic outlines of the heroic tale. It's the individual, confronting the world in all its raw dangers and temptations, coming out of his journey a wise and self-reliant go-getter who now knows how to get things done.

Put another way, the two offer up parallel tales of personal growth in a Hobbesean world in which life is "nasty, brutish, and short" but conclude in a Lockean vein in which the individual, now a fully fleshed out, sovereign person who's tested himself against the world, can come together with others of like sovereignty to form a society based on cooperation, not coercion.

In the one important difference between the two, the individual in *Clockwork Angels* moves beyond self-reliance, the end-point of "The Fountain of Lamneth," to an awareness of the need for the love and respect of others, what Peart has called in *Far and Away* the one, universal desire that "everybody wants. . . Love and respect are the values in life that most contribute to 'the pursuit of happiness"—and after, they are the greatest legacy we can leave behind. It's an elegy you'd like to hear with your own ears: " 'You were loved and respected.'"[1]

"The Fountain of Lamneth" doesn't address that at all.

In the later and more mature view represented in *Clockwork Angels*, individuals coming together in a Lockean society, in which each gives up a little sovereignty in exchange for the benefits of a government to serve them, the critical ingredient for success is the mutual respect of the sovereigns and the mutual ability to love. Only those who have the capacity to love (that's love, not co-dependency, as we see in "Virtuality" and "Test for Echo") are capable of generating respect. "Neither is any good without the other," Peart says.[2] And only among sovereigns in which respect for another is mutual can you have a genuine Lockean democracy. Otherwise one must necessarily rule over another, coercively.

Ayn Rand puts it this way: "To love is to value. Only a rationally selfish man, a man of self-esteem, is capable of love—because he is the only man capable of holding firm, consistent, uncompromising, unbetrayed values. The man who does not value himself, cannot value anything or anyone."[3]

It's significant that in neither "The Fountain of Lamneth" nor *Clockwork Angels* are there echoes of the bible. Biblical tales, universally, are fantasies of top-down command and control: God flooding the world for 40 days and 40 nights so He can start over with the help of Noah, or God presenting the 10 Commandments to Moses after his 40 days and 40 nights of wandering on Mount Sinai.

Typical of the biblical story genre, these are stories that share with Plato a rejection of the individualistic idea of letting people take responsibility for their own lives. (Noah is commanded to build the ark; it wasn't his idea. Moses is given the 10 Commandments; he did not produce them.) To let people rule themselves is to risk letting every city become a Sodom and Gomorrah. Better to destroy the world and start anew than to let people confront the world in all its rawness so that each has the chance to mature into one's own sovereign, capable of cooperating with others to tame the wilds.

1 Peart's quote on love and respect is in "The Prize" in *Far and Away*, page 294.
2 Peart's point that love and respect are only good in combination with one another is in "The Prize" in *Far and Away*, page 294.
3 Rand's quote about only a person who loves himself can love another is in her essay "The Objectivist Ethics" in *The Virtue of Selfishness*, p. 35.

Rush's tales, by contrast, are narratives about letting people plunge headlong into a state of nature (think "The Necromancer," "Xanadu," "Cygnus x-1," among the many others) and indeed into the Sodoms and Gomorrahs of the world (think "Subdivisions," "The Analog Kid," "Dreamline"), because unless and until you test yourself against all that the world can throw at you, you can't separate yourself from your home to grow into a truly self-actualizing person. And self-actualization in a random universe is the end-point of all of Rush's philosophy.

The Cask of '43

In *The Odyssey*, Homer's epic tale of Odysseus as he journeys back to Ithaca after the Trojan battle depicted in *The Iliad*, the hero washes ashore the island of Scheria, a battered wreck of a man in a battered wreck of a ship with a battered wreck of a crew. But he's soon saved by Nausicaa.

Like Panacea in "The Fountain of Lamneth," the beautiful Nausicaa, dressed in purest white, sees past his bedraggled appearance and helps our hero get back on his journey. But soon enough he's landed on yet another island, Aeaea, and rescued yet again, but this time it's by what you might think of as Nausicaa's evil opposite, Circe.

Equally beautiful but more Rolling Stone than Beatle, more goth than saint, Circe turns Odysseus' crew into pigs and turns our hero into . . . her pleasure slave. But with the help of one of his sharp-witted crew members, whose early insight enables Odysseus to avoid Circe's magic, our hero escapes and once again continues his journey home.

As a beautiful savior who is also at the same time a selfish enchantress, Panacea in "The Fountain of Lamneth" embodies both Nausicaa and Circe, and because of that she's the most realistic character of the three. Like each of us, she has a good side and a bad side. But also like Francesca in *Clockwork Angels*, she is what we make her out to be. Is she a savior? Yes. Is she an enchantress? Yes. She's all of these things, because she's really just a projection of what we want her to be.

Panacea, as her name implies, is a drug, a distraction, a masking, an excuse, a belief. Like the lovely but mechanical angels that hover above the square in Crown City, her role is to give us comfort so we don't have to think for ourselves. She's the government that will do everything for us, like the U.S. government came very close to doing in the late 1970s with its alphabet soup of agencies, bureaus, and departments, as long as we do what we're told to do. She's the religion that will make everything right for us as long as we worship the God we're told to worship. She's the Madeira that will keep us sedated as long as we keep the goblets coming and the liquor flowing. She's the relationship that will save us from being alone as long as we subordinate a good part of ourselves to her. Indeed, she's like Calypso, the first goddess to bed Odysseus, who had become enchanted with her harp playing and had spent some seven years with her in the caves of Ogygia as her lover until the urge to return home became too strong.

The time our hero in "The Fountain of Lamneth" spends with Panacea is the critical moment of the story's narrative arc, because it's at that moment, as we hear about in "Freewill," that he must choose how he will live his life. Will he choose free will or will he dance to the powers he cannot perceive? Will he choose free will or will he choose a ready guide in a celestial voice? Will he choose free will or will he be a prisoner in chains to a venomous fate?

Well, he's a hero, not a victim, so he chooses correctly: he rejects the soft, comforting, addicting allure of Panacea and throws himself back out into the world, and his immediate reward is . . . the cold, desolate gray road of uncertainty and discomfort. "Another foggy dawn / The mountain almost gone / Another doubtful fear / The road is not so clear."

Nor is there a reward waiting for him when he finally reaches his destination, the Fountain of Lamneth. "Now, at last I fall before / The Fountain of Lamneth / I thought I would be singing / But I'm tired . . . out of breath."

But his disappointment isn't a cause for despair, as it would be for others ("Many journeys end here"). Instead, it's a cause for joy, because his confrontation with the world in all its rawness has enabled him to discover who he is, so he can say at the end, as those who've never been tested cannot, "Tears spring to my eyes / Though I've reached a signpost / It's really not the end."

What's important for our hero is *how* he got to where he is, not the fact that he got to the Fountain of Lamneth. It's the same message as in "Prime Mover," which says the point of the journey is not to arrive and the point of departure is not to return. The point is the journey itself. We can't be autonomous, and thus sovereign, without the experience of confronting the world. That confrontation is the friction that creates the pearl, the chaos out of which comes order, and the argument that results in agreement. Anything that would keep us from taking that journey must be resisted. That means resisting moralities that tell us what to do, governments that prescribe from on high, or relationships that turn on dependency.

In easily the most well-known story about Rush, at the single most critical point in the band's career, the three musicians chose to live by this maxim of resisting power that would otherwise steal their autonomy.

Just after the release of *Caress of Steel* in 1975, the critical community panned the album largely because of the two concept pieces on it, "The Necromancer" and "The Fountain of Lamneth," and the band's record label and others pressured them to make their next album more commercially acceptable.[1]

At the same time, audiences at their shows were dwindling, and the

---

[1] The panning of Caress of Steel and the resulting "Down the Tubes " tour are both amply recounted in all of the Rush biographies, including *Contents Under Pressure*, page 42, *Merely Players*, page 25, and *Rush: Visions: The Official Biography*. New York: Omnibus Press, 1988, page 27.

dates and the size of the venues they could get for their tour—dubbed the "Down the Tubes" tour—were shrinking. As Peart put it in an essay he wrote to accompany the band's *A Farewell to Kings* tour book, "It was a pretty depressing string of small towns and small clubs, and a lot of unwelcome pressure from certain quarters about making our music more accessible and more salable. It was uncertain for a time whether we would fight or fall."[1]

But rather than give in to the pressure to go commercial, the band doubled down on the direction they had chosen and came out with . . . *2112*, their most non-commercial album ever. It not only included another concept piece, "2112," but it put that piece front and center, making it the entire first side of the album. "We got mad!" said Peart. "We came back with a vengeance with '2112.'"

The rest is history, as they say. The album caught fire and went gold within months, eventually going platinum and then later triple platinum and the title piece, "2112," is now widely recognized as one of the first classics of progressive metal, and on the basis of the success of the album, the band members say, Rush's record label gave them *carte blanche* to do what they want musically without interference and the result is the success the band has seen over its long history.

Thus, the band that exhorts you to trust yourself and resist power that would rob you of your autonomy built its career around that idea, living by its own example.

So in "The Fountain of Lamneth," when the Greek-like chorus in the denouement says, "Draw another goblet / From the cask of '43 / Crimson misty memory / Hazy glimpse of me," you're hearing the siren song of temptation. It's the temptation we all face: the warmth, comfort, and sensuality of Panacea's embrace, the allure of quaffing another goblet of wine and putting off the journey in the cold outside.

Who can resist such temptation? Some of us in fact can't, at least sometimes. But until we're faced with this choice between free will and dancing at the end of another's puppet strings, we can't claim our sovereignty. To renounce our freedom in exchange for comfort is to despair of our capacity to perfect ourselves and, by extension, create the best of all possible worlds. To choose freedom, on the other hand, is to embrace our sovereignty and take our place in a Lockean democracy, our future unlimited.

But what's not acceptable is to have this chance at self-determination withheld from us, our heroic tale never told but rather replaced with a fantasy narrative of command and control.

The God-fearing would make it a sin to drink or to take pleasure in the sensuality of life. The answer for them is to call these activities sins and direct you down a dichotomous path of abstinence and self-denial and exhorting you to renounce the pleasures of the flesh. You can't be trusted with your desires, and therefore you must make yourself a stranger to them.

1 Peart's remarks about the "Down the Tubes" tour is his essay "A Condensed Rush Primer" in *A Farewell to Kings Tour Book*, released September 6, 1977.

The Platonist, seeking to organize all of life under sets of rules to produce a society as close to the ideal as possible, would prescribe what journeys you can take, what jobs you can do, and even what class you fall into. After all, it's not for you to decide any of these things; the philosopher-king makes these decisions based on his wise and benevolent vision for what is best for society.

But these regimes of command and control are based on fantasy narratives of the cowed who would try to mold the world on the basis of their fears rather than on the basis of their dreams and reject the idea of allowing you to govern yourself on the basis of how the world actually is.

So, drink the wine and experience the allure of Panacea. Don't be afraid of your desires, because they are an important part of who you are and they drive you to where you are going. After all, we're all on this spinning top in the here and now and we might as well enjoy our life while we're here. As Rush says in "Dreamline," we're only immortal for a limited time. No one gets points for succumbing to despair.

But we're not just about our desires; we're also creatures of reason. And thus we must edit our actions. As we saw in "Prime Mover," the key lines are "rational resistance to an unwise urge" and "rational responses force a change of plans." We are passion and reason, heart and mind, united, as we learn in "Hemispheres," the concept piece that followed "The Fountain of Lamneth" and "2112."

It's this point of friction between what we want to do and what we end up doing that makes each of us the remarkable person that we are, and unless we throw ourselves out into the world and test our limits, we can't develop ourselves and become, in effect, our own prime mover. And if we can't do that, then the world itself cannot proceed on its journey to become, in actuality, the best of all possible worlds.

Appendix I. Rush as Religion, Metaphysics, Ethics, Physicalism, Economics, Psychology, Sociology, Political Commentary—and Music

Enough people dislike Rush's music or are indifferent to it to keep the band
from ever rivaling popular favorites like The Beatles or the Rolling Stones in the
public imagination. But the band stands out from the crowd due to the sheer
depth of its work as philosophy. Looking at the band as an avatar of Aristotelian
values, as I've done, is just one way to approach all the ideas the band talks about
in its music. There are many other ways, and a number of scholars have dived
in from their unique perspectives to tease out what they see in the band, and
the result is a rich and fascinating exploration of just how thoughtful the band's
work is.

The results of that deep dive by about two dozen academics were collected
and published in 2011 in *Rush and Philosophy* (Chicago: Open Court Press) by
editors Durrell Bowman and Jim Berti. Bowman is a musicologist whose Ph.D.
dissertation from UCLA was on Rush's music and Berti is an educator in upstate
New York.

I published reviews of a third of the scholarly essays in *Rush and Philosophy* for
my web site, *Rush Vault*, and by supplementing *Rush: Life, Liberty and the Pursuit of
Excellence* with them here, you can get a good picture of what underlies a lot of the
ideas discussed in the book along with other lines of philosophical thought that
aren't addressed but are equally valid interpretations of Rush's music.

Why is Rush's music in some ways more like a concert grosso by Arcangelo
Corelli than a jazz improvisation by John Coltrane? What does Rush have to

say about the mind-body problem—you know, whether mental states are ultimately reducible to physical states? How is Rush's music like cognitive behavioral therapy? Is "The Trees" really a political critique of quotas? What kind of virtues do we find in the band's music that complements Aristotle's table of virtues quite nicely? How do people who know one another so well communicate without actually saying anything to each other? Is there some kind of chemical reaction that goes on that acts as a form of communication? It's all really thoughtful stuff.

The reviews show what a thoughtful, satisfying dive into the world of ideas the band's music represents, and they might even pique your interest enough to do your own digging into the band's music and philosophy.

Reviews

List of reviews:
Rush Music: Spontaneous as a Baroque Jam Session
Why Rush isn't cool
Plato: 'Rush Non in Forma Petra Musica'
Applying Plato's ideal forms to Rush
The Trees: More Than Meets the Eye?
Is Rush criticizing government quotas?
Rush's Rosier Shade of Reality
Forget Freud. Go to your happy place
Rush's Table of Virtues
Aristotle forgot a few virtues, but Rush knows what they are
The 'Rand'omness of Rush's Libertarianism
For the last time, Rush isn't that libertarian
Is Rush Helping Humanism Out-maneuver Religion?
The short answer is yes
It's Just Chemistry: Rush Try to Make Sense of Reality
Don't let language get in the way of understanding
Philosophy of Mind has a Headache; Cygnus has Aspirin
Are we mind or body? Yes

1. Rush Music: Spontaneous as a Baroque Jam Session

Why Rush Isn't cool

What's coolness? Well, it's the way John Coltrane plays the saxophone, for one thing. It's not that he's the best sax player there is. In fact, some music critics say his playing from a technical standpoint can be awkward at times. Rather, it's how he uses the instrument for self-expression. There's nothing artificial about it.

Now compare that to, say, a performance of Arcangelo Corelli's "Concert Grosso Op. 6" by the Boston Symphony Orchestra. You might very much enjoy the piece, even love it, but no one would ever use the label "cool" to describe the music or the symphony that performs it.

What makes something cool or gives it cachet is how natural or "unlearned" it is. The person who picks up the sax with a bit of swagger and just starts playing is cool; the person who meticulously sets up his music stand, sits up straight in his chair, and then, very didactically, goes through a piece with studied precision, is not. In fact, we would even call it nerdy.

It's not that cool musicians never practice. It's that their musicianship is more natural. Perhaps they were born into families for whom music comes naturally. They thus possess a self-confidence that comes from their early immersion in music, an imperceptible learning from their earliest days.

That's very different from the person who's had no such early immersion and so very self-consl

ciously and diligently practices to refine one's skill.

John Reuland of Princeton University in his piece, "Nailed It!" says music critics pin the nerd label on Rush because there's nothing natural or self-expressive about their music or how the band plays it. The music has been described as baroque— complex and tightly composed, not spontaneous or natural, and the band doesn't do much improvising when it plays it live. In fact, it strives to replicate a piece as precisely as it can each time it performs it. Of course, that's partly because it has to; there just isn't the musical space for them to get spontaneous if the song is going to hold together.

The nerd label transfers to Rush fans because they appreciate the band's music in much the same way that lovers of the symphony appreciate classical music. They admire the complexity of the composition and the virtuosity of the performance. They admire the music as an artifact to be studied and understood.

It's this notion of music as artifact that sets up something of a class divide between music critics and Rush fans. The artifact has a whiff of western whiteness about it. The artifact is the piece of music that can be analyzed, studied, appreciated, and replicated, and anyone with enough diligence can look at the notations on the sheet of music, so precisely laid out, to learn the piece and strive to come as close as possible to replicating it.

Not so with cool music, with its roots in black culture. It's spontaneous, emotional, natural. Each time it's played it might come out differently, because it's the experience that's key, not the artifact.

Thus, you might say music critics, who hail from the upper class (in spirit if not necessarily in actuality), have always looked down on Rush and its fan base, because they're so outside the naturalness of black music. Being nerdy has been defined as being hyper-white, so on this view Rush and its fans are hyper-white, the very opposite of black coolness.

What the upper class shares with black coolness is just coolness. A person born into an upper class family can be cool—natural or casual—even in a stiff social setting, because class is embedded in their DNA, and everyone knows it. They have cultural legitimacy that stems from their early immersion in the things that the upper class know. They have no need to aspire to know what the upper class knows, because from their early immersion in their identity, possession for them is a kind of birthright.

But for someone outside this class, possession of such knowledge is aspirational, and that's very uncool.

Reuland draws on some statistical work of others to point out that much of Rush's fan base is comprised of post-industrial, post-countercultural working and lower middle classes. And many of them—as much as two-thirds—are self-identified as amateur musicians. So for these working-class musicians, it's a worthy pursuit to try to nail down Rush pieces with precision. They're aspiring to possess Rush's music as an artifact. And thus they're willing to spend hours practicing at their drum set to try to nail down the time signature changes of "YYZ."

Such autodidacticism is admirable. It's hard work. And if you practice a piece and post a video of your playing on YouTube to get feedback on how close you came to replicating the real thing, you're opening yourself up to critical review. That's not always pleasant. But that's how you become skilled.

That's a very western thing to do. From the standpoint of some, it's a hyper-white thing to do. That's another way of saying it's a very uncool thing to do. But when you do in fact master a piece, you've accomplished something that's real and measurable, because you can measure how well you did against something that's concrete: the music as an artifact. And if you've done that, you can take satisfaction in knowing you improved yourself, and now you're ready to take it to the next level. And that's something even the cool can't take away from them.—*Published February 26, 2012*

2. Plato: 'Rush Non in Forma Petra Musica'

Applying Plato's Ideal Forms to Rush

Anyone who's taken a college-level philosophy class will be familiar with Plato and his Forms. These are standards of objective perfection for everything that exists in life. Take a car. A car is excellent not just because you think so but because it embodies qualities of excellence that are universal and objective. These qualities might be the way it handles, how smoothly it accelerates and decelerates, and so on. No car can match exactly the objective Form of the car, because no car is perfect, but those that come closest we call excellent; those that are furthest away we call pieces of junk.

For much of its career, Rush's music has been called pieces of junk: pretentious, humorless, dull. In short, it's a long, long way from the standard of perfection, the objective Form of rock.

In fact, if you were to create a chart depicting the albums closest to and furthest from the objective Form of rock, you would probably put Radiohead's *OK Computer* and something by Led Zeppelin at the top of the chart and pretty much everything by Rush at the bottom.

Thus, when critics slam a Rush concert, in their minds they're not just saying, "Oh, God, this is sooo bad," they're saying, "Anyone who knows anything about rock understands what makes truly good rock, and Rush is different from that."

What are those standards that signify excellence? No one really knows, of course, but if you ask critics they would probably say something like, "Good rock is played with emotion and heart, not mathematical precision, and its about girls, parents, and school and doesn't take on big philosophical ideas."

But this whole idea of objective standards doesn't really make any sense, says Northwestern philosophy teacher George Reisch in "Rush's Metaphysical Revenge." Reisch is also the general editor of the Popular Culture and Philosophy series for Open Court Press, which includes *Rush and Philosophy*.

Whenever a piece of music comes out that critics widely laud for its excellence, such as Sgt. Pepper's Lonely Hearts Club Band, it assumes an iconic status and is held up as a benchmark against which other pieces of music are measured.

But did *Sgt. Pepper* create a new standard or simply meet the existing form of rock?

Reisch says critics tend to grab onto a great new album like *Sgt. Pepper* and treat it as if it actually embodies the existing Form of rock, making it impossible for anything that takes a different approach to measure up. Thus, music like Rush's, which doesn't follow critics' views of the rules of rock, can't measure up by definition. Rush's music is automatically considered "corrupt, illegitimate, or somehow offensive to the status quo," he says.

But once we dispense with the whole notion of objective Forms, it's perfectly legitimate for rock bands to do things differently. If Rush wants to talk about the categorical divide between cognition and emotion, as it does in "Closer to the Heart," than it can do that without being considered an illegitimate form of rock, because there's no such thing as a legitimate or illegitimate form of rock.

When we "kick away the platonic metaphysics" of objective Forms, as Reisch puts it, the only standard of excellence by which we judge rock is our own. Reisch points to a comment once made by Billy Corgan of the Smashing Pumpkins that fans over the years have consistently overruled critics by voting for Rush in popularity and music magazine polls and contests. With these votes, fans are in effect saying, "Rock belongs to the people, not to the critics."

And that's just another way of saying there is no objective Form of rock.— *Published February 25, 2012*

3. The Trees: More Than Meets the Eye?

Is Rush criticizing government quotas?

Durrell Bowman in one of his pieces for *Rush and Philosophy* called "How is Rush Canadian?" assesses "The Trees" to determine whether the piece is just a comic book-like tale about trees acting like people, as Neil has said, or a thinly disguised critique of Canadian content laws.

Those laws, enacted in the 1970s, when "The Trees" was written and recorded, require Canadian broadcasters to include a certain percentage of Canadian content in their programming to maintain their license. Given the individualistic strain in the band's music, especially at that time, it stands to reason that it would oppose that kind of governmental intervention in what should be a purely artistic and market-based matter.

Bowman makes a strong case for the piece as veiled criticism of the law. Lyrically, it stands as a clever metaphor for the kind of mediocrity that comes from any kind of "collectivist" effort. You have the large and powerful Oaks whose boughs overshadow the much smaller Maples. The Maple, of course, is the Canadian national symbol, and the American Oak has long been a subject of myth in American tall tales. Between these two symbols is the well-established tension between Canada and the United States, over the latter's overpowering size and influence on its neighbor. ("MAPL" is also the acronym for testing whether content qualifies as Canadian. "M" stands for music, "A" for artist, "P" for production, and "L" for lyrics.)

From an individualist point of view, the government's requirement that Canadian broadcasters include a minimal amount of Canadian content in their programming is exactly the kind of "leveling" that makes libertarians and free-marketers apoplectic. Individuals should rise and fall on their own merit, not made equal by cutting the competition down to size.

But Bowman goes beyond lyrical analysis to look at what the song does musically to reinforce the idea that the piece is a critique of the content laws. The natural bird sounds in the opening vocal section, for example, speak to the idea that, before the law was enacted, the Oaks and Maples coexisted in a state of nature. When Geddy a little later sings "the Oaks ignore their pleas," after the Maples have filed their complaint, he shifts his vocal emphasis to the first and third beats from the first and second and also fourth and sixth beats. This suggests the idea of taunting or laughing, Bowman says, or, as he puts it, it's like Geddy saying, "nya nya nya."

Bowman covers all sections of the song in this way. In his analysis of the closing section of the song, after the Oaks have been cut down to match the size of the Maples, he says the fading pitches of G#, C#, and B present an "ominous effect, encouraging us to mock the song's sociopolitical 'accomplishment.'"

Bowman acknowledges Neil's contention that the song is nothing more than a quick creative dash that was sparked by a comic he saw in which trees were acting like people. But Bowman makes a plausible case for there being more than meets the eye when it comes to the song. In other words, Neil says it's just a comic piece but he might be winking while he says it.—*Published August 7, 2011*

4. Rush's Rosier Shade of Reality

Forget Freud. Go to your happy place.

It seems obvious, but the way we feel impacts how we see the world. As Geddy sings in "Totem," "I believe that what I'm feeling changes how the world appears."

Certainly the ancient Greeks understood that: Epicetus said that if you walk around in a funk, then you would view everything around you in a negative light. Conversely, if you walk around in a good mood, you would view the world in a positive light.

And yet for generations it never occurred to therapists that they might suggest a dose of happiness to a client who's feeling down. Rather than suggest to a person who's clinically depressed that they go identify what they like to do and then go do it, therapists would sit the person down on the couch and say, "Let's talk about your problems," as if reliving everything that's been bad in one's life would make one feel better.

Drug therapy was another approach. It was accepted practice to prescribe amphetamine for depression. Probably not one of psychotherapy's finer moments, considering the drug's addictive qualities and its nasty side effect of causing users to commit suicide.

The idea that the way to feel better is simply to identify what activities make you happy and then go do them, and do them as much as you can, is called cognitive-behavioral therapy, and it's largely accepted wisdom now in the therapist community.

You might wonder what took them so long to come to this view, because Rush has been dispensing cognitive-behavioral therapy since they cut their first record in 1974, says SUNY Albany clinical psychology professor Mitch Earleywine in his essay "Rush's Revolutionary Psychology."

"Just as a revolutionary new breed of psychotherapy was helping people think straight and feel better, Rush was doing the same," he says.

Independence, rationality, personal responsibility—these are recurring ideas in the band's music and they're also the kind of ideas that are at the core of modern psychology's cognitive-behavioral school, he says.

In a sense, listening to Rush is like spending time with someone who helps you see for yourself that you should strive for thoughtful open mindedness ("Witch Hunt"), clear-headedness ("Vital Signs"), balanced thinking ("Hemispheres"), independence of mind ("Subdivisions"), and perseverance ("Carve Away the Stone," "We Hold On") among a very large catalogue of virtues.

"Rush pairs music with words in a way that trains listeners in some of the key ideas in modern psychology," he says, "leading us to think clearly, responsibly, and happily."

Although he doesn't frame it in this way, Earleywine's analysis suggests Rush's music works as cognitive-behavioral therapy on two levels. On one level, it gives us context or perspective for viewing the world (ignorance is bad; it leads to midnight vigilantism. Blind conformity is bad; it impoverishes the world by submerging unique ideas). On the other level, the act of listening to the music itself makes us feel better, which helps put us in a positive frame of mind, which in turn makes the world look better to us. It takes us off the Freudian couch, in other words, and gets us out in the world with rose-colored glasses on.

Earleywine could have pointed to another essay in *Rush and Philosophy*, "Ghost Riding on the Razor's Edge" by the book's coeditor Jim Berti, which describes the impact Rush's music had on him.

"A few months back, I was experiencing my own personal Hell, a dark period that [brought me close to] physical and mental breakdown. As I have done so often during rough patches of my life, I turned to Rush to help me through. The album Vapor Trails, especially the song 'How It Is,' took on a greater significance . . . hearing Peart's story [of facing a string of personal tragedy] told through music was the perfect combination of emotional and physical release for me."

Yep, that sounds better than psychotherapy and an amphetamine prescription.—*Published June 12, 2011*

5. Rush's Table of Virtues

Aristotle forgot a few virtues, but Rush knows what they are

The holy grail of ethicists is *eudaimonia*, the classical notion of happiness. In this context happiness is broadly defined. It's not about having a good time or walking down the street with a smile on your face; it's about achieving a state of well-being. By developing all of what makes us excellent as human beings—courage, hard-work, fairness, empathy, prudence, and so on—and internalizing all of those virtues so that they become our character, we become happy.

Purdue University philosophy professor Neil Florek in "Free Wills and Sweet Miracles" says Rush's early work reinforces many of the virtues that go into a happy life. In pieces like "Something for Nothing" and "Freewill," the band is both celebrating and teaching the classical table of virtues. But, of course, with Neil Peart penning the lyrics, the band doesn't stop there; Peart adds his owns twists to the classical ideals: persistence and what Florek calls prudent non-conformity.

These Rushian virtues, which would sit alongside justice, courage, moderation, and the other classical virtues, are necessary to be happy. Persistence is necessary because, without it, we'll never overcome the internal and external barriers we all have to becoming happy people. Think of people brought up in religious households and taught to believe their fate is in God's hands. It takes time, as Rush says in "Marathon," to break free of our upbringing to think for ourselves. And non-conformity is a virtue because we need the drive to be different to break free of institutionalized biases. "I'll decide if our fate's in God's hands, thank you. I'm not just going to accept that because you say it is."

Rush's eudaimonic person is also an empathetic person. In pieces like "Red Sector A," "Afterimage," and "Everyday Glory," it's not just us striving as individuals to achieve happiness; it's important that we bring others along with us, too. We have to do what we can to help others achieve happiness.

Florek labels this focus on the classical virtues (with the band's additions) "pre-tragic" and contrasts it with what he calls the band's "post-tragic" phase, the period after Peart's personal tragedies and the band's hiatus in the mid-1990s.

In the post-tragic phase, the classical virtues have collided with reality and the question of what defines happiness can't be answered solely by reference to the classical virtues like moderation, courage, and justice. Where's the justice in loved ones dying well before their time? Hence songs like "The Stars Look down."

What is the meaning of this? / And the stars look down. / What are you trying to do? / And the stars look down. / Was it something I said? / And the stars look down.

Florek calls "The Stars Look Down," from Vapor Trails, probably the bleakest of any in Rush's catalogue, although the song "Vapor Trail" isn't far behind. But if those songs represent the nadir of Rush's outlook on happiness, other songs on *Vapor Trails* and on its follow-up album, *Snakes and Arrows*, at least carry the virtue of persistence and try to eke out an answer for someone who's facing inexplicable loss. The answer Peart comes up with are two other virtues to be added to the classical table of virtues: hope and love.—*Published June 11, 2011*

6. The 'Rand'omness of Rush's Libertarianism

For the last time, Rush isn't that libertarian

Commentators like to point to the celebration of libertarian ideas in Rush's music but Steven Horwitz, the Charles A. Dana Professor of Economics at St. Lawrence University in Canton, N.Y., says Rush's music is more consistently a celebration of individualism than libertarianism, although that's not to deny the deep strains of libertarianism in the band's music.

In "Rush's Libertarianism Never Fit the Plan," Horwitz describes libertarianism as the view that people should be free to live their lives as they see fit, while respecting the rights of others to do the same. Government's only job is to prevent us from harming others, which would deny others their freedom, equal to our own freedom. "As the old saying goes, my right to swing my fist ends at the beginning of someone's face."

With this as our view of libertarianism, it's easy to see why commentators would stick that label on the band. "Anthem," "2112," "Something for Nothing," and "Natural Science, among many others, express various strains of the ideology, and Horwitz points out that Neil himself has, at various times, described himself as a "left libertarian" (a libertarian who believes in a social safety net), although Alex and Geddy have never slotted themselves into the libertarian camp.

Horwitz doesn't mention this, but a number of high-profile libertarians in the United States have said they're big fans of the band, including Neel Kashkari, the U.S. Treasury official under President George W. Bush who in 2008 got the infamous Term Asset Relief Program (TARP) off the ground (that was the big bank bailout that, ironically enough, libertarians and others criticized as too much government intervention), and Rand Paul, the senator from Kentucky who received a letter from Rush's management during his 2010 run for office asking him not to play Rush's music at his campaign events.

Of course, Ayn Rand was a libertarian and Neil's appreciation for her work, at least in his early years with the band, is well known. (Ayn Rand and Rand Paul: what's up with that?)

Horwitz's point is that the libertarian strands in the band's music are undeniable but that to call the band libertarian would require ignoring a significant portion of the band's output. Horwitz didn't identify the songs that either run counter to or else just don't fit nicely into libertarian ideology, but he might have pointed to a number of songs that appear to be critical of rampant materialism, which is a by-product of free economic markets ("Superconductor," "The Big Money"), environmental disaster caused by that rampant materialism ("Second Nature," "Red Tide"), and the need we have for other people in our lives ("Hand Over Fist," among others).

The ideology the band espouses more consistently is individualism, Horwitz says, which is compatible with libertarianism (you can't have inventors and entrepreneurs without it) but the two aren't reducible to one another.

Throughout the band's body of work, the idea that it's individuals, as their own power centers, striving to project their self-worth, is paramount. "What you do is your own glory" in "Something for Nothing," "He's noble enough to win the world" in "New World Man," "Nobody gets a free ride" in "Marathon," and so on. The list goes on and on.

Horwitz doesn't pursue this strain of thought, but to say the band celebrates the individual doesn't mean there's no recognition of how rough life can get when you're out there on your own striving. Roll the Bones from 1991 is almost entirely devoted to how chance and unforeseen circumstances can upend people, and a good amount of the band's output in the last dozen years or so touches on the precariousness of our lives in a world where "the stars look down" while you get buffeted about mercilessly.

But, in the end, it's better to be buffeted about as a self-empowered individual than to be, like the Maples in "The Trees," reliant on the state to enforce equality by cutting the tall down to size.—*Published June 9, 2011*

7. Is Rush Helping Humanism Out-Maneuver Religion?

The short answer is yes.

Humanism is a secular ideology in which morality and decision-making are based on reason without appeal to anything that smacks of religion or the supernatural, so there are no gods; there are only humans who, using all of their skills and creativity in a free and supportive environment, strive to create a world in which as many people as possible can flourish.

For people who are fed up with intolerance, religious divisiveness, or passivity ("Oh, it's God's will"), humanism is deeply attractive. But, ironically, it's also the absence of anything that appeals to the unknowable or mystical that keeps humanism "out-maneuvered" by religion, says Chris McDonald in his essay "Enlightened Thoughts, Mystic Words."

McDonald is becoming a familiar figure to Rush listeners. His book about the band as an avatar of middle class values and aspirations, *Rush, Rock Music and the Middle Class* (Indiana University Press: 2009), stands as the first extended-length look at the band that goes beyond biography to focus solely on the band's music and lyrics from an academic standpoint.

In "Enlightened Thoughts," he makes the case that humanism is deeply embedded in Rush's work and that, given the rational, "academicized" discourse in which humanism is ordinarily expressed (in other words, it's dull), that's probably not a bad thing. As he says in one of the subheads of his piece, "Humanism needs its evangelists, too," and the music of Rush is not a bad evangelist to have on your side.

McDonald uses much of his essay to build the case for Rush as an avatar of humanism. Since the problems of religion play such a big role in Snakes and Arrows, the album provides a rich vein to mine nuggets that either espouse humanistic ideas ("I have my own moral compass to steer by" in "Faithless") or question religious ones ("We hold beliefs as a consolation / A way to take us out of ourselves" in "Armor and Sword").

But humanistic ideas are threaded deeply throughout the band's catalogue. McDonald spends some time looking at a trio of songs from the band's early years that, in their totality, represent a highly unusual celebration of eighteenth-century secular political movements: "Beneath, Between and Behind," which talks about the promise, and the later decay of that promise, of the American revolution, "Bastille Day," which celebrates but also casts a critical eye on the French revolution, and "A Farewell to Kings," which talks about replacing feudal society with something that has the promise of being better (democracy) but that comes with its own risks of disappointment and excess.

In between the early songs and *Snake and Arrows* is a consistent evangelism for humanism or for the pursuit of self-excellence, a humanistic ideal: "Something for Nothing," "2112," "The Trees," "Marathon," "Mission," "Available Light," "Cut to the Chase." The list is long and deep.

In McDonald's view, what these songs do is provide a way of talking about humanism that transcends the "academicized" discourse that entraps humanistic ideals. "If humanistic ideals are to replace religious ones, the same feeling of sacredness, power and mystery [that is leveraged by religion] must still attend them," he says.

That's a view shared by many humanists, who say there's nothing inconsistent about humanism's focus on rationality while encouraging people to talk about it in poetic terms, because people need to feel wonder and have a sense of spirituality about things to motivate them. It's about inspiration.

And Rush—"so secular, so critical of faith and superstition"—yet also employing the tropes of religion (like its borrowing from the Lord's Prayer in "Something for Nothing") steps into this vacuum to "inspire the wonder in us."—*Published June 7, 2011*

8. It's Just Chemistry: Rush Try to Make Sense of Reality

Don't let language get in the way of understanding

René Descartes ushered in modern philosophy with his acknowledgement in 1637 that everything we perceive in the world is subject to doubt. You act like you're my friend but how do I know you really just aren't interested in using me to advance your career? In other words, I really know nothing for certain about the reality of the world external to myself; I only know what's inside my head.

When you take this idea to its extreme, you become a solipsist: the only reality is what's inside your head; everything else is a projection of that. In a sense, everything outside of you is simply your dream.

The opposite of solipsism is behaviorism. Since you act like you're my friend, then you must be my friend, because the only reality is your behavior. If you stop acting like my friend after you become a vice president with my help, then you're simply no longer my friend.

Todd Suomela, a Ph.D. student in communications and information technology at the University of Tennessee, in his essay "The Inner and Outer Worlds of Minds and Selves," says much of what Rush was trying to express during its techno phase in the 1980s concerns this divide between our inner reality and the world around us. Although Suomela doesn't point to the image of the three orbs on the cover of Hold Your Fire, released in 1987, he might as well have because that image expresses the "alone-yet-together" character of the human experience. Alex, Geddy, and Neil are each individuals, encased in their own sphere, but they travel in a cluster as a unit. They're separate but together at the same time.

And so it is with all human experience. Each of us is a sphere that travels alone through the world but we interact—try to communicate—with one another without any certainty that we're understanding one another correctly or even that were seeing the world in the same way.

Think of President Barack Obama pushing through health care reform in the United States a couple of years ago. Supporters say the law encompasses free-market solutions to the problem of out-of-control medical costs in the country. Critics say it's a form of socialism. Which is the truth? The language in the law is the same for supporters and critics alike. Both sides are reading (or reading about) the same words, yet one side takes away one meaning and the other side takes away the completely opposite meaning. It's almost like people are living in separate worlds. What is the truth, and how can people of such different views find a way to agree on what constitutes the truth?

You can see this problem expressed in lyrics like "truth is after all a moving target" in "Turn the Page" on *Hold Your Fire* or in the classic "Limelight" line in which Neil thinks the person approaching him might just be some star-struck celebrity hound: "I can't pretend a stranger / Is a long-awaited friend."

Into this problem comes Ludwig Wittgenstein, the Austrian-born philosopher whose posthumous work, Philosophical Investigations, suggests our doubt about the world arises out of the artifice of our language. Each of our thoughts are unique, yet we're forced to communicate them using a set of agreed-upon words that can't capture the essence of what we're thinking, and indeed, that corrupt our own understanding of what we're thinking because we think in these words, which are imperfect. As Suomela says, "The grammar of our expression forces a certain mode of thought upon us."

Thus, imagine the orbs on the cover of *Hold Your Fire* agreeing to a set of words to describe things, yet none of these words really captures what the orbs are trying to say, and in fact, the use of the words actually clouds the orbs' thinking on the matter. You might say it's the insufficiency of language that keeps the orbs separate. Maybe if the orbs could communicate perfectly, there would be no doubt about the reality outside each of them.

So, Rush is wrestling with the same problem we all are. As Neil writes in "Show Don't Tell" on *Presto* from 1989, "Who can you believe? / It's hard to play it safe."

Since there really is no answer to this problem, you might conclude that we're doomed to live in doubt. But do we have to despair? Drawing on Wittgenstein, Suomela suggests not. "We don't need to be certain of what an opinion actually is in order to go on living in a language community with other people," he says. In other words, we can and do make it work, by not relying on language.

But what do we rely on? The answer is probably our thoughts, our intuitions, even if we don't have the language to express them. Like good friends, or an old married couple, who don't need to talk to one another to know what's going on with one another, we stay in communication in other ways. You might just call it chemistry. "Signal transmitted / Message received / Reaction making impact / Invisibly / Elemental telepathy / Exchange of energy / Reaction making contact / Mysteriously / Eye to I / Reaction burning hotter / Two to one / Reflection on the water." ("Chemistry," *Signals*, 1982)—*Published June 5, 2011*

9. Philosophy of Mind Has a Headache; Cygnus Has Aspirin

Are we mind or body? Yes

Philosophy of mind is an academic discipline in which one of the central problems is the different natures of mind and body. We're physical beings, and indeed, many of our mental processes can be reduced to physical states that we can measure. For example, by using various types of scans, we can actually see changes taking place in our brain in real time based on what we're experiencing. But there remains a central part of our conscious experience—our feelings—that we can't reduce to measurable physical action. It's possible to map physical changes to our brain when we look at, say, the color red, but what we can't map is how looking at red makes us feel. Some philosophers of mind, known as physicalists, say we'll eventually be able to reduce even these subjective states to measurable physical actions. But there are other schools that think some states of consciousness are simply not reducible to something that's measurable. That is, it's not a question of developing measuring tools fine enough to measure those states, because they're simply not the type of states we can measure. The problem is that, if that's the case, then can we ever say iffy things like mysticism, ESP, and fairies aren't real? Who can say without a shadow of a doubt that elves don't reside among us in a parallel universe?

Liz Stillwaggon Swan, a post-doctoral fellow of history at Oregon State University, wades into this debate in her essay called "A Heart and Mind United," and uses the duality idea explored in "Cygnus X-1: Hemispheres" to help us clarify one way to look at the issue. In the piece, we first follow Apollo, the god of reason, who helps us take care of our basic needs—food, shelter, clothing—before we shuck him aside after life gets boring to instead follow Dionysus, the god of love. But as soon as winter sets in, it becomes clear that dancing in the woods won't keep us warm at night or our stomachs full. Then along comes Cygnus, through a black hole, who helps us find a way to combine the two views of living, and we live happily ever after as people who know how to unite heart and mind in structuring our lives.

The parable is simply a cautionary tale about taking an either/or view of the world. It's not necessary to reduce our thinking to purely physical terms, as physicalism tries to do, and neither is it necessary to reject physicalism and admit the existence of the supernatural. In other words, you can allow that some things aren't measurable without having to also allow the existence of anything we can dream up, like fairies.

"The solution," she says, "is to develop, in connection with the natural sciences, a deeper kind of physicalism—one that allows for the variety of human experience without taking on supernatural baggage. If we are committed physicalists, then we should strive for a deeper understanding of human nature that recognizes us as fully emerged from and enmeshed in the natural world, not partly separated from, and beyond, it."

The key here is that we're fully emerged from the natural world. That means our irreducible thoughts are also emerged from the natural world, even though we can't measure them. But fairies? While our thoughts about them are real, albeit non-quantifiable, they themselves aren't necessarily real.

Swan calls "Hemispheres" the uniting of heart and mind, and that's what the editors of *Rush and Philosophy* use as the subtitle to their book. The subtext is, the music of Rush means to a lot of people the uniting of heart and mind.—*Published June 4, 2011*

Appendix II. The Meaning of Rush's Clockwork Angels Runes

Separate from the music, one of the interesting aspects to Rush's 2012 *Clockwork Angels* album is the ancient runes depicted on the cover. They're arrayed like numbers on a clock face, each rune symbolizing a chapter in the 12-track narrative of *Clockwork Angels*.

In the sense that *Clockwork Angels* is a critique of religion, the use of pagan symbols to denote chapters makes sense, because the runes are in effect replacing religious symbols in how we're supposed to take the action in each chapter. That puts the pagan runes on the same footing as religious symbols.

Depictions of the runes were widespread on the Internet prior to Rush's release of the album, in June 2012. That set off something of a scramble among Rush fans to figure out what they mean. I like to think I was the first one out with definitions for the complete set, which I posted on my web site, *Rush Vault*, in May. The post continues to be the most popular of the web site.

On the following page I present my take on the runes: their definitions and how they're supposed to fit into the narrative, which is based loosely on Voltaire's religious satire, *Candide*.

Note that the rune for 3 o'clock is out of order as depicted on the clock face. Rush lyricist Neil Peart says the order of the runes evolved over time and they don't line up perfectly with their order in the narrative.

The Runes on the Clock Face

Hour	Song	Element
12 o'clock	"Caravan" (copper)	related to Venus, Aphrodite, and beauty
1 o'clock	"BU2B" (sulphur)	as in "fire and brimstone" of hell
2 o'clock	"Clockwork Angels" (metallurgy)	annealing, or metal transformation
4 o'clock	"The Anarchist" (winter)	cold, forbidding, discontent
5 o'clock	"Carnies" (zinc)	known as philosopher's wool, and changes its nature
6 o'clock	"Halo Effect" (gold)	what society holds in highest esteem
3 o'clock	"Seven Cities of Gold" (mercury)	or quicksilver, linked to animal spirits
7 o'clock	"The Wreckers" (water)	associated with intelligence, adventure
8 o'clock	"Headlong Flight" (oil essences)	plant oils used in metal purification
9 o'clock	"BU2B2" (quicklime)	associated with the devil
10 o'clock	"Wish Them Well" (lead)	reincarnation, time to move on
11 o'clock	"The Garden" (earth)	as in "salt of the earth"

12 o'clock "Caravan" (copper):

Copper relates to beauty, yet the protagonist of the story, Owen Hardy, wants to leave the farm he's been happy living on up to this point. He's a young man and wants to see the world, so he's blind right now to the beauty, the bucolic setting, that's surrounded him through his young life. The world lit only by fire, from the lyrics, appears to refer to the flying steamships. If they're anything like a steam-driven locomotive, these things are powered by red hot bricks of coal and belch extremely hot vapor clouds.

Neil in a June 13 interview with Jim Ladd on the SiriusXM Deep Tracks program says the world is governed by a benevolent watchmaker, who wants to make sure everyone is content but also wants to make sure no one rocks the boat. The young man isn't content and he goes on to rock the boat.

1 o'clock: "BU2B" (sulfur)

The idea that we live in the best of all possible worlds is from the German philosopher Gottfried Leibniz (1646–1716). Leibniz was a mathematician and said that we had to live in the best of all possible worlds, because the world was created by God, who is omnipotent, and an omnipotent being would only create the best of all possible worlds. So, why does this world contain evil if it's the best of all worlds? Because we need evil to bring out the best in us. Just as we need danger to bring out the courage in us, we need evil to bring out our humanity.

The idea that we should accept our individual fates as inevitable flows out of Plato's Republic. Plato divided society into separate classes: A leadership class, a warrior class (also known as an auxiliary class), and a worker class. Leaders plucked people out of the worker class and put them into the auxiliary class, and they plucked people out of the auxiliary class and put them into the leadership class. Whatever Plato's Republic was, it was not a democracy.

The leaders wanted people to be content, and they wanted people to believe that this is the way the world is. There's no choice in the matter. If you're a worker, you deserve to be a worker and you should be content with that. The leaders will rule benevolently on your behalf, but you mustn't rock the boat. The leaders believed it was okay to lie to the people—tell a noble lie—if it's in the best interest of the society. In the Republic, the idea that people are born into a class and destined to live in that class is a noble lie that the leaders tell the workers, all in the name of social harmony.

2 o'clock: "Clockwork Angels" (metallurgy)

The term "Chronos" relates to time. Think of time-related words like "chronology," "chronicle," "anachronism," and "chronic."

Chronos was the Greek god of time, which based on culture is depicted in different ways. The Greeks depicted him as a kind of serpent with three heads. The Romans depicted him as a naked man in front of the Zodiac wheel. And in later Western cultures he was depicted as Father Time, the bearded timekeeper.

The angels representing land, sea, and sky are the offspring of Chronos and Ananke, the goddess of inevitability.

The rune is metallurgy, which could refer to the metal gears and wheels inside the clock tower that make the hands and the clockwork angels go around. The clockwork angels represent icons, almost like religious idols, to which we pray good things will happen to us. They are containers for our hopes and dreams. By investing in them symbolic power to watch over us, like angels, they reduce the need for us to feel like we have to manage our lives on our own. Instead of using our reason to take matters in our own hands, we just say the angels will look out for us and we feel comforted by that, but of course we're abdicating our moral responsibility to a mere idol. Neil on the June 13 Jim Ladd show says the angels are indeed icons, created by the government, to comfort people and also to entertain them.

4 o'clock: "The Anarchist" (winter)

The idea of winter recalls Shakespeare's "winter of discontent" in Richard III, which defines the anarchist quite well, since the alchemist is motivated by discontent. In the lyrics of the piece, he speaks of his envy and how he never got his fair share. But winter also represents a change of season for the main character. He gets to the city and is dazzled by it, lands a job as a carnival worker and everything is going well for him. But then he confronts the anarchist, who throws his bomb detonator at him. The protagonist catches it just at the moment everyone turns to look at him. He's caught with the detonator in his hand and is falsely thought to be an anarchist bent on destroying everything. So, he takes flight and ends up on the frontier of civilization: the seven cities of gold, which ends up being covered in a "Sahara of snow." In other words, in the arc of his journey, winter has descended.

5 o'clock: "Carnies" (zinc)

The protagonist, Owen Hardy, sees the anarchist with a bomb, bent on destroying everything and creating chaos. The anarchist tosses the detonator into the protagonist's hands, and at just that moment others see the protagonist and suspect he's the would-be perpetrator of chaos. He's a victim of mistaken perception. Zinc relates to transformation. It's one of the metals alchemists were able to change simply by burning it. It transforms into what's known as the flower of zinc, an attractive fluffy white material. It might be that the protagonist, in an instance, has been transformed against his will, from an onlooker into the outcast.

6 o'clock: "Halo Effect" (gold)

All that glistens is not gold. This is the mid-point of the story arc. Enter the love interest. The protagonist had a love in his earlier life but he put that behind him. Now he finds himself seduced by his own fantasies, which he projects onto a beautiful dancer he meets in the teeming city. In fact, the woman is not at all who he thinks she is, and once he sees past his fantasies, he sees he hasn't found true love at all. Maybe the woman he loved in his earlier life is in fact the love that he's been seeking. Neil says "halo effect" represents a psychological term for the effect beautiful people have on us. We tend to project onto beautiful people what we want to believe about them, and that blinds us to their true nature. Eventually we're disillusioned.

3 o'clock: "Seven Cities of Gold" (mercury)

We come to mercury, which is all about speed. It also relates to animal spirits, which are everywhere as he journeys to the outer edge of civilization and reaches what might be thought of as the Wild West, where Eldorado is believed to exist, the place where opportunists gather to strike it rich or die trying, and where you take the law into your own hands. As Alex has put it, "You can hear the danger of the big city as our traveler approaches. Then when Neil comes in and we break out the riff, you're there--you're in the city with all of its excitement and opportunity and trouble." Neil has said he had Cormac McCarthy's "No Country fir Old Men" in mind when he wrote this part of the story.

7 o'clock: "The Wreckers" (water)

The symbol has many meanings, including multiplication, but it also means water and looks like waves, or rough seas, and that's what "The Wreckers" is about. The protagonist's ship is caught in a hurricane and it sees a beacon of light, so it steers there in the hopes of finding safety. But the light is a trick and the ship is destroyed on unseen reefs and only the protagonist survives. Neil has said he had in mind a small band of Englishmen hundreds of years ago who lived on the southwest coast of the country. They would set up a light in a dangerous part of the coast to attract ships at night caught in stormy weather seeking safety. The ships would crash on the unseen rocks, and the Englishmen would plunder anything of value.

8 o'clock: "Headlong Flight" (oil essences)

We come now to the symbol for oil essences, which are used in the transformation process. It might be that the protagonist, having endured betrayal and cruelty and the worst of human treachery, has finally scratched his itch for adventure and now has a better idea of what's important in life. But he also recognizes that his adventures were essential for him to get to this point in his life, thus he says he'd do it all again if he had the chance. Parenthetically, Neil has said he himself has no desire to live his life again, so he's taking a point of view that's alien to him.

9 o'clock: "BU2B2" (quicklime)

Here we have the short musical interlude, the purpose of which is to confirm that the protagonist now understands the world has no plan, we live in an existential hell, but even with that understanding, he still chooses to live on the basis of his plan. Neil describes this interlude as a soliloquy, the follow-up to the first soliloquy in the story, BU2B2.

10 o'clock: "Wish Them Well" (lead)

Now we have lead, which is associated with rotting away and coming back to life again as something new. The protagonist bears no ill will to those who've done him wrong. Although the world appears godless, he still chooses to turn the other cheek. In a way he pities the people who've tried to hurt him, because he knows they're in essence living in their own hell, whereas he has escaped that by governing his passion with reason. His goal is to put toxic people behind him, rather than let himself get worked up over other people's behavior.

11 o'clock: "The Garden" (earth)

We've come to the symbol for earth, and we see the protagonist in the manner of the salt of the earth. He's with the ones who are genuinely close to him, loved and respected, which are the universal goals we all seek, even in a world that has no plan. Again, the world is godless, but he has created his own Eden, spending his days cultivating his garden.

The story in some ways seems like "Prime Mover" fleshed out, because that piece from 1987 is about the benevolent Platonic watchmaker who creates the world—sets it spinning— and then leaves us to make the best of our time in the world. In "BU2B," the boy realizes we're spinning and no one is in control, not even the watchmaker, so all that we can do is enjoy the ride as best we can. That doesn't mean throwing caution to the wind. The adventurer tries that in the first part of *Clockwork Angels*. Rather, it means combining a sense of adventure (emotion, passion) and a willingness to go for it with intelligent, thoughtful preparation and measured reaction to events as they unfold. But it also requires integrity. Treating others with respect and love (wishing even your enemies well), so that you are worthy yourself of respect and love.

BIBLIOGRAPHY

Banasiewicz, Bill. *Rush Visions: The Official Biography*. New York: Omnibus Press, 1988.

Berti, Jim, and Durrell Bowman, eds. *Rush and Philosophy*. Chicago: Open Court, 2011.

Bruner, Edward M. and Victor Witter Turner, eds., *The Anthropology of Experience*. Chicago: University of Illinois Press, 1986.

Burns, Jennifer. *Goddess of the Market: Ayn Rand and the American Right*. London: Oxford University Press, 2009.

Costelloe, B.F.C., and J.H. Muirhead, trans. *Aristotle and the Earlier Peripatetics: Being a Translation from Zeller's 'Philosophy of the Greeks,'* Vol. II. London: Longman, Greens, and Co., 1897.

Critchley, Simon. *The Book of Dead Philosophers*. New York. Vintage, 2009.

de Botton, Alain. *Religion for Atheists*. New York: Pantheon, 2012.

Dos Passos, John. *U.S.A.* New York: Library of America, 1996.

Gillespie, Nick and Matt Welch. *The Declaration of Independents. How Libertarian Politics Can Fix What's Wrong with America*. New York, PublicAffairs, 2011.

Gray, John. *Hayek on Liberty*. 3rd ed. New York. Routledge, 1998.

Grube, G.M.A., trans. Plato: *Republic*. Indianapolis: Hackett, 1974.

Haidt, Jonathan. *The Righteous Mind*. New York: Pantheon, 2012.

Hayek, Friedrich. *The Constitution of Liberty*. Chicago: University of Chicago Press, 1960.

Hayek, Friedrich. *The Road to Serfdom*. Chicago: University of Chicago Press, 2007.

Hegarty, Paul and Martin Halliwell. *Beyond and Before: Progressive Rock Since the 1960s*. New York: Continuum, 2011.

Homer. *The Odyssey*. Richard Lattimore, trans. New York: Harper Perennial Classics, 2007.

Kant, Immanuel. *Critique of Pure Reason*, Norman Kemp Smith, trans. New York: St. Martin's Press, 1965.

Kant, Immanuel. *Groundwork of the Metaphysic of Morals*. H.J. Paton, trans. New York: Harper Torchbook, 1964.

Kant, Immanuel. *Prolegomena to Any Future Metaphysics*, Lewis White Beck, trans. Indianapolis: The Bobbs-Merrill Co., 1950.

Kelly, Kevin. *What Technology Wants*. New York: Viking Adult, 2010.

Lee, Stephen. *European Dictatorships, 1918-1945*. 3rd ed. New York: Routledge, 1987.

Lee, Stephen J. and Paul Shuter. *Weimar and Nazi Germany*. Portsmith: Heinemann, 1996

Leibniz, Freiherr von Gottfried Wilhelm. *Theodicy: Essays on the Goodness of God, the Freedom of Man and the Origin of Evil*, E.M. Huggard, trans. Project Gutenberg, 2005: http://www.gutenberg.org/catalog/world/readfile?fk_files=1507027

Locke, John. *Two Treatises of Government* and *A Letter Concerning Toleration*, Ian Shapiro, ed. New Haven: Yale University Press, 2003.

Locke, John. *An Essay Concerning Human Understanding*, Peter H. Nidditch, ed. London: Oxford University Press, 1979.

Lukianoff, Greg. *Unlearning Liberty: Campus Censorship and the End of American Debate*. New York: Encounter Books, 2012.

McDonald, Chris. *Rush, Rock Music and the Middle Class*. Bloomington: Indiana University Press, 2009.

McKeon, Richard, ed. *Introduction to Aristotle*. 2nd ed. Chicago: The University of Chicago Press, 1973.

McLuhan, Marshall. *Understanding Media: The Extensions of Man*. New York: McGraw-Hill, 1964.

Mill, John Stewart. *Utilitarianism*. 2nd ed. Indianapolis: Hackett, 2003.

O'Rourke, P.J. *On the Wealth of Nations*. New York: Atlantic Monthly Press, 2007

Peart, Neil. *Far and Away: A Prize Every Time.* Toronto: ECW Press, 2011.

Peart, Neil. *Ghost Rider: Travels on the Healing Road.* Toronto: ECW Press, 2002.

Peart, Neil. *Roadshow: Landscape with Drums.* Toronto: ECW Press, 2007.

Peart, Neil. *The Masked Rider: Cycling in West Africa.* Toronto: ECW Press, 1996.

Peart, Neil. *Traveling Music: The Soundtrack to My Life and Times.* Toronto: ECW Press, 2004.

Peikoff, Leonard. *The Ominous Parallels: The End of Freedom in America.* New York: Plume, 1983.

Popoff, Martin. *Contents Under Pressure: 30 Years of Rush at Home & Away.* Toronto: ECW Press, 2004.

Popper, Karl R. *The Open Society and Its Enemies: The Spell of Plato.* Princeton: Princeton University Press, 1962.

Price, Carol and Robert M. Price. *Mystic Rhythms: The Philosophical Vision of Rush.* Berkeley Heights: Wildside Press, 1999.

Rand, Ayn. *Anthem.* New York: Signet, 1938.

Rand, Ayn. *Atlas Shrugged.* New York: Signet, 1957.

Rand, Ayn. *For the New Intellectual.* New York: Signet, 1961.

Rand, Ayn. *Philosophy: Who Needs It?* New York: Signet, 1984.

Rand, Ayn, and Peter Schwartz. *The Ayn Rand Column,* 2nd. ed. Second Renaissance Press: New York, 1998.

Rand, Ayn. *The Fountainhead.* New York: Signet, 1943.

Rand, Ayn. *The Virtue of Selfishness.* New York: Signet, 1961.

Rasmussen, Douglas B. and Douglas J. Den Uyl. *Liberty and Nature: An Aristotelian Defense of Liberal Order.* Chicago: Open Court, 1991.

Ross, Alex. *Listen to This.* New York: Farrar, Straus and Giroux, 2010.

Ross, W.D. Aristotle: *Metaphysics,* vols. I and II. Oxford: Oxford University Press, 1948.

Smith, Adam. *An Inquiry into the Nature and Causes of the Wealth of Nations.* Kathryn Sutherland, ed. London: Oxford University Press, 1993.

Smith, George H. *Atheism, Ayn Rand, and Other Heresies.* Buffalo, N.Y.: Prometheus Books, 1991.

Stump, Paul. *The Music's All That Matters: A History of Progressive Rock.* London: Quartet Books, 1998.

Telleria, Robert. *Rush Tribute: Merely Players.* Kingston: Quarry Press, 2002.

Vasari, Giorgio. "Raphael of Urbino," in *Lives of the Artists*, Vol. I. Oxford: Oxford University Press, 1998.

Voltaire, *Candide*. 2nd ed. Robert M. Adams, trans. New York: W.W. Norton & Company, 1991.

Von Mises, Ludwig. *Human Action*. 4th ed. San Francisco: Fox & Wilkes, 1963.

Wagner, Jeff. *Mean Deviation: Four Decades of Progressive Heavy Metal*. Brooklyn: Bazillion Points, 2010.

Wall, Mick. *Enter Night: Metallica: The Biography*. London: Orion, 2010.

Whitman, Walt. *Leaves of Grass*. E. Sculley Bradley and Harold W. Blodgett, eds. New York: W. W. Norton & Co., 1985.

Zernike, Kate. *Boiling Mad: Inside Tea Party America*. New York: Times Books, 2010.

Zeyl, D. J., trans. Plato: *Timaeus*. Indianapolis: Hackett, 1974.